SPLENDOURS OF THE ANCIENT ANDES

MARIA LONGHENA • WALTER ALVA

Thames & Hudson

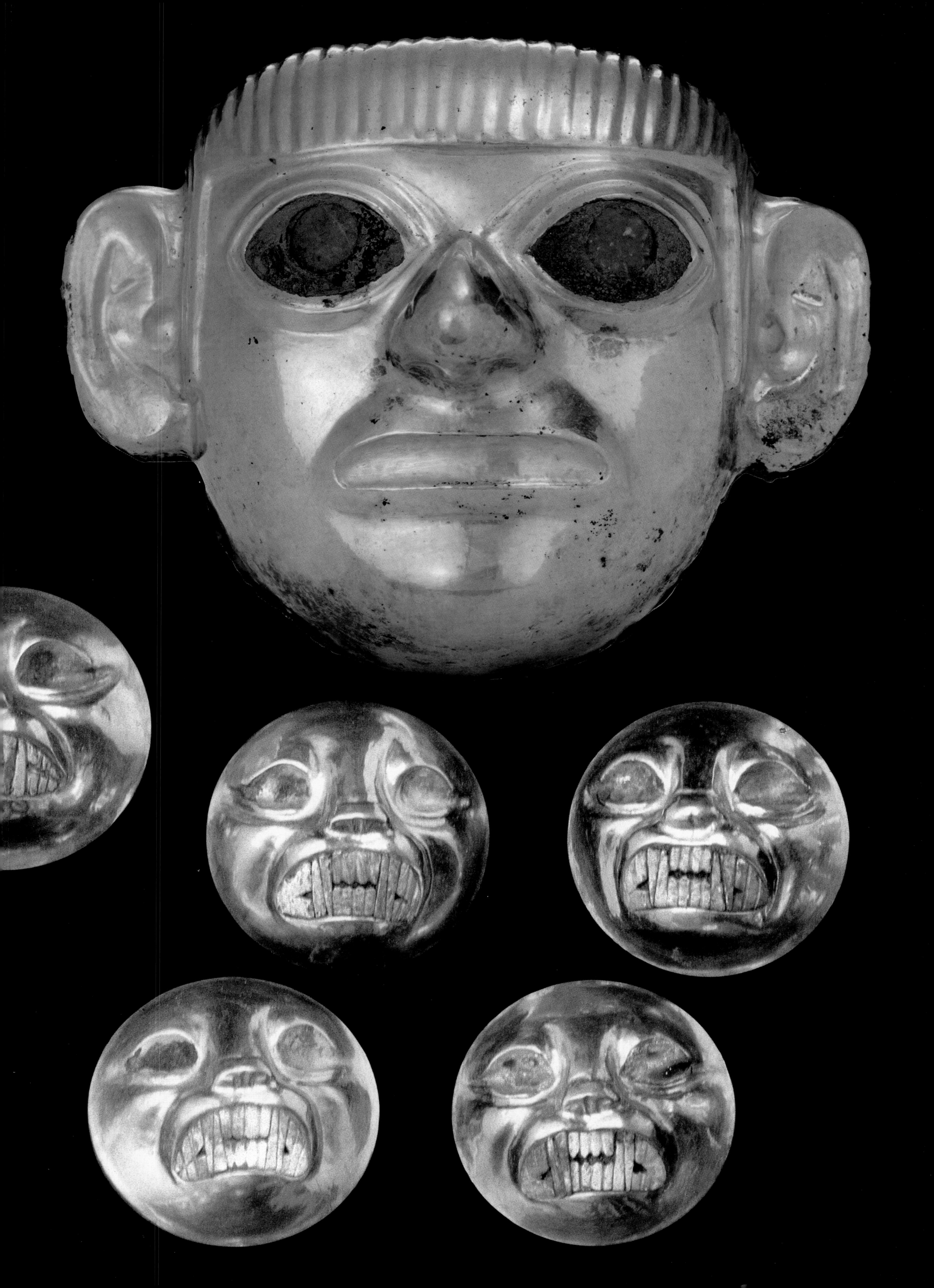

Text
Maria Longhena
Walter Alva

Editorial co-ordination
Valeria Manferto De Fabianis
Fabio Bourbon

Art Director
Patrizia Balocco Lovisetti

Graphic design
Anna Galliani

Drawings
Monica Falcone
Roberta Vigone

Translation
C.T.M., Milan

CONTENTS

The Editor would like to thank Arturo Chipoca of the Peruvian Embassy in Rome and Rossana Becerra of Promperú in Lima for their valuable help

First published in Great Britain in 1999 by Thames & Hudson Ltd, 181A High Holborn, London WC1V 7QX

British Library Cataloguing-in-Publication Data
A catalogue record for this book is available from the British Library

ISBN 0-500-01929-0

Printed and bound in Italy

(Note: numbers of captions refer to the page on which the illustration appears)

1 An ear ornament made by the Sicán goldsmiths: the central figure resembles the god-hero, Nylamp.

2–3 A gold Chimú burial mask.

4 and 4, 5 These gilded copper beads inlaid with shell come from Sipán, where intact tombs were found containing many fine examples of Moche art.

5 (above) The eyes of silver and lapis lazuli are the most striking features of this small gold head. They appear dilated, perhaps to reproduce the effect of coca.

6 These Moche ear discs are made of gold, inlaid with a mosaic of pieces of lapis lazuli and shell.

7 An example of the most accomplished expression of Moche ceramics: the portrait vessel. The person shown was probably of high rank.

Preface

by Walter Alva

8 (below) The curious iconography of this pendant from Guayas in Ecuador may allude to the daily journey of the sun from east to west, symbolized by the two opposed spirals.

8 (above right) This beautifully made object is the handle of a tumi, *a ceremonial knife. It is made of gold and turquoise and depicts the god-hero Nylamp, a figure taken from the historical and religious traditions of the Sicán culture.*

9 Metalworking can be traced back to a very early period in the Andes. In Colombia, the art reached high technical and aesthetic levels as shown by this graceful Quimbaya container in the form of human figure, called a poporo.

The central section of the Andes mountains in South America forms, with Mesoamerica, the cradle of the New World civilizations. The cultural evolution that took place here spanned over five thousand years and ended with the birth and development of the two great empires of the Aztec and Inca peoples, who had to confront the European Conquistadors.

But before the rise of the Aztecs and Incas, hundreds of other peoples and ethnic groups had lived throughout the continent over the millennia. Split down the centre by the massive Andean mountain chain that separates the Pacific coastal strip from the Amazonian plateau, South America saw many fascinating Pre-Columbian civilizations flourish and die. In the central Andes of present-day Peru, pre-Inca peoples developed advanced techniques of irrigation, agriculture and fishing to control and exploit the wide variety of local environmental and climatic conditions. These include the driest deserts in the world, jungle, coastal oases, mountain valleys, tundra and permanently snow-capped peaks. During their extraordinary evolution, often in a hostile environment, the indigenous peoples domesticated animals such as the llama and learned to cultivate grains such as maize and tubers such as the potato, later to save Europeans from famine. These cultures built huge temples, sanctuaries, residential complexes, forts, palaces and roads and they learned how to produce beautiful pottery, textiles and jewelry with a high degree of skill – true works of art that are being brought to light after centuries of oblivion.

Thanks to their rapid territorial expansion, the Incas concentrated this development into an empire that covered a huge part of the Pacific coastal area until the 16th century. Based on state control of production and redistribution, the amazing organization of the Inca empire has even inspired contemporary political parallels. Archaeological research from the end of the 19th century, and in modern times in particular, continues to uncover new and remarkable aspects of civilizations that have left such wondrous remains as the city of Machu Picchu, the gigantic and enigmatic symbols etched in the Nazca deserts, the temples of Chavín and the splendid funerary goods of the Moche lords.

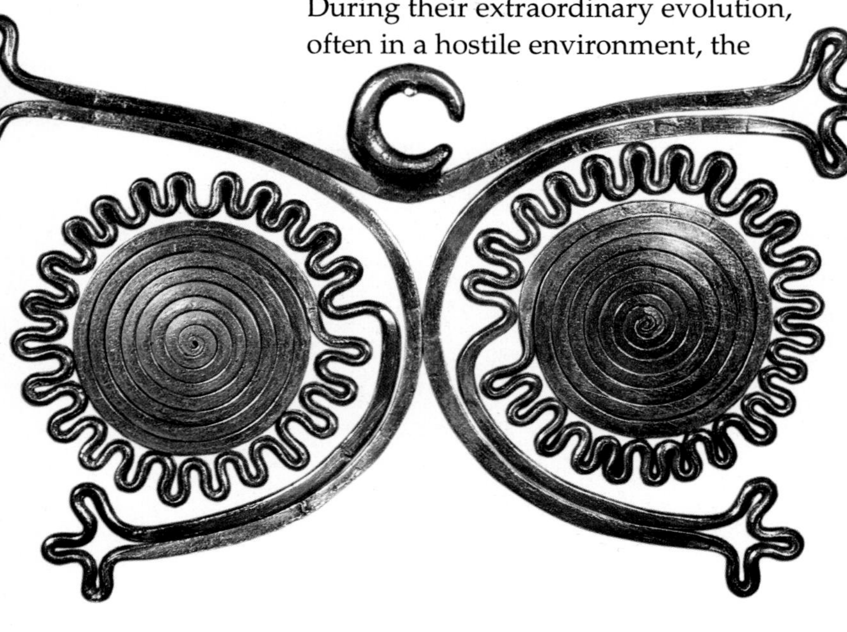

10–11 Machu Picchu, the most celebrated archaeological site in the Andes, nestles spectacularly between the Old Peak and the New Peak. Its agricultural terracing, temples, houses, fountains and magnificent setting, directly over the Urubamba valley, make it a marvellous place to visit for both tourist and scholar.

12–13 The Inca rulers built numerous civil and military outposts far from Cuzco, particularly along the coast, in order to decentralize the political and administrative power of their empire, Tahuantinsuyu. Tambo Colorado, seen here, is one of the best preserved.

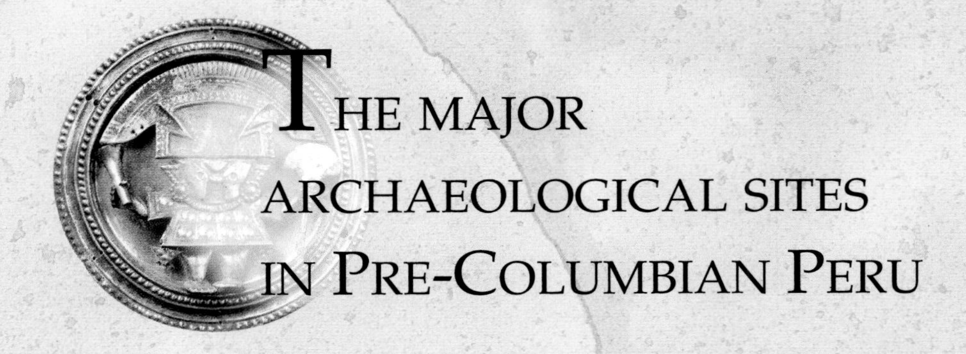
THE MAJOR
ARCHAEOLOGICAL SITES
IN PRE-COLUMBIAN PERU

COLOMBIA
BRAZIL
HUACA DEL DRAGON
CHAN CHAN
ECUADOR
ULASA
PARAMONGA

N

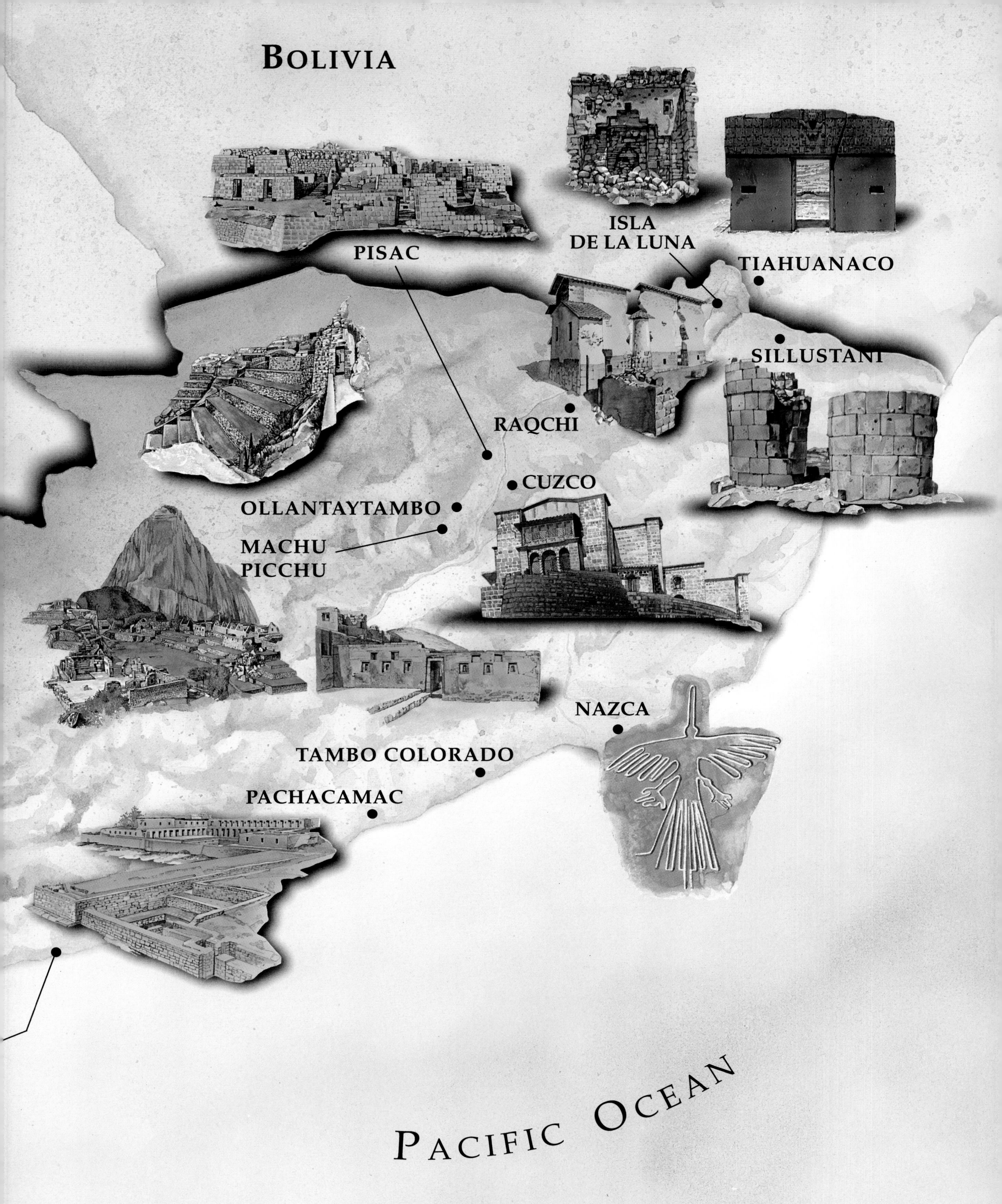
BOLIVIA
ISLA
DE LA LUNA
PISAC
TIAHUANACO
SILLUSTANI
RAQCHI
CUZCO
OLLANTAYTAMBO
MACHU
PICCHU
NAZCA
TAMBO COLORADO
PACHACAMAC
PACIFIC OCEAN

HISTORY OF THE ANDEAN CIVILIZATIONS

16 Manco Capac, seen here in a painting dating from the Colonial period, was the traditional founder of the Inca dynasty. Surrounded by legends and stories, it is impossible today to know whether he was a historical person or a mythical figure.

Introduction

17 The oral traditions of Tahuantinsuyu have been preserved and passed down to us by the Spanish chroniclers. They recount that Mama Ocllo and Manco Capac were the ancestors of the Inca dynasty. Various legends mention these figures, possibly wholly mythical, and state that they came from the region of Lake Titicaca. These portraits were painted in the 18th century by an unknown artist.

In 1512, exactly twenty years after Christopher Columbus first landed on the American continent, a Spanish navigator called Vasco Nuñez de Balboa left the Darien Isthmus, today known as Panama, to lead an expedition south into the region between the Andes and the coast of the Pacific Ocean. A native of Darien, impressed with the greed of the Conquistadors, had suggested that Balboa head south, for there he would find a fabulous and immensely rich kingdom called El Dorado. Balboa's trip quickly came to an end when he fell victim to a plot, but some years later the search for El Dorado was continued by Pascual de Andagoya. In 1522, Andagoya headed down the coast of Colombia and Ecuador until he found himself, according to the inhabitants, in an extremely powerful empire. Andagoya named this mysterious land Birú, after the name of a small river in the native language. These two expeditions were the first approaches by Europeans to the continent known today as South America and to the world of the Andes.

But who were the people who lived on those dry coastal plains and on high mountain plateaus? Who were the lords who had created the huge empire and to whom the subjected peoples gave the honorary title of Inca? In discussing the birth and development of the Andean civilizations up to the time of the Spanish Conquest, it is important also to consider briefly the geographical and climatic characteristics of the countries where their remains have been discovered.

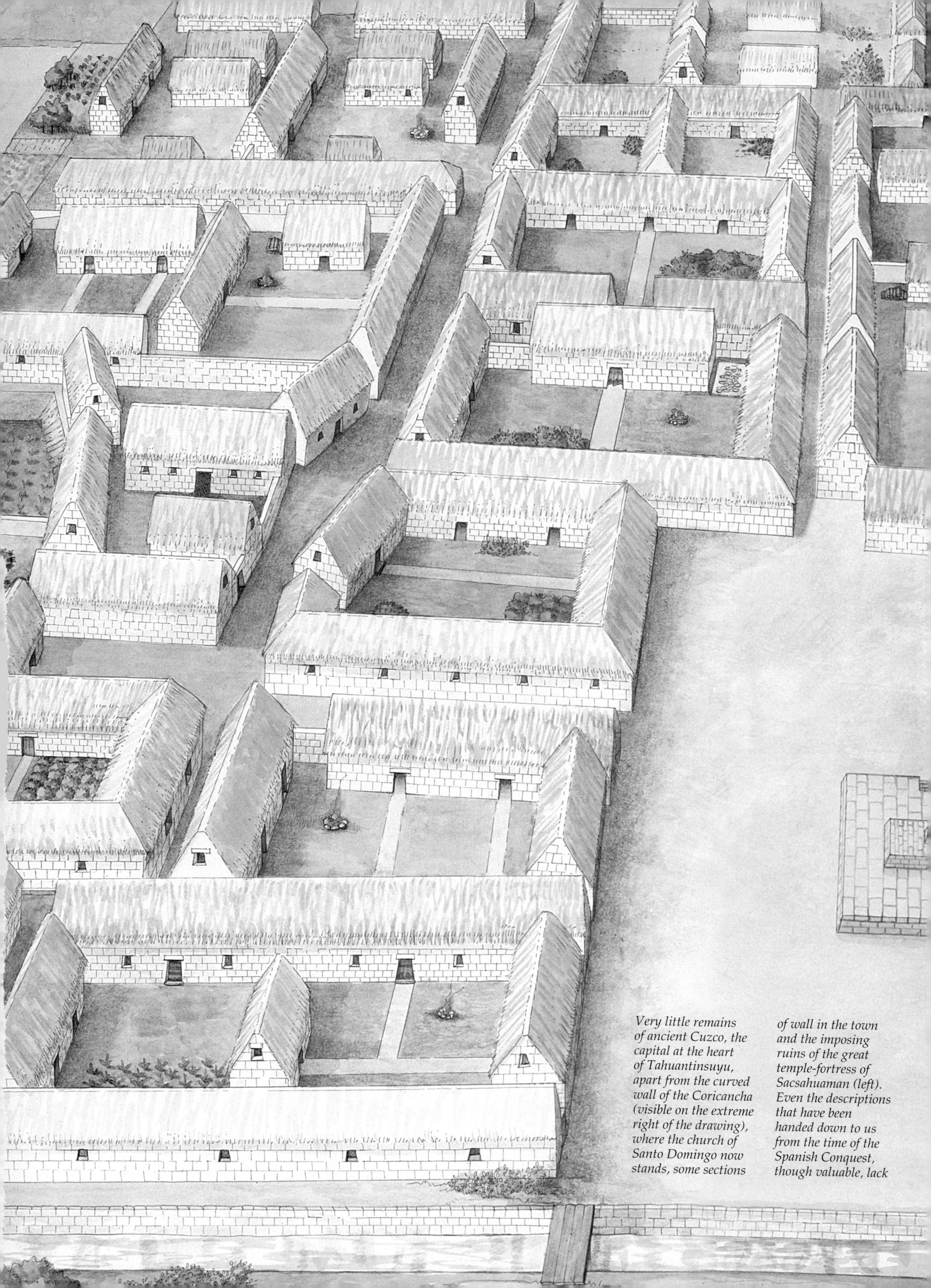

Very little remains of ancient Cuzco, the capital at the heart of Tahuantinsuyu, apart from the curved wall of the Coricancha (visible on the extreme right of the drawing), where the church of Santo Domingo now stands, some sections of wall in the town and the imposing ruins of the great temple-fortress of Sacsahuaman (left). Even the descriptions that have been handed down to us from the time of the Spanish Conquest, though valuable, lack

19 (below) Female figurines of this type are found frequently in ancient Peruvian art. The figure is naked and rather stiff, with the hair parted in the centre and tied tightly back.

19 (right) Similar to the previous figurine in pose and execution, this Inca statuette of a male figure shows the typical elongation of the ear lobes and simple cylindrical head-dress which were the standard symbols of high rank among the Inca. The slight swelling in his left cheek indicates that the man is chewing coca leaves.

Preceramic Period 4000–1800 BC

During this long period, the nomadic groups of hunter-gatherers of the Andes began domesticating plants and animals, in an increasingly settled lifestyle. The most ancient collective burial sites and the first ceremonial centres belong to this period and are evidence of an organized society. Sites on the coast include Huaca Prieta and Aspero; sites in the highlands were Kotosh and La Galgada. The sites are characterized by terraced buildings which were probably used as temples. There is no evidence of pottery but there were other means of artistic expression, such as weaving, which has survived in the form of fragments of vegetal fibres and cotton.

The oldest fragment of woven vegetal fibres found in Peru (3500 BC)

The beginning of cotton cultivation (2500 BC)

Early Ceramic Period 1800–900 BC

The Early Ceramic Period represents an important period of transition during which arts, building techniques and other aspects of society that had appeared in the Preceramic Period were developed. The adoption of pottery-making and metalworking were fundamental. The ceremonial centres of the coast and the highlands became more complex. Temples were built in a U-shape. The site of Garagay was built on the coast and has one of the first examples of multicoloured wall-paintings. Cerro Sechín, in the Casma valley, is one of the most famous sites of this period; it was founded in the 2nd millennium BC.

The oldest ceramic fragment found in Peru, at Kotosh (1800 BC)

Approximate date of fragments of wood found at Cerro Sechín (1519 BC)

Date of copper sheets found at Mina Perdida (1250 BC)

Early Horizon 900–200 BC

The first of the three 'horizons' that the history of Pre-Columbian Peru is conventionally divided into covers the birth and diffusion of the great pan-Peruvian cults that influenced the formation of the cultures that followed. The religious centre of Chavín de Huántar expanded from around 900 BC; its monoliths are carved and incised with the symbolic imagery of the jaguar and other monstrous beings connected with the Amazonian forests but also species from the coast. At the moment, we know neither the origins of the religious cult that brought about the first great unification of Peru nor the identity of the people who promoted it. Metalworking also became widespread during this Horizon.

The older phase of the ceremonial centre of Chavín de Huántar; construction of the Old Temple, also known as the 'Castillo' (900–500 BC)

The more recent phase of the site during which the New Temple was built (500–200 BC)

Beginning of the decline of Chavín and diffusion of the Paracas culture on the south coast (200 BC)

Early Intermediate Period 200 BC–AD 700

The regionalism that characterized various moments of Andean history began during this period. The cultural and perhaps political unification created by Chavín came to an end and the territory broke up into a series of small 'kingdoms' or 'states' which corresponded to civilizations or cultures. Of these, the Moche (also called Mochica) emerged in the northern coastal area, and the Nazca prospered along the southern desert coastal strip. Archaeological research shows remarkably advanced societies based on agriculture and fishing, that produced pottery, woven textiles and objects made from precious metals. Tombs of high-ranking individuals containing manufactured objects of high quality suggest the existence of a rigidly organized society.

Cahuachi becomes the capital of the Nazca cultural area (100 BC)

Probable first construction phase of the Pyramids of the Sun and the Moon at the site of Moche (AD 100)

Middle Horizon
AD 700–1000

A new phase of unification took place during this Horizon. The small states that had emerged over the previous centuries were absorbed by the political and cultural power of the Huari empire. For the first time, a road network and defensive walls appeared, as well as true cities based on a grid layout. From a religious and cultural point of view, the Huari were influenced by another power, the theocratic centre at Tiahuanaco near Lake Titicaca. This site may have represented an attempt at bringing new life to the cult of the Staff God originally found at Chavín. This period also brought magnificent examples of monumental sculpture, polychrome pottery and textiles woven with great skill.

Peak of the city and empire of Tiahuanaco (AD 500)

Political and cultural emergence of the city of Huari, perhaps the capital of the empire of the same name (AD 600–700)

Collapse of the Huari and Tiahuanaco centres due to unknown causes (AD 1000)

Late Intermediate Period
AD 1000–1450

Around AD 1000, unknown events brought about the decline of Huari power while a new political and cultural division occurred across Peru. New civilizations emerged, particularly along the coastal areas, from the ashes of the Moche and Nazca peoples and new, important ceremonial centres were built on the ruins of the Huari centres. The powerful kingdom of the Chimú (or Chimor) people rose on the north coast and the huge city of Chan Chan grew to become one of Pre-Columbian Peru's most impressive centres. Artistic techniques included the working of gold and silver and the use of feathers for ornamentation. Further south, the burial sites of Chancay and Ica-Chincha contain evidence of complex funerary rites and a refined textile industry. In 1450, the advance of the Inca empire put an end to the opulent Chimú civilization and all the small states of the Late Intermediate Period.

Peak of the Sicán culture in the northern coastal valleys (AD 1000–1100)

Founding of Chan Chan (c. AD 1000)

Peak of the Chimú culture in the northern coastal valleys (AD 1350–1450)

Minchançaman, king of Chan Chan, capitulated to the Incas and the Chimú kingdom fell (AD 1463)

Late Horizon
AD 1450–1533

This Horizon corresponds to the period of establishment and expansion of the last great unifying force in Pre-Columbian Peru – the empire of the Incas, more properly called Tahuantinsuyu. Thanks to a rigidly organized state and a powerful army, the first Inca kings managed to expand their power in a very short time. They subdued and subjected a number of different peoples to create an enormous empire whose road network and megalithic constructions are still visible. The first kings are known only through stories handed down orally and they may have been legendary rather than historical. We are more secure with the Inca dynasty beginning with Inca Pachacutec. In 1533, the Inca Atahualpa was betrayed, captured and put to death by the Spanish captain, Francisco Pizarro.

Mythical beginning of the Inca dynasty with king Manco Capac (*c.* AD 1200)

The reign of Pachacutec, first Inca king whose existence can be historically proven (AD 1438–1471)

Death of king Atahualpa and fall of Tahuantinsuyu (AD 1533)

Death of the last representative of the Inca dynasty, Tupac Amaru (AD 1572)

26 This Inca figurine is remarkable for the four decorative bands inlaid with different materials, including precious Spondylus shell and gold. It probably represents a semi-divine being, perhaps related to the fertility of the land.

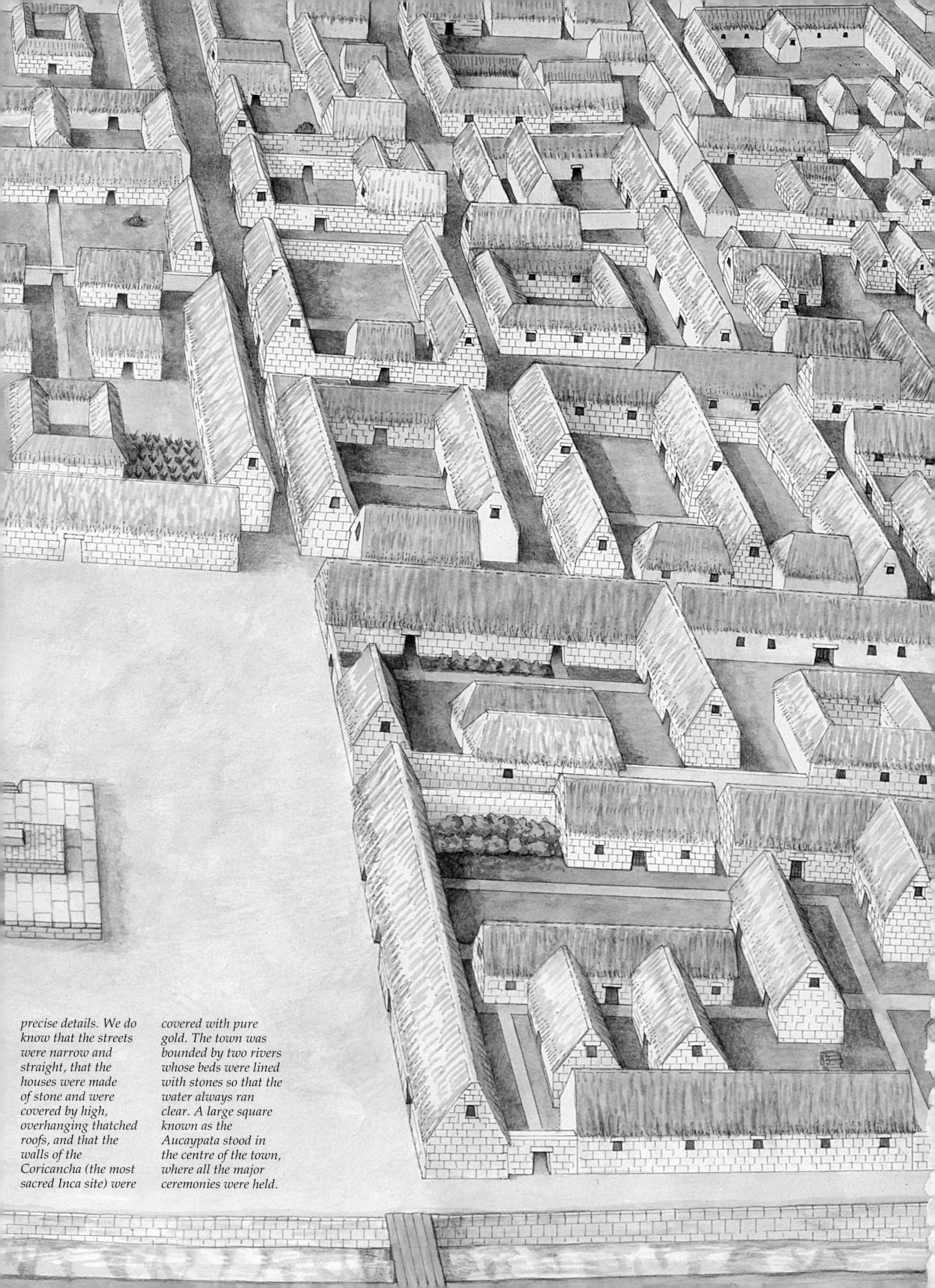

precise details. We do know that the streets were narrow and straight, that the houses were made of stone and were covered by high, overhanging thatched roofs, and that the walls of the Coricancha (the most sacred Inca site) were covered with pure gold. The town was bounded by two rivers whose beds were lined with stones so that the water always ran clear. A large square known as the Aucaypata stood in the centre of the town, where all the major ceremonies were held.

THE PRECERAMIC PERIOD AND THE BEGINNING OF THE CERAMIC PERIOD

Today Peru covers an area of around 1,285 sq. km (496,221 sq. miles). In the north it is wedged between Ecuador and Colombia; in the east it is bounded by the Amazonian rainforest of Brazil and the Bolivian highlands; in the south the tip of the country touches Chile. Peru is therefore a huge country characterized by a great diversity of landscapes and climates – the tall, snowy mountains of the Andes, high plateaus, the Amazon rainforest and the dry Pacific coastline – which endow the country with an extraordinary variety of colours, plants and animals.

The Peruvian coast is a desert strip around 3,000 km (1,863 miles) long, interrupted here and there by green oases created by mountain rivers whose flow depends on the seasonal rains of the mountains.

The dry climate of the coastal region gradually gets damper and rainier as the land rises towards the Andean slopes. A geographical area called the Sierra lies between 2,285 and 3,445 m (7,500 and 11,300 ft), where the temperate climate and fertile soil have benefited human settlements and agriculture for thousands of years.

The Altiplano is a huge, flat, steppe-like area at an altitude of between 3,765 and 4,267 m (12,350 and 14,000 ft) straddling the eastern and western sides of the peaks of the Andes, which rise to a height of 5,945 m (19,500 ft). In this area of cold climate, also called the Puna, lies Lake Titicaca. The lake, now partly in modern-day Bolivia, has played an important role in the Pre-Columbian history of Peru.

The vast, hot and humid expanse of the Amazonian rainforest lies on the eastern slopes of the Andes chain and is known as the *selva.* Its main characteristic is intense rainfall that feeds many rivers, principally the Amazon itself.

The mystery surrounding the origins of the Peruvian people is still as far from being solved as is that of the arrival of the first humans on the American continent across the Bering land bridge. Archaeologists use the term Preceramic Period to indicate the interval between the first human settlements and the appearance of ceramics in about 1800 BC. Traces of human presence, in the form of manmade stone objects, and the bones of Pleistocene fauna have been found together in a cave at Pichimachay in the province of Ayacucho; radiocarbon dating has placed the objects in a period around 18,200–14,700 BC.

Not all scholars agree that the 'stone tools' found at Pichimachay were manufactured, and therefore the theory that the site was a human settlement is placed in doubt. Others, however, consider the finds in the Ayacucho valley to be irrefutable evidence of the presence of a nomadic population during the period 20,000–15,000 BC.

Bones of animals and humans associated with stone tools dating from before 15,000 BC have been discovered in other caves and shelters at Telarmachay, Lauricocha and Guitarrero. On the basis of palaeontological and archaeological evidence, it can be suggested that the first inhabitants of the Andean mountains moved down through the isthmus of Panama and Colombia, despite the obstacles of the barren mountains and harsh climates, until they reached the highlands and descended towards the coast.

These nomads hunted large animals such as the mastodon and horse and, once these species had become extinct around 10,000 BC, deer and the ancestors of the domesticated llama and alpaca. They also gathered tubers, fruits and wild plants in the mountainous areas, and molluscs in the rivers and fish from the sea. There are a few examples of art from this remote period in the form of rock paintings and bone ornaments.

Theories of movements of early populations

.... Theory of Montandon
----- Theory of Paul Rivet
—·— Theory of Mendes Correa
\\\\ Theory of Ales Hrdlička

29 Weaving was one of the oldest crafts practised in Pre-Columbian Peru. This fragment of cotton dates from the earliest period of the Paracas culture: the influence of Chavín can clearly be seen in the characteristic images of the Staff God.

Around 6000 BC, the inhabitants of the Andes began to cultivate certain plants. Consequently, groups of people began to create permanent settlements and abandon their nomadic lifestyle. Llamas and alpacas began to be domesticated in the highlands and settlements started to appear. The first traces of agriculture proper date from around 4000 BC in the Sierra, and later in the coastal region.

Although species of domestic animals in the Pre-Columbian Andean world were limited to alpacas, llamas, dogs, guinea pigs and a few others, the variety of plant crops, many unknown in Europe until after the Spanish Conquest, was very wide. Among the most important were corn (*Zea mais*), many members of the cucurbit family, such as gourds, cucumber and melon, the bean (*Faseolus lunatus*), the avocado, peanuts, chili, tomatoes and the potato.

Around 2500 BC, Andean peoples began to cultivate cotton, which became their primary material for weaving. Weaving was the oldest and most important means of artistic expression for the peoples of Pre-Columbian Peru.

Following the rise of agriculture and an increase in population, the first ceremonial and public buildings began to appear at the end of the Preceramic Period, between 2700 and 2000 BC. These were built from stone and adobe (sun-baked bricks). The architectural forms were at first very simple but gradually increased in complexity during the Early Ceramic Period. The spread of inhabited centres, particularly along the coast, is evidence of a new, organized society, governed by an individual or a small group. Ordinary people may have paid a part of the fruits of their agricultural labours to priest-kings, who managed the economy of the village and conducted religious ceremonies for which temples were built. Some small, simple buildings associated with the temples have been excavated, which were used for domestic purposes.

Archaeological research has shown that pottery first appeared in Peru around 1800 BC. The earliest shapes were fairly limited – jars, bowls and bottles – but their elaborate and refined styles are evidence of a fairly advanced society. From the 17th century BC, the inhabited centres in the coastal areas increased in size and were transformed into huge ceremonial sites. It is thought that around a thousand people might have lived in the houses around the large, pyramidal buildings used for worship. Research has also established that agriculture was intensified and techniques for irrigating fields were devised; these were duties performed by one part of the population. As in previous centuries, a restricted élite officiated at religious ceremonies. Fishing was still as important as in the Preceramic Period and remained an integral part of the economy of the coastal cultures. Over the centuries, pottery and weaving evolved into widespread and sophisticated crafts, as shown by the quality of votive and funerary offerings discovered.

Tombs dating from the Preceramic Period show evidence of stratified societies: the structure of tombs containing richer grave goods differs from the others, and it is apparent that the deceased buried in them had enjoyed a certain status in the community. This is shown, for example, by the presence of 'exotic' objects alongside those of local production, which must have been obtained through exchange with distant places. Examples include mirrors made from anthracite and the shells of *Spondylus princeps* from the warm waters of the coast of Ecuador.

One of the most surprising and interesting aspects of the Early Ceramic Period is the fact that the ceremonial sites built between 2000 and 1500 BC are among the largest built at any time in Peru. Three architectural styles particular to the coastal region began to diverge from the ancient model that had characterized public buildings in the previous period. These styles had clear structural differences despite developing from a common root. An interesting aspect of the first style is the use of friezes and reliefs as decoration on the walls of temples, some of which can still be seen today. Complexes formed by U-shaped pyramidal platforms, which have their prototype at El Paraiso, were built above all in the valleys of Lurín, Rímac, Chillón and Chancay, and at other sites in the central coast area, such as La Florida and Garagay. The last site is famous for its adobe walls painted in bright colours with figures from the supernatural world.

Many sites in the Casma valley on the north-central coast, such as Sechín Alto and Pampa de las Llamas, contain massive truncated pyramids built on a rectangular base, with patios and circular plazas; here too, the layout is based on a U-shape. In the nearby valleys of Supe and Nepeña, archaeologists have found architecturally similar sites. Cerro Sechín developed towards the end of the Preceramic Period and flourished during the Early Horizon.

COLOMBIA
ECUADOR
PERU
BRAZIL
BOLIVIA
CHILE

1 El Paraiso
2 La Florida
3 Garagay
4 Caballo Muerto
5 Huaca de los Reyes

30 (opposite) Dated to between 1800 and 400 BC, this is one of the oldest examples of pottery known from Peru. Its modest, stylized features give no clue to its precise cultural origin, but it is probably from the northern coast area.

31 (below left) Cupisnique pottery is rich with symbolic imagery; this male figure, perhaps a shaman, seems to be meditating. His broad collar or necklace is probably a symbol of status.

The third regional style, known as Cupisnique, is found further north in the wide valleys of Virú and Lambayeque. It was once considered contemporary with Chavín de Huántar but is now thought to be several centuries older.

The Cupisnique style can be seen at several well-preserved sites in the Moche valley, such as Huaca de los Reyes. Vast, rectangular squares are combined with large, elegant platforms which have a wide, low structure and are decorated with adobe reliefs. On top of the platforms are rows of colonnades, reached by flights of steps.

The Cupisnique style is not only associated with architecture but also with elegant pottery vessels. Pieces are usually black or grey and depict people, anthropo-zoomorphic figures and creatures that are part-jaguar and part-birds of prey. These are ancient examples of a religious imagery which was disseminated further afield by the growing influence of the religious centre of Chavín de Huántar in the following centuries. The pyramidal temples, probably stylized symbols of mountains, were not positioned at random – they all face northeast towards the Andes, in the direction of the sources of the coastal rivers.

Some scholars have suggested that the various temple sites formed the first small 'states' of Pre-Columbian Peru during the Early Ceramic Period. Each centre was an autonomous political and cultural entity ruled by a warrior-king, supported by an élite body of priests whose duty it was to manage religious worship. The population lived in small houses clustered around the temple complexes, and worked the fields, practised various handicrafts or fishing, and traded with the peoples of nearby valleys.

Around 900 BC, the most important coastal sites entered a phase of decline while the power and prestige of a small centre in Callejón de Conchucos in the north-central highlands began to grow: Chavín de Huántar.

31 (above right) An example of the Cupisnique style, this tall, monochrome pot is decorated with relief and incised motifs. It has a stirrup handle and a short spout.

32 This ceramic vessel has somewhat hybrid characteristics: the spherical shape combined with a stirrup-handle resembles the Chavín-Cupisnique style but the snake-like relief is similar to motifs found in the art of the northern coastal cultures.

THE EARLY HORIZON

The history of Pre-Columbian Peru is complicated and still difficult to trace. No forms of writing have been identified for the periods before the Incas and scholars have to rely on archaeological and iconographic sources of information. On the basis of the finds so far brought to light, the interval between the end of the Early Ceramic Period and the Spanish Conquest has been divided into three 'Horizons' and two 'Intermediate Periods': the first term refers to periods of political and cultural unification, and the second to division and regionalism.

The Early Horizon, also called the Formative Period, is dated to 900 to 200 BC; its initial phase corresponds to the decline of the coastal power centres which had emerged in the earlier period. Around 900 BC Chavín de Huántar began to flourish in the highlands in Callejón de Conchucos, to the east of the Cordillera Blanca.

The majesty of the site, even in ruins, convinced the first Spanish explorers that it had been built by giants, as testified by the accounts of Pedro de Cieza de León. When questioned by Vasquez de Espinoza in 1616, the local inhabitants explained that the site was the remains of an ancient place of worship and pilgrimage.

Archaeologists once believed that Chavín might have been founded around 1300 BC and that its architectural models influenced the coastal ceremonial centres. Recently, however, it has been shown that the coastal centres were actually older and that the cultural influence travelled the other way. In fact, the oldest buildings at Chavín de Huántar do not predate 900 BC.

Nevertheless, the precise meaning of this site, its buildings and the images carved in its stones still remains an unsolved enigma. Archaeology has shown that Chavín de Huántar was established as a centre of religious power between 900 and 200 BC. A temple site called El Castillo, or Old Temple, was built in the typical U-shape plan of older sites. In 400 BC, this was replaced by a newer construction called the New Temple. Some scholars have suggested that these sites were astronomical observatories as well as places of worship. Perhaps Chavín was the centre of the first great Andean civilization, or, more simply, was a centre of theocratic power that had a unifying role for centuries.

Peruvian archaeologist Julio C. Tello considered Chavín as the origin of Peruvian culture and the centre of a religious ideology that influenced succeeding civilizations up until the creation of the Inca empire.

Chavín's most celebrated monuments are three monoliths decorated with reliefs of complex images of monstrous and mythical hybrid beings, which are also found in pottery decoration, textiles and sculpture throughout Peru. Two figures are dominant on the monuments (the Lanzón, the Tello Obelisk and the Raimondi Stela), the 'Jaguar God' and the 'Staff God'.

From the moment Chavín de Huántar was rediscovered, the most renowned scholars of Pre-Columbian Andean cultures have put forward very differing theories as to the origin of the deities worshipped there and their cults. The presence of elements extraneous to the environment of the highlands, such as the caiman, the jaguar and some tropical plants, has led to the suggestion that the temples were built by people who had migrated from the *selva* (the Amazonian forest), having crossed the Andes. However, this theory has recently been undermined by evidence that these motifs were already present at coastal monuments in the Early Ceramic Period. As Chavín developed later than other sites, the 'exotic' images would have been a cultural inheritance from the older centres.

Other scholars have proposed a rather complex but attractive theory: that the cult of the jaguar-like god might be the consequence of contact with the Mesoamerican world, in particular with the Olmec civilization, which was partly contemporary with Chavín. In the current state of our knowledge it is possible to agree with Julio Tello that the religious ideology of Chavín was assimilated by other civilizations, as shown by decorations on ceramics, textiles and stone reliefs.

Other ceremonial centres in the highlands that had flourished earlier also reached their cultural peak at the same time as Chavín: Pacopampa, Kuntur Huasi and Caballo Muerto. Cerro Sechín, a small temple site founded around 1500 BC, experienced its greatest expansion during the Early Horizon and it is here that the oldest examples of monumental stone art are found. Two different styles have been identified in the pottery of Chavín de Huántar: the first, known as Ofrendas, consists of monochrome vessels, either black or grey, decorated with incised zoomorphic patterns including the image of the 'feline god'. The second, Cupisnique, had originated several centuries earlier in the valleys between Virú and Lambayeque. Its livelier style is seen in the curious shapes of globular bottles and vessels. Metalworking also reached a high level during the peak of Chavín; its origins can be traced back to 1500 BC.

Around 200 BC, the New Temple at Chavín was abandoned and destroyed for reasons still unknown. Archaeology has shown, however, that the beliefs that were developed at Chavín continued to permeate Peruvian civilizations.

1 Chavín de Huántar
2 Cerro Sechín
3 Virú
4 Caballo Muerto
5 Kuntur Huasi
6 Pacopampa

Area of expansion during the Early Horizon

33 (below) Formed of a pair of owls joined at the base and by the spout at the top, this charming vessel is a product of the Salinar culture, one of the oldest on the northern coast. During the Early Intermediate Period the pottery of the northern coastal area was typified by globular, 'sculpted' forms, with little attention paid to colour.

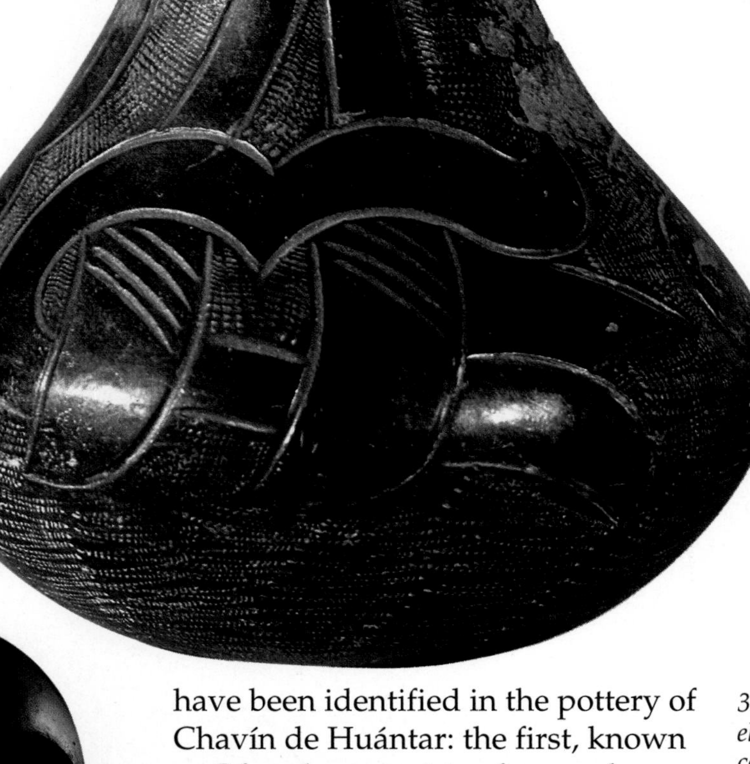

33 (above) This elegant, bottle-shaped container is a good example of Chavín pottery. Abstract, stylized motifs have been incised on the grey-black surface.

THE EARLY INTERMEDIATE PERIOD

Areas of expansion of regional cultures during the Early Intermediate Period

1 Vicús
2 Cajamarca
3 Moche
4 Virú
5 Recuay
6 Lima
7 Pachacamac
8 Huari
9 Paracas
10 Cahuachi
11 Pucara
12 Tiahuanaco

A Vicús culture
B Cajamarca culture
C Salinar culture
D Moche culture
E Virú culture
F Recuay culture
G Lima culture
H Huari culture
I Paracas culture
J Nazca culture
K Pucara culture
L Tiahuanaco culture

34 (left) In addition to zoomorphic images, Vicús pottery also depicts humans. This vessel is in the form of a priest-like person, perhaps a shaman, sitting with crossed legs in a meditative and hieratic position.

34 (above) Owls are popular images in pottery from the northern coast, such as this Vicús bottle with a stirrup-shaped handle. Andean cosmogony linked the night birds to death, the kingdom beyond the tomb, and human sacrifice.

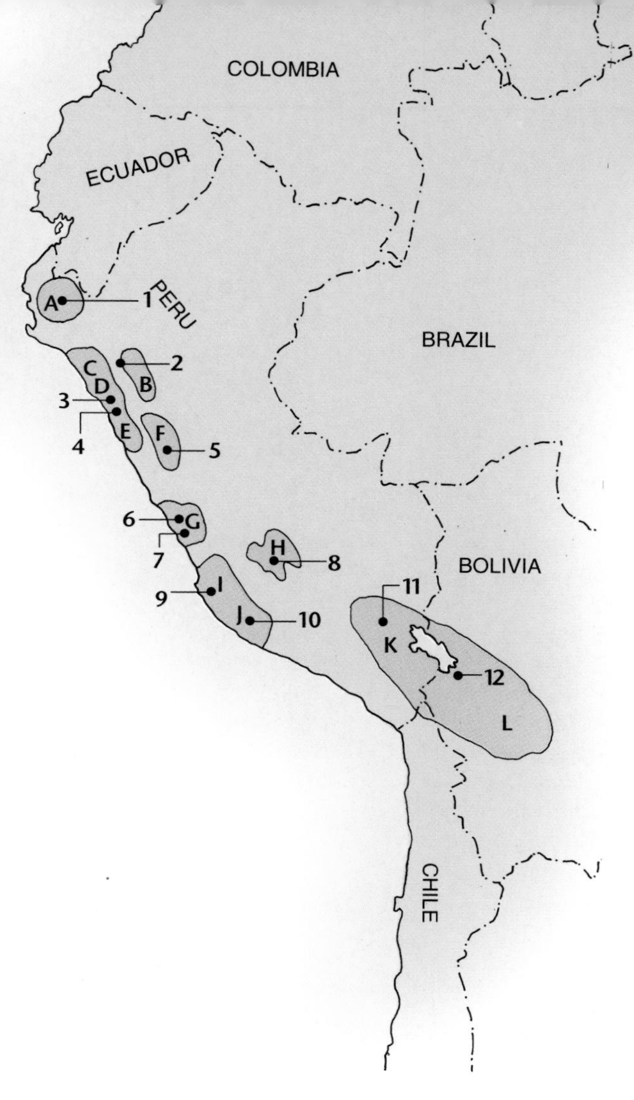

Following the fall of the religious and perhaps political unity exerted by Chavín civilization, regional cultures began to flourish from around 200 BC. These cultures had first emerged some centuries before, and have been associated by scholars with the formation of small, independent 'kingdoms' linked by trade and sharing the cultural inheritance of Chavín. The existence of these kingdoms is in fact documented from about 500 BC: some lasted only a short time while others endured until AD 700, throughout the phase known as the Early Intermediate Period.

Funerary assemblages related to the Vicús culture have been found in the northern coastal area around Piura. The tombs were quite deep, sometimes as much as 14 m (45 ft) below ground level. Two different styles can be discerned in the pottery: the first is simpler and coarser; the other, featuring zoomorphic and anthropomorphic shapes, is of local origin and early Moche in style. Besides the many examples of pottery finds, the Vicús tombs contain large quantities of jewelry and metal objects. Their presence shows that these peoples specialized in metalworking from the beginning of the Early Intermediate Period and that they achieved high levels of quality. The objects are mostly made of copper or an alloy of gold and copper. This metalworking tradition was developed most in the northern coastal area and persisted for many centuries. In the south, however, weaving was the principal craft.

Ruins of settlements and cemeteries of other cultures are found in several valleys of the northern coastal area. Pottery attributed to the Gallinazo culture (also called Virú) has been discovered in the Virú and Moche valleys. Inhabited sites and tombs along the Chicama, Moche, Nepeña and Lambayeque rivers have yielded fine ceramic containers produced by the Salinar culture: these show a strong influence of Cupisnique art, especially in the use of globular shapes. The largest Salinar settlement is Cerro Arena, which includes residential structures but lacks any buildings of a ceremonial nature. The elegant and curious Virú, Vicús and Salinar ceramics were not objects for everyday use but were utilized in burials and ritual ceremonies, as can be deduced from their elaborate forms, their variety of decorative patterns and from the contexts in which they were found.

35 (left) Images of sea creatures and birds stand out among the great range of animal motifs found in Vicús pottery, as seen in this well-made container with a stirrup-handle.

35 (above) The Vicús culture may have had links to Ecuador. The vessel seen here with a stirrup-shaped handle and short spout takes the form of a crab and demonstrates the Vicús love of marine imagery.

36 (below) Among the pottery objects produced by northern cultures during the Early Intermediate Period were musical instruments. This drum from Virú has a handle with anthropomorphic features.

37 (opposite, above left) Pottery models of buildings were also produced by the Salinar culture, as demonstrated by this interesting example. Note the geometric frieze around the top of the building.

36 (above) This curious vessel also belongs to the Virú culture. It consists of globular bottle with a long, thin spout, combined with a model of a building, possibly the stylized image of a temple, with a minuscule human figure inside.

37 (left) This simple but expressive human head was produced by the Salinar people. A preference for sculptural qualities and globular shapes were characteristic features of northern coastal pottery throughout the Early Intermediate Period.

37 (above) At first sight this Salinar bottle might perhaps be considered a piece of contemporary art because of the purity of its shape. As with other finds of the Early Intermediate Period, this example was not intended for everyday use but was a funerary offering.

38 (below) Although the ancient Moche people had no system of writing, the images they created in their ceramics provide much information about their customs and many aspects of everyday life. The vessel illustrated here shows a warrior with a shield, large ear discs and a head-dress.

From the beginning of the 1st century AD, a civilization began to flourish in the homeland of the Salinar culture. Moche's numerous archaeological remains confirm that it was supreme along most of the northern coast, as seen, for instance, in the vast diffusion of its pottery style. As no one knows what these people called themselves, the name Moche (or Mochica) was given to the culture by archaeologists after the valley that was their home. We do not know if the cultural supremacy of the Moche peoples over their neighbours also corresponded to a political and military power, but the variety and richness of their ceramic forms, the interesting examples of monumental architecture and their tombs do allow us to define several traits of Moche society and to propose some interesting theories.

The Moche economic system, like those of previous eras, was based primarily on agriculture which was supplemented by marine resources. Systems of irrigation, probably inherited from the Gallinazo civilization, were perfected and connected several valleys. Many scholars believe that an élite caste of warrior-kings, perhaps also fulfilling the role of priest, headed a rigidly hierarchical social organization and controlled the land to the north of the Moche valley.

The magnificent tombs recently discovered at Sipán almost certainly contained members of this caste. Unfortunately in most cases their sumptuous burial furnishings have been plundered by local tomb-robbers, or *huaqueros*. The most outstanding example to have survived is the tomb of the so-called 'Lord of Sipán', next to whose richly equipped body were laid out the remains of those who accompanied him in death, as well as a dog and llamas sacrificed to ease his journey beyond the tomb and to propitiate the gods. The Moche also built monumental temples, with the finest examples found in the Moche valley. The largest is the Huaca del Sol, which takes the form of a pyramid rising in a series of adobe platforms, probably originally reaching a height of over 40 m (130 ft).

39 'Portrait vessels' are some of the finest ceramics produced by the Moche. This beautiful example has an added metal nose ornament, which was a sign of status.

40 The importance of personal ornamentation for the Moche is clear from a study of their ceramics. This figure, sitting with his legs crossed, is wearing a round hat and two large bracelets.

At one time the temple platform supported a shrine, to which access was probably only permitted to the members of the cult. Although no evidence of this shrine has been found since it was made of perishable materials, various pottery models have survived.

The walls of the Temple of the Moon and the contemporary Temple of Pañamarca in the valley of Nepeña are covered with interesting murals. It is thought that the first was built before the emergence of the Moche civilization when the valley was still inhabited by the Gallinazo peoples. The most interesting wall-paintings were discovered in the 1990s in the temple of El Brujo in the Chicama valley north of the modern city of Trujillo. This is an adobe pyramid, about 30 m (100 ft) high, which was built and modified in a series of phases between AD 200 and 800. The adobe wall reliefs depict very powerful scenes: for instance, one of the most impressive shows a procession of life-size men, naked and joined by a rope around their necks. Perhaps they are prisoners or victims about to be sacrificed. This scene is very similar to decorations on Moche pottery featuring warrior figures and the anthropo-zoomorphic god Ai Apaec.

The pyramidal buildings are comparable to Mesoamerican structures and functioned not only as temples but also as the burial place of cult representatives and members of the reigning élite.

Most of our information about Moche society and religion comes from the images on their pottery, which scholars consider form an 'illustrated dictionary'. It should be remembered that such vessels come from places of worship or burial sites and were used for purposes of ritual and not in everyday life. There are two distinct types of Moche pottery: one is globular and takes the form of animals or gods, generally with a stirrup-shaped handle, while the other is decorated with painted scenes such as episodes from battle, the capture and sacrifice of prisoners, hunting, and enigmatic magico-religious rites whose protagonists are priests and hybrid anthropo-zoomorphic gods. Ai Apaec is one such god, a sort of demon with feline fangs similar to the jaguar god inherited from the Chavín culture.

Like the Vicús, the Moche perfected the techniques of metalworking and excelled in this art, as shown by the finds from the tomb of the Lord of Sipán. This tradition survived in the Lambayeque valley over the centuries and after the Inca conquest

Chimú goldsmiths were brought to the court at Cuzco to continue their art for their new overlords.

Archaeological evidence for the Moche culture shows it to have been a complex society whose economy was based on agriculture, fishing and numerous crafts. Nobles almost certainly received tribute in goods from the people. The cultural and political decline of the Moche seems to have occurred around AD 600, and is believed to be the result of a series of El Niño events and drought.

40–41 The Moche were skilful metalworkers as well as potters. This object, found in a tomb, is a golden cloak with a decoration like a rayed sun at its centre. The techniques of creating precious ornaments in gold and silver was inherited by the Chimú who, in their turn, passed them on to the Inca people.

41 (right) Much of our information about the clothing and personal ornaments of the Moche people comes from the images on their pottery. The sash worn by this elegantly dressed person is probably a mark of social rank.

41 (above) The small figure on the top of this spherical pot has a hieratic bearing and an expression typical of someone in a trance-like state, perhaps the result of taking a hallucinogenic substance. He may therefore be a shaman or a priest.

During the Early Intermediate Period a more modest culture than the Moche appeared in the central coastal region. Scholars have named it the Lima culture as its area of influence included the site of Peru's modern capital. Current research shows that the Lima culture was not unified, but was rather a series of artistic styles with common features that developed in different valleys and which have been named after different ceremonial centres. One of these is Maranga, which exercised political and religious control over the Rímac valley. The Rímac artistic style, also known as 'Nievería', produced pottery vessels with twin spouts connected by a flat bridge handle, typical of the southern coastal area, but similar to Moche pottery in their rounded shapes.

Other cultures flourished elsewhere but are less well known due to the scarcity of finds that would allow us to define their characteristics. At Cajamarca in the Sierra, production of white kaolin pottery decorated with finely

42 (above) Despite its superficially stylized features, this Recuay terracotta figurine has been fashioned with skill and elegance. It depicts a warrior with a shield, ear ornaments and a very elaborate head-dress. The llama probably symbolizes an animal about to be offered as a sacrifice.

42 (below) This fine example of a Recuay vessel is in the form of a building with tiny people inside; it may be a model of a house.

painted geometrical and zoomorphic motifs developed at a late date: the tripod pots produced here were a form unknown elsewhere in Peru and suggest a foreign influence, perhaps from Ecuador.

In the Callejón de Conchucos where centuries earlier the sanctuary of Chavín de Huántar had flourished, the Recuay culture inherited the tradition of stone sculpture. But the large monolithic statues produced during this period, generally of warriors or mothers with babies, show none of the skill of Chavín; instead they are like great blocks that have been only roughly formed into reliefs. The same characteristics are seen in the sculptures that adorn the so-called 'architraves' of buildings that have today disappeared. A recurring image is a central male figure, naked but with his hair arranged in a stylized fashion, flanked by two felines or birds of prey and holding a trophy-head in one hand. Certain motifs in Recuay stone art have clear links with Chavín traditions although they have none of the expressive force of the earlier culture. The most interesting finds are pottery containers left in tombs. Like those from Cajamarca, these are made from kaolin and are decorated with positive and negative painted patterns. The images show that the animals worshipped were the serpent, the condor and, once again, a feline.

Different forms of stone sculpture have been found in the highlands near Lake Titicaca. Here, at 3,910 m (12,840 ft), the centre of Pucara developed in the Early Intermediate Period. It gave its name to a culture that extended its influence north as far as Cuzco, and south to what is now Bolivia and perhaps along the Chilean coast. The site of Pucara is large and impressive, consisting of six different centres of monumental buildings. These include stepped pyramids, sometimes associated with small, sunken temples, and walls that enclose monolithic altars.

Pucara also presents us with intriguing mysteries, both surrounding its origins and the iconographic message of its stelae. Numerous stone sculptures have been found in areas used for worship and burial: the sculptures are for the most part small, painted figures with life-size heads, while the stelae clearly demonstrate the practice of the cult of trophy-heads connected with ritual decapitation – a custom that was widespread in the Andes. The stelae are decorated with reliefs on both faces. Depictions of fish, serpents and people with bird-like faces or jaguar shapes are especially striking. These clear signs of an artistic inheritance from Chavín have prompted scholars to theorize that the founders of the ceremonial centre of Pucara set out to perpetuate the cult and traditions of Chavín. In turn they transmitted them to Tiahuanaco, which later flourished on the shores of Lake Titicaca.

It is not known precisely what happened at Pucara around 300 BC; archaeological excavations have not revealed signs of a fire or any other type of destruction but decline nevertheless set in and the site was abandoned around AD 200.

43 (left) Stone sculptures were one of Pucara's most important means of artistic expression. They were often huge in size, but Pucara artists also produced small figurines with anthropomorphic features, such as the one seen here.

43 (below) The strange creature depicted in relief on this Pucara stela has the head of a fish with a rather snake-like body. In fact the skeleton of the creature shown has been identified as a species of freshwater fish found in Lake Titicaca.

The chronicler Pedro de Cieza de León described the monuments of Tiahuanaco as 'well worthy of admiration and being seen' and considered that the site had actually been Antigualla, 'the oldest city in all Peru'. Several scholars, including Arthur Posnanski, fascinated by the many singular aspects of the site of Tiahuanaco and the mysteries that surrounded it, concluded after years of historical and archaeological research that the centre was founded roughly 10,000 years ago. Orthodox archaeologists are sceptical of this claim and have identified several chronological phases in the history of the site between 300 BC and AD 1000, based essentially on the evolution of pottery types. However, it has not yet been possible to establish precisely the chronological sequence of the construction of the different megalithic complexes, most of which appear to have been built from around AD 200. The Kalasasaya, Akapana, Pumapunku and the Semi-Subterranean Temple are the most important – but who built them and why did they decide to erect so many huge constructions, for which it was necessary to transport tons of andesite extracted from quarries 300 km (186 miles) away? Without doubt, Tiahuanaco inherited many aspects of Pucara's material culture but its enormous size and the mysterious images in its stone monuments inevitably recall the original site: Chavín de Huántar.

A frieze on the architrave of the so-called Gateway of the Sun has a central figure of a hybrid god holding two snake-like sceptres in his hands. This is the same image as is found on the Raimondi Stela, although with some variations. Archaeologists have called the figure the 'Gateway God' or 'Staff God'. Tiahuanaco is thought by many to have been a ceremonial centre linked to the ancient cult associated with this god and designed for the observation of the stars. Perhaps it was founded as a religious sanctuary and place of pilgrimage when Chavín was abandoned – but there are still many questions surrounding its buildings and enclosures.

The importance of Tiahuanaco during the Middle Horizon and its relations with the powerful Huari empire will be considered in the next section.

44 Enigmatic and threatening, the 'Staff God' stands over the Gateway of the Sun at Tiahuanaco. Scholars believe that this image is associated with a cult passed on from Chavín de Huántar.

45 The strange figure on this gold plaque from Tiahuanaco is difficult to identify: it may perhaps be a god or a warrior.

Archaeological remains of the Early Intermediate Period indicating high levels of cultural achievement have been found not only in the highlands and the northern coastal area, but also along the southern desert coastal strip. Here too the term 'civilization' is valid, although we know little about the peoples that lived in the Ica and Nazca valleys from 500 BC on.

Archaeologists long considered the Paracas culture to be completely distinct from the Nazca but now it is now generally agreed that there was a single tradition that developed without a break throughout the period between 500 BC and AD 600.

In the 1920s, the archaeologist Julio Tello was intrigued by elegant embroidered textiles in private collections in Lima and set out to discover where they came from. In 1925 he began a project of excavation on the arid slopes of Cerro Colorado on the peninsula of Paracas. Here he made an exceptional discovery: two large cemeteries with graves that had been preserved intact due to the location and the arid climate. As a result of Tello's discoveries, it is possible to distinguish two distinct components in the Paracas cultural tradition, known as 'Cavernas' and 'Necropolis', each of which has its own types of burial, grave goods and cranial deformation of the deceased. Tombs of the phase known as 'Paracas Cavernas' are subterranean and bottle-shaped and were dug to a remarkable depth in the rock of a terraced hilly area. The tombs were collective, containing up to 40 men, women and children whose social caste is clear from the offerings that accompanied them. The poorest individuals wore a plain, coarse cotton shirt or dress and their only grave good was a simple gourd filled with food. High-status individuals were wrapped in elegant, decorated materials and buried with ceramic containers, gold jewelry, combs and other beautifully made objects. A stone wall signalled the presence of the tomb at the mouth of the vault. Pottery of the Paracas Cavernas phase was decorated with resinous pigments applied after firing and displays a range of different styles. The oldest style is represented by globular pots with stirrup-shaped handles and an incised feline that inevitably suggests a link to a cult derived from Chavín, but one which seems to have faded with the succeeding Necropolis tradition.

46 (below left) The two burial sites on the Paracas peninsula contain large numbers of graves of different types. The mummy bundles in them were wrapped in splendid decorated cotton textiles like those shown here.

Burials belonging to this tradition were found at the northern tip of Cerro Colorado. They took the form of underground rooms, with walls, excavated quite shallowly. Inside them Tello discovered 429 mummy bundles – the mummified bodies of adult men in the flexed position wrapped in several layers of textiles, some of which were up to 20 m (65 ft) in length. Each body was placed

in a basket, forming a huge bundle. Each mummy bundle contained rich offerings, such as pottery objects in a style different from those found in the 'Cavernas' tombs.

The extraordinary discovery of the Cerro Colorado tombs and their treasures shed new light on the cultural development of the southern coast. The most significant artistic element were the textiles which were very sophisticated, accomplished in technique and incorporated a wide variety of colours and imagery. These, together with the pottery, have allowed many aspects of the civilization and its religion to be reconstructed. The Paracas civilization was the first example of a complex society on the southern coast of Peru, flourishing from around 550 BC to AD 100.

46–47 Paracas pottery was painted with natural pigments applied after firing. This seated figurine retains traces of its original colours.

47 (right) Unlike the pottery of the northern coast, that found in the south of Peru from the Early Intermediate Period on shows a strong interest in decoration using a wide range of colours, as seen in this attractive Paracas vessel in the shape of a human figure.

48 (centre) Strange animals and mythical beings are depicted on the multicoloured and accomplished pottery of the Nazca. This vessel with a double spout is in the form of the so-called Killer Whale, one of the most common deities in Nazca iconography.

48 (below right) The rounded forms and asexual appearance of this terracotta Nazca figurine recall the well-known 'baby face' images found in Olmec art.

In addition to these cemeteries, remains of villages and ceremonial centres that appear to be part of the Paracas cultural tradition have also been found in the valleys of Chincha, Pisco, Ica, Palpa and Río Grande de Nazca, but our knowledge of the civilization and its religion is derived from the decorations on the high quality objects that were deposited in the graves. Two parallel traditions in Paracas pottery production have been identified in the 1st century AD. The first, in the Cañete, Chincha and Pisco valleys, takes the form of simple monochrome vessels and is known as Topará.

48–49 Perhaps one of the most mysterious of the large pictures traced out in the dry surface of the desert is the 'Astronaut'. Some of these gigantic geoglyphs created by the Nazca are only visible from a high altitude. This figure is one of only a few anthropomorphic geoglyphs found.

49 (opposite below) The strange feline painted on this brightly coloured vessel is also from the Nazca religious pantheon. The same zoomorphic and monstrous motifs are found in Nazca textiles.

The second, known only in the Ica and Nazca valleys, has bright polychrome decoration and was perhaps the source of the typical pottery production of the Nazca.

Nazca society extended its influence over the south coast area between AD 100 and 700, although there seems to be no real division between the Nazca and Paracas cultures, except for elements of a technical nature. The Nazca retained the same artistic images and expressions, and indeed developed and expanded them, continuing a long cultural tradition and deep-rooted ideology.

During the first decades of the 20th century, a desert valley at the feet of the Andes linked to the Nazca culture revealed one of the most fascinating mysteries of the American continent: the geoglyphs on the Pampa de San José. The geoglyphs are markings etched in the desert surface and they represent the most enigmatic traces left by any of the peoples of the Early Intermediate Period (although some scholars considered them the work of an earlier age).

In addition to the geoglyphs, evidence of Nazca material culture has been uncovered in excavation projects. The most important is at Cahuachi, considered to have been the 'capital' of the ancient civilization between AD 100 and 500, although the long years of archaeological research have not revealed a proper town layout that would allow the site to be defined as such. It seems instead to have

been an important ceremonial centre and probably the seat of a theocratic oligarchy that held religious, political and administrative power. Nazca society was highly specialized and its main economic resources were fishing and agriculture.

The Nazca used a complex and ingenious irrigation system that transformed arid and desert-like terrain and valleys into fertile and productive land. Nazca weavers excelled in producing textiles, especially early on when there were still strong links with the Paracas traditions. In time, pottery became more important and was very accomplished, both technically and in the use of colour. The painted vessels produced by the Nazca are regarded as a sort of pictorial dictionary of their religious pantheon. Numerous hybrid and monstrous figures recur, including the 'Killer Whale' and the 'Mythical Anthropomorphic Being', which has unequivocal Chavinoid features.

Pottery decoration also attests to the importance of the cult of the 'trophy-head' which was linked to the ritual practice of decapitation. Unlike the Vicús and Moche cultures, goldworking remained limited to simple techniques.

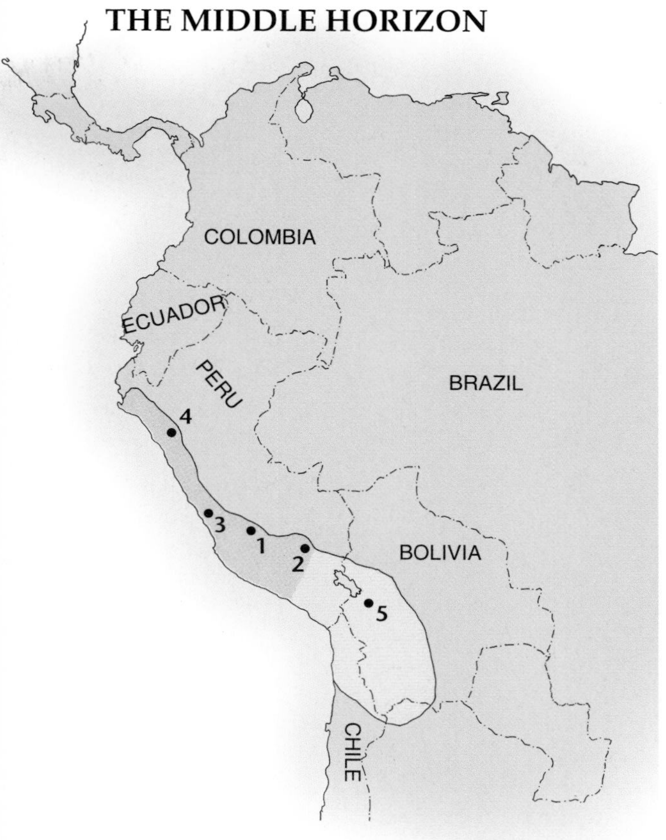

During the Middle Horizon, between AD 600 and 1000, Peru experienced a phase of political and cultural reversal: the small, regional 'kingdoms' or 'states' that had flourished in the previous period were forced to succumb to two unifying forces, defined by some scholars as 'civilizations' and by others as 'empires'. The growth in importance of the ceremonial centre of Tiahuanaco in an earlier age has already been mentioned, but beginning around AD 600–700 it was transformed into the main seat of what could be called a 'hegemonic state' which imposed its religious and cultural influence on smaller centres in distant regions. During this phase, the ancient cult of the Staff God

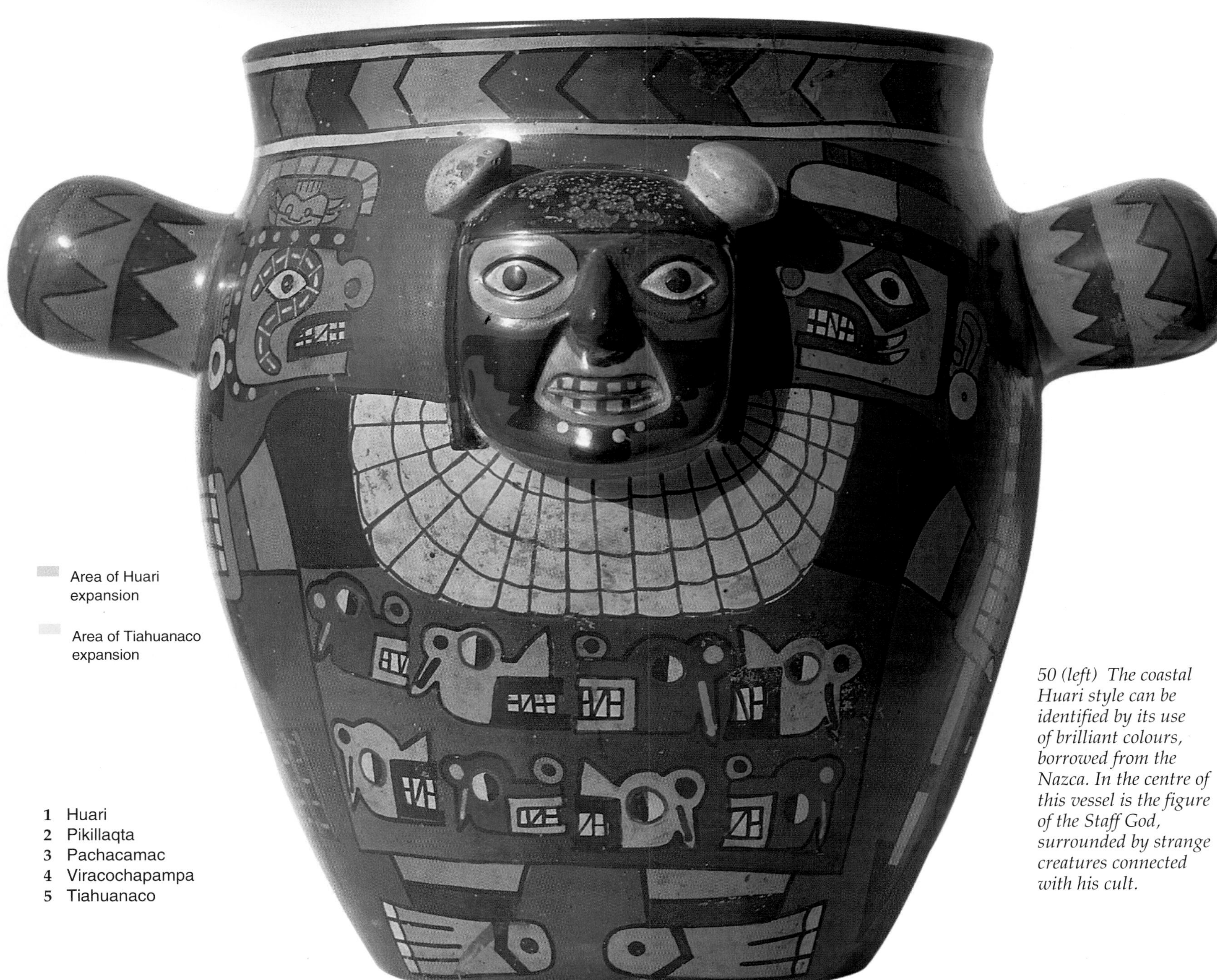

50 (left) The coastal Huari style can be identified by its use of brilliant colours, borrowed from the Nazca. In the centre of this vessel is the figure of the Staff God, surrounded by strange creatures connected with his cult.

50 (opposite above) *This Tiahuanaco-style beaker is painted with an aggressive and frightening image of the Staff God, whose cult spread throughout Peru in the Middle Horizon.*

51 (above) *Feline features, often monstrous, also appear in textiles.*

became widely diffused. The area of of Tiahuanaco's ideological and cultural influence extended to the extreme south of Peru and to the region of Atacama in northern Chile; to the southeast it reached the peninsula of Cochabamba and, if less strongly, even to northwestern Argentina. Due to the fragmentary archaeological evidence, it is almost impossible to establish whether Tiahuanaco's expansion was 'imperialist' or simply the diffusion of a religious cult linked with a form of commercial and cultural hegemony. It has been suggested that groups of warrior-priests set out from Titicaca to establish power centres in subjected provinces, so giving rise to a true theocratic empire. Yet the absence of proof of a military conquest suggests that the expansion was of a peaceful and religious nature, unifying Peru and its neighbouring areas in the worship of the Staff God.

Very different, according to the current state of research, was the rise of the other unifying force during the Middle Horizon, the Huari civilization. The Nazca, Moche and Cajamarca cultures and the small kingdoms and centres that had established themselves during the Early Intermediate Period were absorbed and subjected by this new political and military power that imposed novel artistic expressions and its own economic system, the product of an efficient, centralized structure. This transformation was radical and profound, especially in the area of central Peru. The centre of diffusion of this powerful force was the site of Huari in the region of Ayacucho, 700 km (435 miles) from Tiahuanaco. From here a group of peoples carried out a policy of expansion and conquest, subjecting other populations and creating a single, large empire.

The most outstanding innovation from this period was the emergence, perhaps for the first time in Peruvian history, of settlements on a grid layout which replaced the older

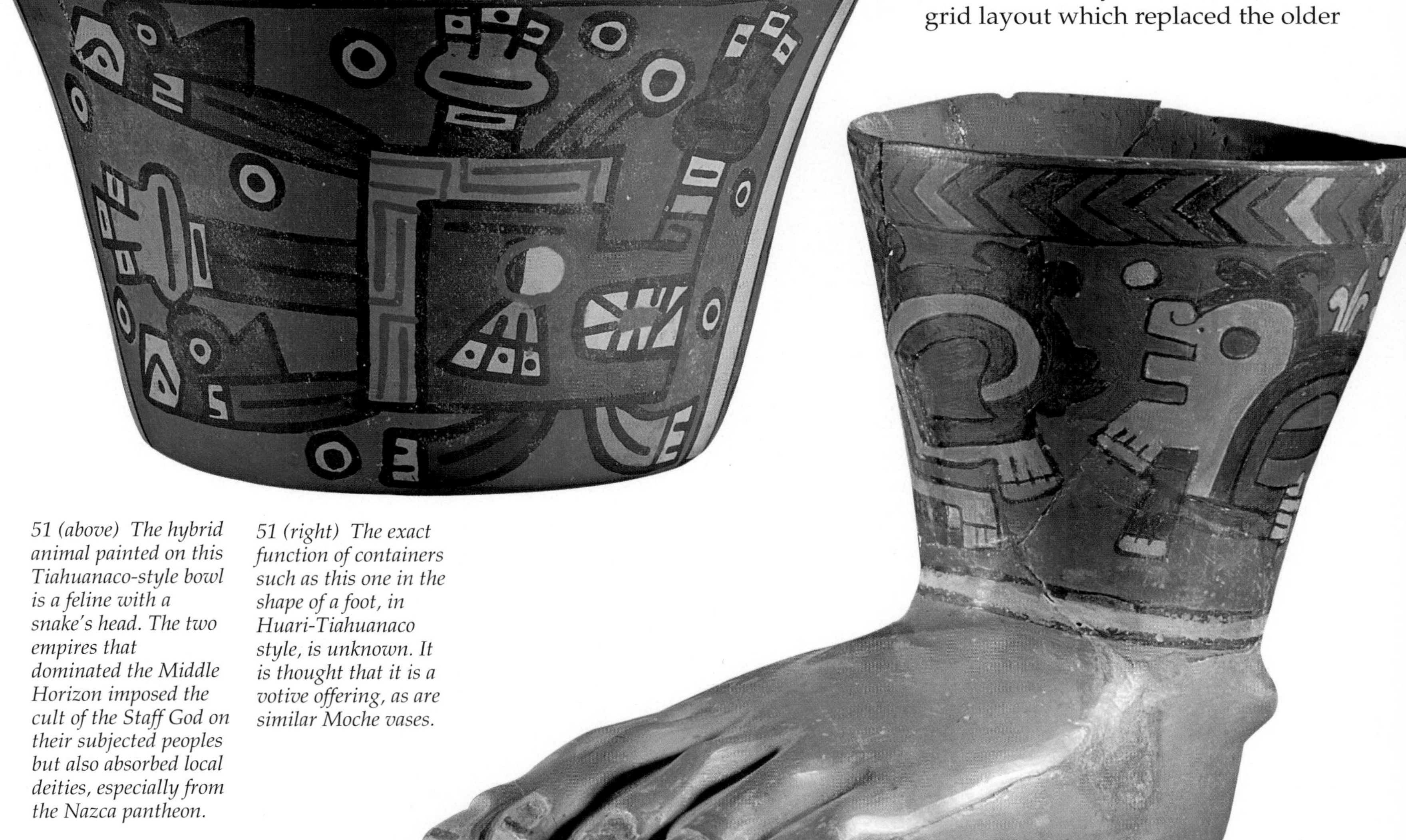

51 (above) *The hybrid animal painted on this Tiahuanaco-style bowl is a feline with a snake's head. The two empires that dominated the Middle Horizon imposed the cult of the Staff God on their subjected peoples but also absorbed local deities, especially from the Nazca pantheon.*

51 (right) *The exact function of containers such as this one in the shape of a foot, in Huari-Tiahuanaco style, is unknown. It is thought that it is a votive offering, as are similar Moche vases.*

52 (below) *Although simple, the stylized figure painted on this Huari bottle is rather striking, with the emphasis on the eyes, hands and teeth.*

52 (above) *Despite its expression, perhaps indicating a hallucinatory state, this figure appears relaxed and content. The rounded shapes of the body are emphasized by the vertical painted lines.*

designs based on ceremonial centres. Important complexes, such as Cajamarquilla, Pikillaqta and Viracochapampa, were built on the same layout as Huari along the north coast and in the Sierra. The large defensive walls that surrounded Huari cities are evidence of the strong militarization of the new society and empire.

But just as significant were the innovations associated with religious ideology. Symbols found in the fine textiles and multicoloured pottery objects include not only elements that were derived from ancient cults of the conquered peoples, but also represent the introduction of another deity. Scholarly interest in this mysterious and omnipresent figure is strong because his features are those of the Staff God of Tiahuanaco, suggesting that there was a strong link between these two centres of power during the Middle Horizon.

We do not yet know in which direction the influence travelled, whether it was of a political, military or commercial nature, and which of the two centres – Tiahuanaco or Huari – was dominant. What is certain is that the cult was imposed to such an extent that it replaced all others that had flourished in previous ages.

53 (left) Instead of the usual images of gods or monsters, this attractive vessel is in the form of a bird, depicted with remarkable realism. The feet and tail form a tripod support.

53 (below) This Huari-style figurine combines expressive force with a stylized design. The hands and arms are only hinted at in paint, in contrast with the precise modelling of the facial features. The expression and dilated eyes suggest the man is perhaps a shaman in a state of trance.

Elegant objects created by Huari craftsmen have been found even in the most peripheral areas of the empire, including large polychrome pottery containers, high-quality textiles, often decorated with feathers, jewelry, figurines made from semiprecious stones, particularly lapis lazuli and turquoise, and stone sculptures – evidence of another link with the monuments of Tiahuanaco.

Around AD 1000 almost all Huari urban centres were abandoned. Clearly a crisis undermined the foundations of the empire which brought about a political collapse, yet many aspects of the ideology and material culture were absorbed by the civilizations that followed during the Late Intermediate Period. Recent research, which will be discussed in the next section, has shown that the Inca empire derived several of its characteristics from the imprint left by the Huari and Tiahuanaco cultures. With the fall of Huari, the second unifying force of the Andean world came to an end and another phase of regionalism began; this is known as the Late Intermediate Period.

54 One of the most famous objects in Sicán art is the tumi, *a sacrificial knife made of gold or copper in the shape of a crescent moon. The fine example seen here is surmounted by a gold figurine of Nylamp, the mythical cultural hero of the Sicán civilization. The earrings and head-dress are inlaid with turquoise.*

Following the collapse of the Huari empire, many small 'kingdoms' sprang up, each with its own culture, particularly along the coast. Much fascinating evidence has been produced by excavations in this area and chroniclers have left some historical accounts recording the characteristics of, and events relating to, these peoples, who were later subjected by the Incas.

The oldest of these cultures is today called Sicán. Its development was centred in the Lambayeque valley in northern Peru and its boundaries have only been defined with certainty in the last few years. It seems that the oldest Sicán remains date from around AD 700–800, while symbolic imagery and types of pottery indicate that its cultural roots can be traced to the Moche. The peak of Sicán coincided with the Late Intermediate Period.

Oral histories handed down over the centuries tell how the Sicán people arrived from the sea, guided by their god-hero Nylamp, and settled in the Lambayeque valley. Two versions of a single tradition have come down to modern times concerning this significant founding event: the first was written by chronicler Miguel Cabello de Balboa in 1586 and the second by Ruviños y

Andrade two centuries later. Nylamp, also called Nymlap, arrived on a raft accompanied by a group of his family and retainers. He is thus a culture hero and the founding father of an ethnic group which became a new and flourishing culture. Archaeology has provided support for this oral tradition in the form of pottery and metal artifacts found in several ceremonial centres, such as Huaca el Corte, and in boot-shaped tombs.

The peak of the Sicán culture began around AD 900. This was the period in which monumental architecture was erected, large chamber tombs were dug, arsenical copper was intensively used and trading relations with the Ecuadorian coast were established. Many objects incorporate the symbolic image of a figure that corresponds closely to the description given to us by the Spanish chroniclers of the hero Nylamp, also known as the 'Sicán Lord'. He has bird-like features, including two small wings, a crescent-shaped headdress covered with feathers, and a hooked nose and pointed eyes. These features are clearly seen in the famous 'Illimo Tumi', a beautiful sacrificial knife in the shape of a half-moon. Legend has it that the mysterious man who arrived from the sea belonged to a blood-line that boasted a divine bird as its ancestor.

55 (above) Sicán tradition claims Nylamp as the founding father of this people. He is supposed to have arrived by sea on a raft with a group of retainers. This terracotta bottle includes the image of Nylamp in relief in the centre.

55 (left) The skill of the Sicán goldsmiths is evident in this gold bowl. A tiny bird with turquoise eyes perches on the handle.

56 (below) Found in a Chimú tomb, the precise function of this enigmatic wooden object is unknown. The hand is holding a sort of disc, carved with mythological scenes.

56 (right) The Chimú produced wooden objects of high quality. This figure, made from the wood of the algarroba tree, is inlaid with the motif of small fish made of mother-of-pearl. It was found with three similar figures at the site of Huaca Tacaynamo. The position of the arms of the four figures has suggested to archaeologists that they are litter bearers.

Some archaeologists believe that the Sicán culture disappeared after a prolonged drought and that its survivors were incorporated into the 'kingdom' of Chimú from about 1375. In this case, too, chronicles and archaeological evidence support one another in that Chimú (also called Chimor) was certainly the most powerful and materially the richest of all the small kingdoms of the Late Intermediate Period.

A series of urban centres was built and the Chimú overlords probably allowed each of these to develop autonomously, both economically and culturally, while they centralized administrative power. This political system was aimed mainly at the control of water for irrigation and it was certainly effective, as shown by the richness of the funerary goods and the size of the residential areas of the towns.

The largest site is Chan Chan, which covers an area of 20 sq. km (almost 8 sq. miles). Its remains are rightly considered one of the archaeological marvels of the Andes. Chan Chan contains walled enclosures surrounded by temples, roads, cisterns and houses. The walls of the most important buildings are decorated with magnificent adobe decorative friezes.

The Chimú perfected the art of metalworking, inherited from their predecessors, the Moche and Sicán peoples. They excelled in the production of vessels, gold and silver masks and jewelry, and in the art of feather-working. Their pottery, although continuing the typologies of the Early Intermediate Period, lost its originality.

Their monochrome containers, red or black – according to firing conditions – shared the globular form and stirrup-handle of the Moche culture but lacked the variety of shapes and range of colours. The huge numbers of pottery objects found suggests that they were mass produced in moulds for daily rather than ceremonial use.

While weaving reached extremely high levels of skill in the southern coastal regions, the craftsmen of the northern coast, particularly in the Lambayeque valley, placed more importance on working gold, silver and arsenical copper.

57 (above) A small masterpiece, this Chimú wooden ear ornament is decorated with a complex mosaic made from different coloured shells. The brightly coloured figure in the half-moon hat resembles one of the main characters in the mythological history of the Sicán and Chimú peoples.

57 (left) Another product of Chimú artists, the surface of this wooden box is divided into six rectangles containing stylized zoomorphic figures. A series of holes around the upper edge and on the lid suggest a cord was threaded through to fasten it.

58 (right) The Chancay pottery repertoire includes large containers in simple shapes, such as the example shown here with red-brown geometric motifs painted on a pale background. Chancay objects mainly come from burial sites.

58 (left) This small anthropomorphic container is also Chancay. The facial features have been created with great delicacy.

Chroniclers of the Colonial era tell of the existence of three other kingdoms along the coast, which, like the Chimú, were subjected by the Incas in 1450. Of one of these, called Cuismancu, no archaeological trace has yet been found and so its existence cannot be confirmed. The kingdom of Collique has been identified with the area of the Chancay culture on the central coast. The site that has yielded most remains is the cemetery of Ancón, but the originally richly provisioned

La Centinela was probably the 'capital' of the Chincha kingdom. The accomplished weaving of this people reveals the legacy of the Nazca and Paracas tradition, but their pottery was decorated with simple geometric patterns.

While the Chimú culture has left significant architectural remains, those belonging to the other small coastal 'kingdoms', although interesting, are too scanty to offer much insight into these peoples who lived along the central and south coasts in the Late Intermediate Period. Excavations continue, however, and in future it is probable that further pieces will be added to the historical and cultural jigsaw of events that preceded the rise of the last great unifying force in Pre-Columbian Peru, the Inca empire.

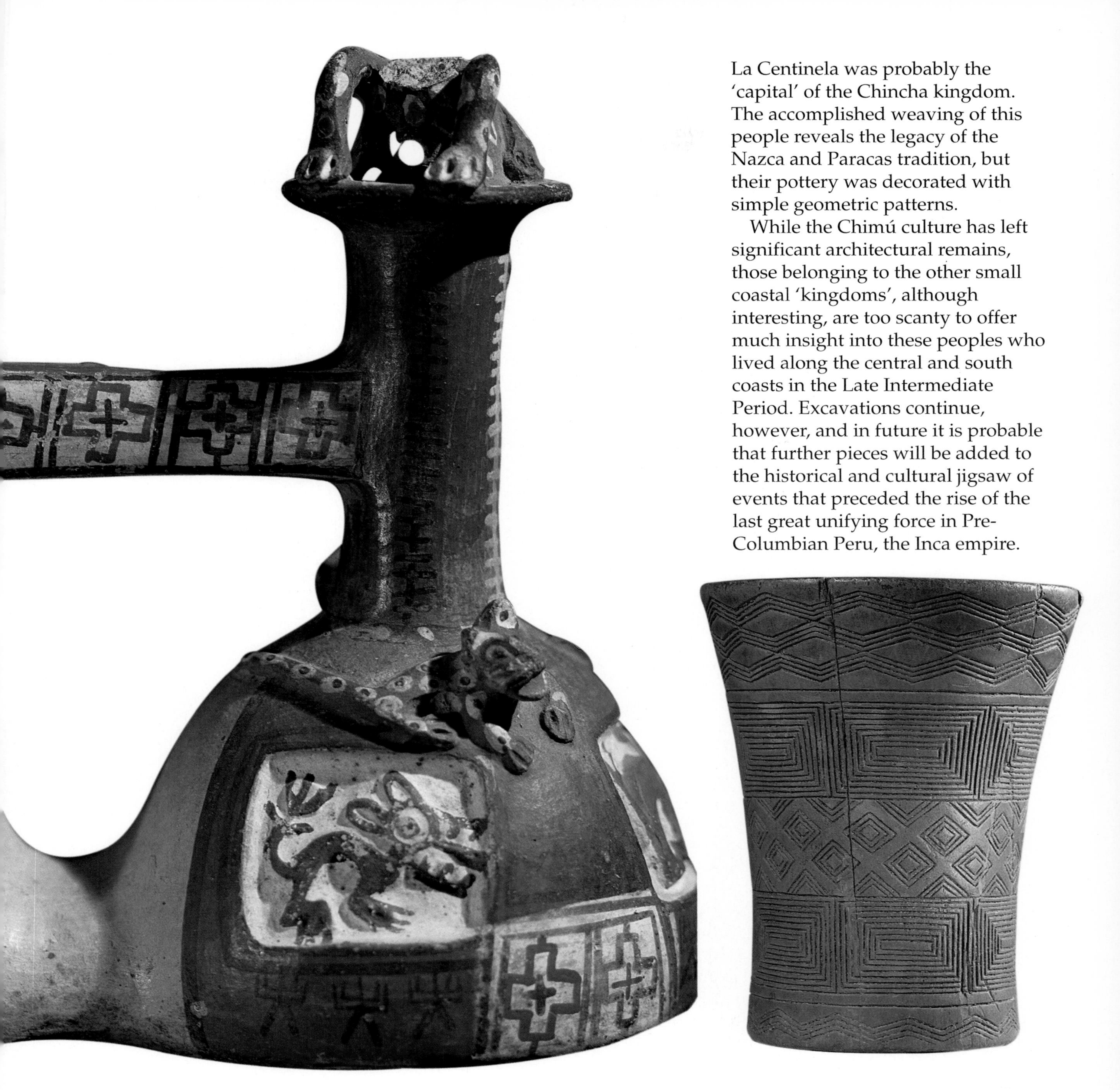

tombs have been plundered over the last two hundred years. Here, as at Paracas, the tombs contained many mummy bundles wrapped in a flexed or seated position and wearing wooden masks. Typical of the Chancay culture are the *cuchimilcos*, anthropomorphic pottery figurines of different sizes with stylized features; these were used as amulets or for worship.

Remains of the other culture mentioned by the chroniclers have been found in the area along the south coast previously inhabited by the Nazca. The kingdom of Chincha flourished in the fertile valley of the same name and in the valley of Ica. An anonymous 16th-century document provides information about this people, describing them as extremely organized and divided into groups of farmers, fishermen and merchants. The merchants travelled up and down the coast on balsa rafts and created a trading network between Ecuador and the highlands. The archaeological site of

58–59 This double container known as a 'salt-cellar' is a typical example of the fusion of Inca and Chancay styles, seen also in the geometric decoration in red and brown.

59 (right) This vessel is a kero, *a type of wooden beaker used for ritual libations. It has been dated to the Inca period but the style of the geometric decoration reveals the strong influence of southern coastal cultures and resembles motifs painted on Chancay pottery.*

THE LATE HORIZON
THE INCA EMPIRE

Maximum extent of the Inca empire
— Communications network

1 Tulcán
2 Quito
3 Chachapoyas
4 Cajamarca
5 Moche
6 Chavín
7 Pachacamac
8 Tambo Colorado
9 Machu Picchu
10 Ollantaytambo
11 Cuzco
12 Nazca
13 Tiahuanaco
14 San Pedro de Atacama
15 Cumcó

Although archaeological research over the last decades has unearthed a wealth of information about the Pre-Columbian Andean world, the origins of the Inca civilization still remain shrouded in mystery. What is known is that one of the small kingdoms formed during the Late Intermediate Period in the region of Cuzco managed to establish itself through force and then by cultural dominance. We know a great deal about the so-called Inca 'imperial age' because of the detailed information of the Spanish chroniclers of the 16th century, but evidence of the formation of the Inca ethnic group is scarce.

Inca history is permeated with legends that have been handed down orally. The most frequently told legends at the court of Cuzco at the time of the Conquest concerned the ancestor couple of the Incas. Their names were Manco Capac, the hero-civilizer, and his sister and wife, Mama Ocllo. These mythical figures were sent from the waters of Lake Titicaca by their father, the sun god Inti-Viracocha, and travelled to Cuzco to bring a new culture there. Another version relates that the founders of the line were four semi-divine brothers called the Ayar who tried to colonize the region of Cuzco with their sister-wives. Following a series of adversities, only one of the brothers, Ayar Manco, survived with his wife, Mama Ocllo, who together founded the capital of the future empire. Many other stories were told to the Spaniards and though we can be sure that historical fact is hidden in these myths, it is very difficult to separate one from the other.

60 (opposite above) The chronicles of Guaman Poma de Ayala tell of four legendary-historical periods, also called 'generations'. This drawing taken from his account shows the first of these periods: the Wari Viracocha Runa ('white peoples'), who were descendants of Noah sent by God to populate the Earth. The text contains elements of Andean traditions mixed with Christian beliefs.

60 (opposite below) Manco Capac was the legendary founder of the Inca dynasty. This ancestor figure of the Incas may have come from the region of Lake Titicaca. In this drawing taken from the accounts of Guaman Poma de Ayala he is shown wearing an unku *decorated with geometric patterns called* tocapu.

60–61 These portraits painted in oil by an anonymous 18th-century artist show the dynasty of Inca rulers, descendants of Manco Capac and Mama Ocllo. No historical proof of the first seven kings exists, and they may simply have been legendary characters.

There is a similar problem concerning the dynastic succession of the Inca emperors. The list as it existed in the centuries following the Spanish Conquest contained thirteen names, of which the first was Manco Capac and the last Atahualpa. Yet it is only from the ninth emperor, Inca Yupanqui (Pachacuti or Pachacutec), who came to power around AD 1438, that dates and events can be related to historical facts.

It seems that, until the middle of the 13th century, the Incas were just one of the many ethnic groups that lived in the valleys around the site of the future Cuzco. It was only during the following decades that they organized a form of rule based on their military successes over the peoples in the neighbouring valleys. Around 1400 they succeeded in creating a true 'state'. The determining factor in their rapid development was the ever-growing threat from the war-like Chanca people settled in the valley of the river Pampas who had formed a powerful confederacy some time earlier. Some scholars think that the Chanca were descended from the ancient Huari civilization. Intimidated by the rise and expansion of the new power in the southern valleys and having expelled the Quechua tribes from their own lands, the Chanca tried to put pressure on the Incas in an attempt to slow their military and economic rise, but it was they who were defeated in a bloody battle sometime between 1430 and 1440. Pachacuti ascended to the throne around this period, putting an end to the disputes with the bellicose Chanca. After his victory he was awarded the honorary title 'Inca'.

Little archaeological evidence exists relating to the legends of the birth and consolidation of the Inca kingdom following their defeat of the Chanca and other hostile peoples such as the Colla and the Lupaca. Several interesting theories have been put forward, however. As a result of research carried out during the 1960s, some archaeologists, including the American J.H. Rowe, claimed that the origins of the Inca

civilization should be looked for not in the cultural and geographical area of the highlands of Cuzco but in the region that was once dominated by the Huari and, probably, in the region of Tiahuanaco. In spite of strong criticism by opponents of this theory, it has recently received some support from investigations of finds dating from the Middle Horizon, the age in which the Huari civilization dominated and unified the Andean world. Huari domination strongly influenced an ethnic group today called the Quotakalli that was settled in the northern part of Cuzco valley and known from its pottery. During the centuries following the fall of the Huari civilization, the Quotakalli did not lose their links and affinities with their overlords but maintained their fundamental traits. These eventually found their way into the Killke culture, whose pottery production is classified as belonging to the 'early Inca' period that preceded the 'imperial Inca' age. Indeed, finds relating to the Killke culture seem to belong to a precise moment in history, corresponding to the ascent to the throne of Pachacuti.

In addition to elements that were particular to the region of Cuzco, the Killke culture therefore seems to have been strongly influenced by the Huari civilization. This influence was not limited to material culture and pottery design, but was later also to emerge more clearly in the

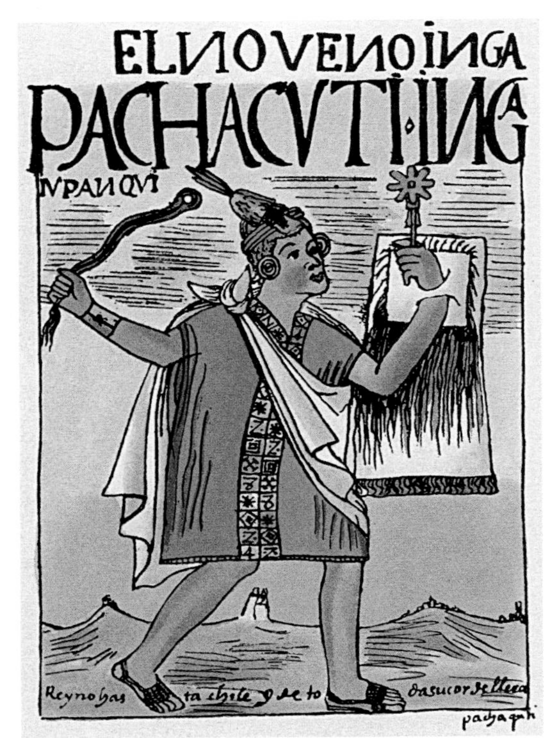

62 (centre) Pachacuti or Pachacutec was one of the most famous rulers in the history of Tahuantinsuyu. In this drawing the king is shown elegantly dressed in his regal tunic, an unku, *and holding a shield. His head-dress is decorated with feathers from the mythical bird, the* corequenque, *according to Garcilaso de la Vega.*

62 (below) A drawing of the meeting of the Camachicoc Apocuna, *or High Council, an element of Inca administration: the emperor is visible in the foreground, surrounded by high ranking counsellors; he carries a sceptre and is wearing an* unku *decorated with geometric patterns.*

62 (opposite right) *This drawing by Guaman Poma de Ayala depicts a battle between two armies. On the left, the Inca army is led by the ruler wearing a plumed helmet; the enemy is a rebellious tribe unwilling to accept Inca dominance.*

63 (centre) *Inca roads often crossed bridges made from vegetable fibres that spanned deep gorges. The drawing shows a* Chaca Camayoc, *an official whose responsibility was to oversee the construction and management of bridges.*

63 (below) *An Inca and his wife, both elegantly dressed, are depicted at the celebration of the last festival of the year linked to the seasonal cycles: the* Capac Inti Raymi, *which took place in December and was dedicated to the sun god Inti. At this festival both llamas and children were sacrificed in the god's honour.*

imperialist and militarist ideology of the Inca world and in its model of political and social organization. No other example of a similar political system has yet been documented in this region. Given the current state of our knowledge, therefore, it can be suggested that the emergence of the last Andean empire – the Inca – was closely associated with strong Huari influence and that unarguable similarities existed between the two. Furthermore, considering the close relationship between the Huari and Tiahuanaco civilizations, it is possible to connect the legends that speak of the origins of the Incas in the region of Lake Titicaca with the archaeological evidence.

Due to the many question marks that still hang over the origin of the Incas, it is difficult to suggest precise dates for the main historical events. In the chronology formulated by J.H. Rowe, which is considered the most reliable, the beginning of the Inca dynasty is put at around AD 1200.

From that moment on, the kingdom continued to grow in strength until the ascent of Pachacuti, supposedly the ninth Inca, to the throne around 1438. This prince's original name was Cusi Yupanqui but, following the crushing defeat of the Chanca, he changed it to Pachacutec Inca Yupanqui.

63 (top) *The* Quipu Camayoc *(master of the* quipu*) was a kind of accountant who used the* quipu *to record information. It was his duty to keep the Inca regularly informed of the economic and financial situation of the empire.*

63 (above) *This fine example of a* quipu *consists of a series of knotted strings hanging from a crosspiece. Using this tool, the Incas were able to record exact numbers of animals and quantities of agricultural products. Recent studies have shown that the* quipu *could also be used for literary purposes and record keeping.*

The king settled in the city of Cuzco and initiated a policy of expansion that took his kingdom to a position of supremacy over the many other groups in the region. As head of the army, with his brother Capac Yupanqui and his son Tupac Inca, Pachacuti embarked on a series of conquests to strengthen his power and to expand the borders of the Inca state. These military campaigns were the first move in the creation of the empire.

Around 1450, the Inca army conquered the territory of the Colla people who lived on the shores of Lake Titicaca; shortly after, they overran the region of Arequipa, reaching the southern coast. To the north they captured territory as far as the city of Cajamarca, almost 1,000 km (620 miles) from Cuzco, in the meantime putting down a revolt by the Chanca. Along the northern coast, the Chimú king, warned of the advance of the Incas, sent an army against them, but his capital, Chan Chan, fell into Inca hands around 1463; the last king, Minchançaman, was forced to capitulate. The advance of the Inca army continued unchecked along the northern coast as far as the area of Quito, which was annexed together with the lands of several Ecuadorian tribes.

Around 1471, when the Inca troops had returned to Cuzco, Tupac Inca succeeded his father as ruler and continued the policy of conquest. At the end of his reign, which lasted at least 22 years, the Inca empire ruled the greater part of the southern Andes, and lands which today are part of Chile, Bolivia and Argentina were included within its borders. Following the assassination of Tupac Inca, his son Huayna Capac ascended the throne. He undertook numerous expeditions to the northern territories of the empire to put down revolts by subjected peoples, many of whom were openly opposed to the conquerors. The ruler was made clearly aware of the difficulties involved in running a large empire that included different ethnic groups speaking various languages and practising local customs. His political and military problems were exacerbated by the arrival of an unknown and incurable epidemic which began to decimate his people. It is thought today that the sickness was smallpox, transmitted to the indigenous population by contacts with the Spaniards who were settled in Darien, now Panama. Huayna Capac, already alarmed by the difficult situation and by the rumours of the approach of bearded white men with strange animals, was himself struck down by the illness and died in 1527.

After its brief but glorious peak, the Inca kingdom entered into a decline caused more than anything by the struggle between the two sons of the dead ruler: Huascar, who was was the designated successor to the throne, and his ambitious brother, Atahualpa. The foolish greed and jealousy that caused this

64 (top) A stylized drawing of Cuzco, as seen through the eyes of Guaman Poma de Ayala. Only a few traces remain of the ancient capital's walls and buildings, incorporated into buildings of the Colonial era.

64 (above left) The tenth king of the Inca dynasty, depicted in this drawing, was Tupac Inca, who reigned c. *1471–93. He was famous for his territorial conquests and maritime expeditions.*

64 (above right) Inca Huayna Capac was the eleventh ruler of the dynasty and reigned c. *1493–1527. After his death, the Inca empire began to fall apart due to the rivalry between his sons Huascar and Atahualpa. The picture shows the Inca armed with a lance and shield and wearing an* unku *and a helmet decorated with the feathers of the* corequenque.

65 (opposite) A view of Cuzco, the Inca capital considered by its inhabitants to be the centre of the world, from the book Civitates Orbis Terrarum. *Clearly visible are the grid layout of the town centre, inherited from the Huari civilization, and, on the left, a palace or temple. The Inca himself is being carried by servants in the foreground.*

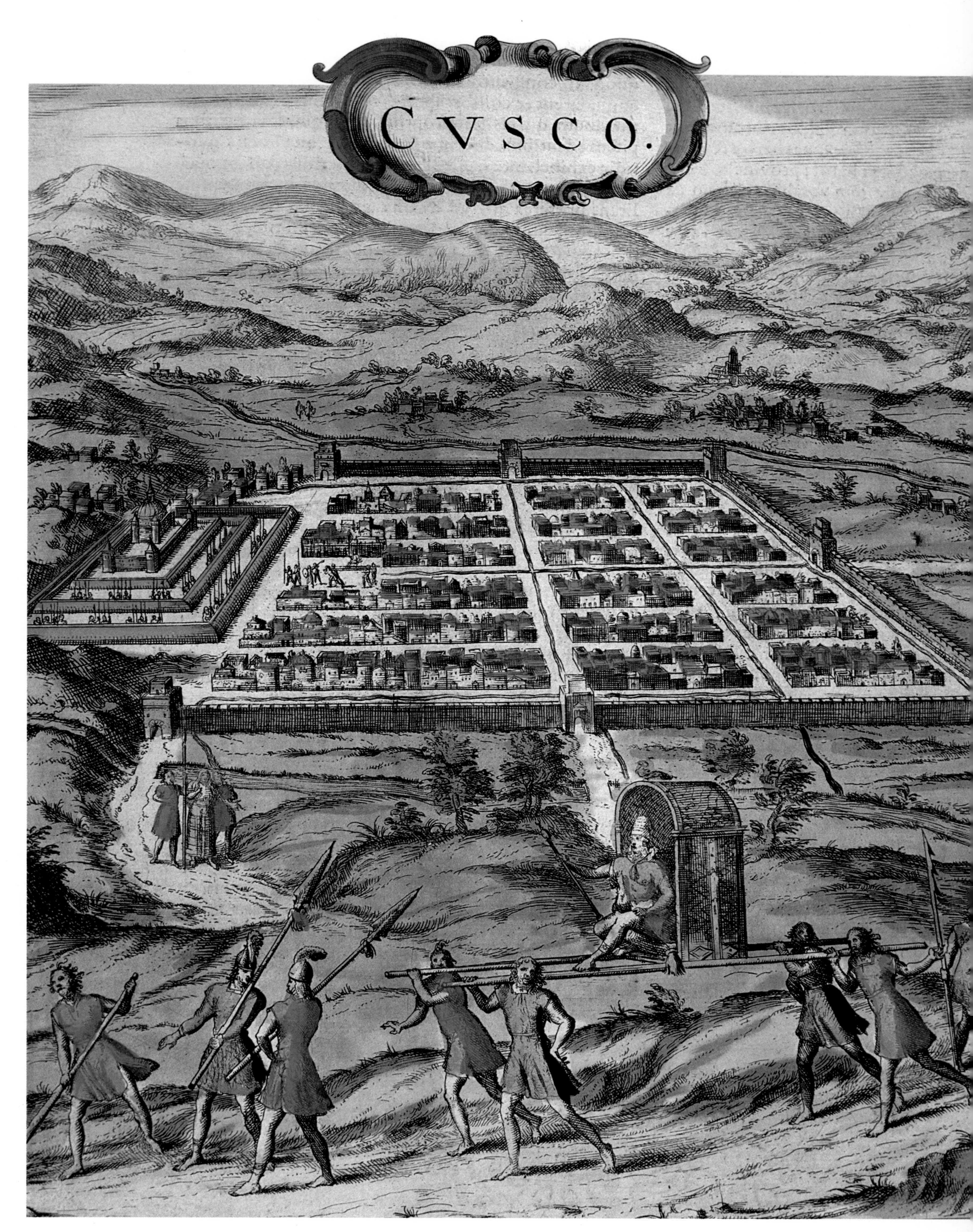
CVSCO.

war contributed to the weakening of Inca power and opened the way for the European Conquistadors, who overran the great Andean empire in very a short time.

But what was the rapid development of Inca power founded on, and what was it that allowed a small state to transform itself into a gigantic empire during the reign of Tupac Inca? It was probably a series of interlinked elements: the absolute power of the rulers; the exceptional organization of the army; and a state and society structured according to a rigid hierarchy. Today we wrongly call the empire 'Inca', but its correct name is Tahuantinsuyu. This is a Quechua word, the language spoken by the Inca people, which literally means 'The Four Quarters United'. 'Inca' was simply the title given to the rulers, who might inherit it at birth or be awarded it for their qualities – it was analogous to the title Caesar given to Roman leaders. It is usual to call the people Inca too – their original name is still unknown – as well as the civilization as a whole.

The empire was divided into four parts, each of which was called a *suyu*. Each *suyu* was further divided into provinces with an urban centre from which a local governor ruled. Cuzco was considered the 'centre of the world' by its inhabitants as it was the ideal geographical centre of Tahuantinsuyu, as well as the centre of power. Yet, despite its organization and extent, the empire was not unified but was rather a vast confederation of ethnic groups with their own cultural and linguistic characteristics, only tied to Cuzco by treaties and alliances. Contrary perhaps to popular imagination, these alliances were often not the result of Inca conquest. One of the methods the Inca rulers adopted to promote their imperialist policies was that of 'reciprocity'. The Inca in person, or an army representative, met with the ruler of another kingdom or tribe and presented him with gifts, including women exchanged as wives. He then proposed the annexation of the lands to the Inca state. If the ruler of the lesser power accepted, the enticing promises were kept and sealed with banquets. If the offer was refused, battle ensued which nearly always ended in an Inca victory and the capture of the leader who had dared oppose the will of his powerful adversary. It is therefore not surprising that the foundations of the political balance of Tahuantinsuyu were weak and that the Inca leader was forced to put down continual rebellions and to devise strategies to maintain the cohesion of his immense territory.

One of these was the imposition of a common language, Quechua, on the political and administrative élite, although the use of local dialects was not prohibited. Quechua was probably spoken by the oldest tribes in the Cuzco region; it was then adopted by the Incas and spread throughout the empire during the 15th and 16th centuries. Today it is still spoken by three million people in the Peruvian Andes. Imperial officials were sent to the different regions to teach Quechua, and the sons of the nobles who governed the annexed provinces were required to go to school in Cuzco to assimilate

66 (right) A group of soldiers and officials pays homage to the ruler. The Inca is seated on a throne placed on a sort of pedestal and covered by a canopy adorned with feathers. Those present all wear symbols of power: the head-dresses and ear-spools are particularly reminiscent of the ornaments worn by the god-hero Nylamp.

66 (opposite, centre) A map of the Inca empire, more correctly called Tahuantinsuyu in Quechua, meaning 'The Four Quarters United': it was divided into four regions or suyus *(Chinchasuyu, Contisuyu, Collasuyu and Antisuyu), each located in a particular direction. Cuzco, naturally, was at the heart of the four regions and was considered the centre of the world.*

67 (below left) The storehouses of Tahuantinsuyu, which held the produce and goods of the empire, were called collcas *and were managed by a functionary called a* collca camayoc. *Here, this official is shown making his report to the Inca by referring to his* quipu *for information.*

Inca culture. Another political strategy was that of the *mitmac*. These were forced migrations in which groups of people, sometimes entire populations, were transferred from their homeland to other regions, often distant and already colonized, so that they could adapt quickly to Inca customs.

The officials of the empire were charged with administering the provinces and taxing the inhabitants. A *quipu* – a recording device perhaps inherited from the Huari – was used for this purpose. It consisted of wool or cotton strings fastened at one end to a cross cord; simple or compound knots tied in the strings represented information.

67 (centre) An administrator of the Inca is depicted in this drawing by Guaman Poma de Ayala. He is shown with two quipu, *his main work tool. The* suyuyoc *were leading representatives of each* apo *or province of the empire. The word* apo *comes from the Quechua word for tribal chiefs.*

67 (above right) The offer of young women was a common means of obtaining favours, cementing alliances and negotiating peace. This drawing shows an Inca dignitary presenting two females during negotiations with the Spaniards.

Studies of the *quipu* have discovered that each was different from the others (for example, the colour and length of the strings) but had a meaning that all versed in *quipu* could understand.

In 1910, the archaeologist Locke discovered an element that was common to all *quipu*: the groups of strings represented numbers and each knot was a value in the decimal system. The *quipu* was therefore a tool for recording quantities and was used above all for assessing the economic assets of the empire.

The cities and provinces were connected to Cuzco and each other by an immense network of roads, many originating in the Huari period, which extended along the coast and into the mountains. The *chasqui*, message carriers used by the Inca, ran dozens of miles each day along paths, across rope bridges over rivers, and up and down steep flights of mountain steps, stopping only at rest places called *tambo*. It is important to remember that the Incas had no animals for transportation or traction, such as mules or horses, which is why they never built carts or similar vehicles, nor did they develop practical uses for the wheel. Goods were carried on people's backs or on llamas.

The different ethnic groups were obliged to convert to the official religion of the empire, the worship of the sun, although local cults were permitted as well as that of the ancient Creator Deity, Viracocha. A new temple dedicated to Inti, the sun, was built beside that of the ancient Creator Deity at the enormous sanctuary of Pachacamac on the coast which had been a place of pilgrimage for centuries. Besides the gods, the Inca himself was also worshipped as the incarnation and son of the sun – this was in addition to his absolute power as sole political and religious leader, comparable with the authority of the Egyptian pharaohs. He reigned assisted by his wife-sister, called Coya, and supported by a swarm of dignitaries and officials whose responsibilities were assigned according to a strict pyramidal hierarchy. According to the chroniclers, land was divided between religion, state and community.

THE CONQUEST AND THE FALL OF THE INCA EMPIRE

68 (opposite) This portrait of Atahualpa, the thirteenth Inca, was painted in the 18th century. His violent dispute with Huascar, his brother, contributed to the weakening of the political power of the empire and facilitated the Spanish Conquest.

69 (below) Here the members of the royal family are seen on a journey, being carried on a litter protected by a feathered canopy.

69 (above left) Francisco Pizarro brought the Inca empire to an end, capturing Atahualpa and condemning him to death in 1533.

69 (above right) The Inca Huascar was taken prisoner on the orders of his brother Atahualpa. Here he is seen with his hands tied behind his back and held by a cord around his neck. The soldier on the right is blowing the Strombus shell trumpet to announce the capture.

On the death of the Inca Huayna Capac, around 1527, a violent struggle for succession broke out at the court at Cuzco between Huascar, the legitimate son and designated heir of the dead king, and Atahualpa, called 'the bastard' as he was the natural son of the king. It should be noted that succession in Tahuantinsuyu was not simply by primogeniture, rather the heir was chosen from among the many sons of the Inca by the members of the nobility on the basis of his merits and abilities. To put an end to the damaging conflict, Huascar was assigned the throne of Cuzco while Atahualpa was elected ruler of Quito, the second city in importance in the empire. This division inevitably brought about the decline and weakening of monarchic power and it was exactly this situation that facilitated the Spanish Conquest.

The captain of the expedition, Francisco Pizarro, had already undertaken several exploratory expeditions along the coast of Ecuador and Colombia and these had persuaded him that the legendary El Dorado spoken of by the natives of Darien was not far away. In 1527 he returned to Spain to obtain the necessary finances to undertake his ambitious project.

In 1532, Pizarro set sail for Peru with fewer resources at his disposal than he had hoped for – no more than 60 soldiers on horseback and 110 foot-soldiers. None the less, his ambition and greed for the fabled treasures drove him onwards. He landed at Tumbes, which, when he had been there ten years earlier, had all the appearance of a rich and bustling city, but he immediately realized that something had changed. Everywhere there were signs of death and suffering caused either by epidemics or war. The inhabitants, now accustomed to Europeans, explained that in the distant city of Cajamarca was the ruler Atahualpa, who was locked in a bitter struggle with his brother. As they progressed towards Cajamarca, the Spaniards soon realized that the people of the empire were very dissatisfied with Atahualpa because of his increasing ill-treatment of them in the form of heavy taxation and the obligation to sacrifice children to protect the health of the Inca. This discontent towards the rulers of the empire clearly favoured the purpose of the Europeans and Pizarro quickly appreciated that these circumstances would make it easier for him to encourage the locals to rise up against Atahualpa.

He and his men left Cajas and crossed the passes of the Andes to reach Cajamarca where Atahualpa was waiting, ready to welcome the bearded strangers from the sea. Atahualpa agreed to meet Pizarro in the main square of the city where he offered the Spaniard chicha in great goblets of gold according to the Inca custom.

The next day, disregarding the hospitality of the Inca, the Spaniards laid a trap for him and on the pretext that he had refused to honour the Cross and the Bible, Atahualpa was captured and his men slaughtered. To obtain his liberty, Atahualpa promised to give the Spaniards as much gold as could be held in one of the rooms of the royal palace. Pizarro accepted and took possession of some of the treasure that had been reserved for the Spanish king, Charles V. Shortly afterwards, in 1533, some members of the élite faithful to Atahualpa killed his brother Huascar who was suspected of collaborating with the Spaniards. Using the excuse of a rebellion by those faithful to the imprisoned king, Pizarro accused Atahualpa of high treason and condemned him to death on the pyre, the penalty for heretics.

For the Inca, cremation was unacceptable as it separated the soul from the body. Atahualpa was instead beheaded in exchange for conversion to Catholicism. To the desperation and dismay of the

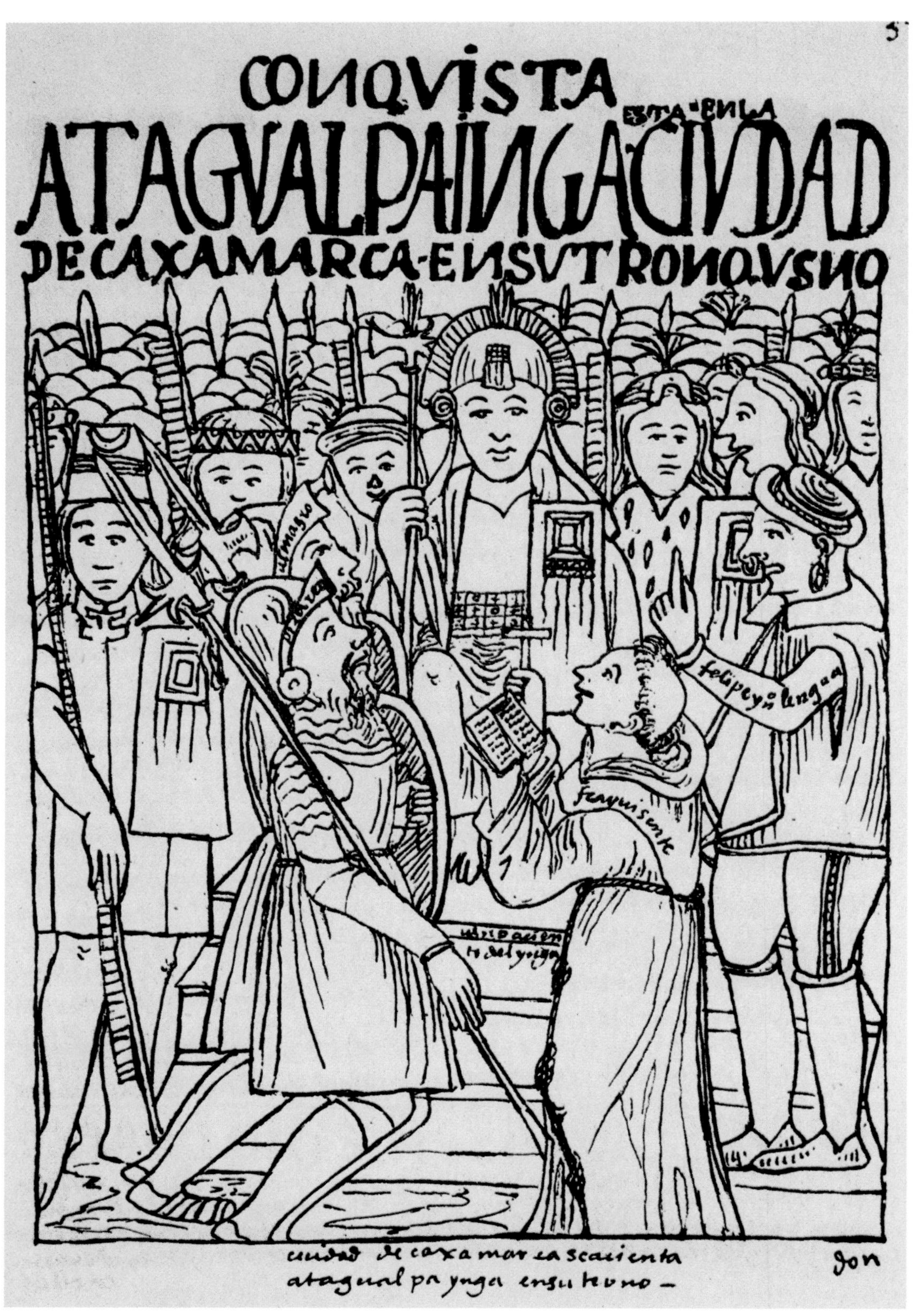

70 (top) In this graphic drawing by Poma de Ayala the death sentence is being carried out on Inca Atahualpa by the soldiers of Francisco Pizarro.

70 (above) Here Atahualpa is shown before his execution, seated with his hands and feet tied. Note the corequenque *feathers on the Inca's head that signify his status. One of Pizarro's guards is sitting next to the last Inca ruler.*

70 (right) Pizarro met Atahualpa at Cajamarca and attempted to convert him to Catholicism.

members of the royal family, Pizarro's next move was to place another member of the dynasty on the throne as a puppet monarch. His first choice, a younger brother of Atahualpa, was poisoned soon after, and he then chose another brother, Manco Inca. The Conquistadors now had an open road to the capital, Cuzco, and could take possession of the treasures they had so long been searching for. In Cuzco they first plundered the gold that lined the walls and gardens of Coricancha, the Temple of the Sun. This was the final blow for Tahuantinsuyu, already weakened by the lengthy internal struggles – and for Inca civilization.

The Spaniards had not yet won the whole battle, however: on one side they found themselves fighting the resistance of Manco Inca and his men, and on the other they had to overcome violent disagreements in their own ranks.

The two captains, Francisco Pizarro and Diego de Almagro, were no longer companions but enemies and they were both assassinated by their opponent's supporting faction. Their successors were obliged to continue fighting the armed resistance of the sons of Manco – Titu Cusi Yupanqui and Tupac Amaru. The first, who had lived with the Spaniards since he was a boy, wanted to create a new Inca state with Spanish recognition and support. His plan failed miserably, however, as his father submitted to the enemy and converted to Catholicism. Tupac Amaru continued his struggle against the Spanish until 1572 when he was captured and beheaded. His death marked the final curtain of the great empire of Tahuantinsuyu that had dominated the Andes for a short period and achieved political, military and cultural pre-eminence. Spanish chroniclers have left us detailed accounts of its history, while others, vaguer and more fragmentary, relate to the peoples subjected by the Incas. The most important were Garcilazo de La Vega, son of a Spanish captain and an Inca princess and author of the Royal Commentaries, and Guaman Poma de Ayala, author of *El primer nueva corónica y buen gobierno.*

71 (above) Tupac Amaru was the last Inca. He was captured and condemned to death by the Spaniards in 1572.

71 (above) This 1602 illustration shows the capture of Cuzco by Pizarro's troops soon after Atahualpa's execution. The soldiers first sacked the Coricancha, the famous 'Temple of the Sun'. A few remains of the Inca city survive, incorporated in buildings of the Colonial period.

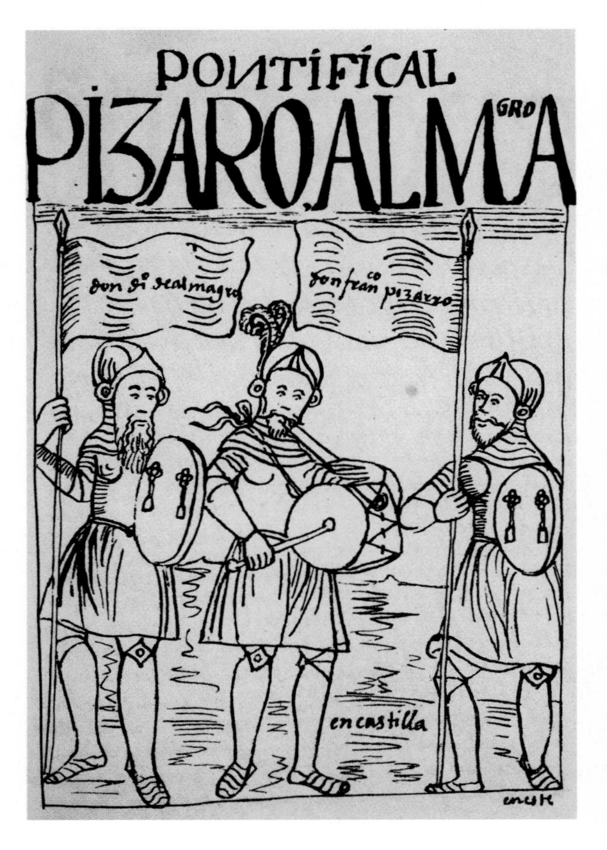

71 (right) Francisco Pizarro and Diego de Almagro were originally companions at the head of the Spanish army but later became bitter enemies. Both died during the internecine struggle that tore the Spanish forces apart after the death of Atahualpa and the dismantling of the Inca empire.

PRE-COLUMBIAN CIVILIZATIONS IN ECUADOR AND COLOMBIA

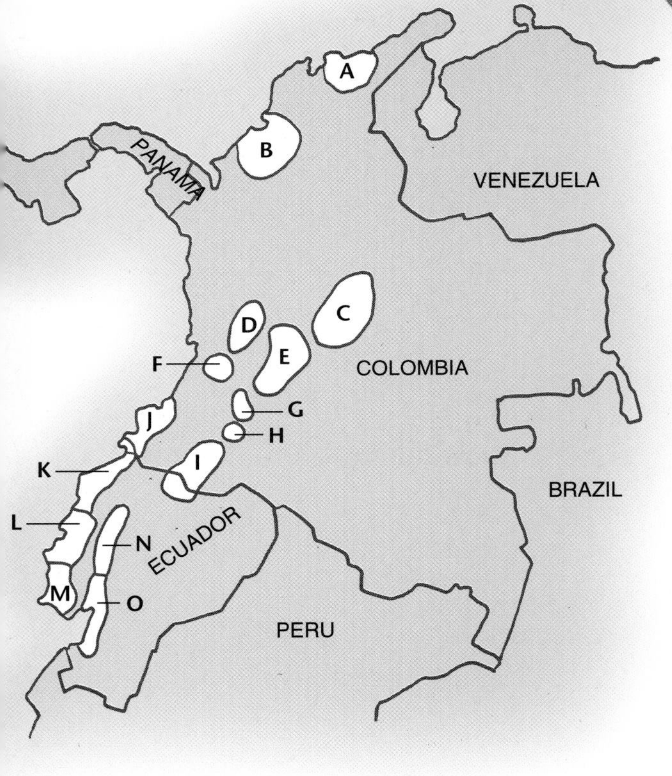

A Tairona
B Sinú
C Muisca
D Quimbaya
E Tolima
F Calima
G Tierra Adentro
H San Augustín
I Nariño
J La Tolita
K Jama-Coaque
L Bahia
M Guangala
N Quevedo
O Milagro

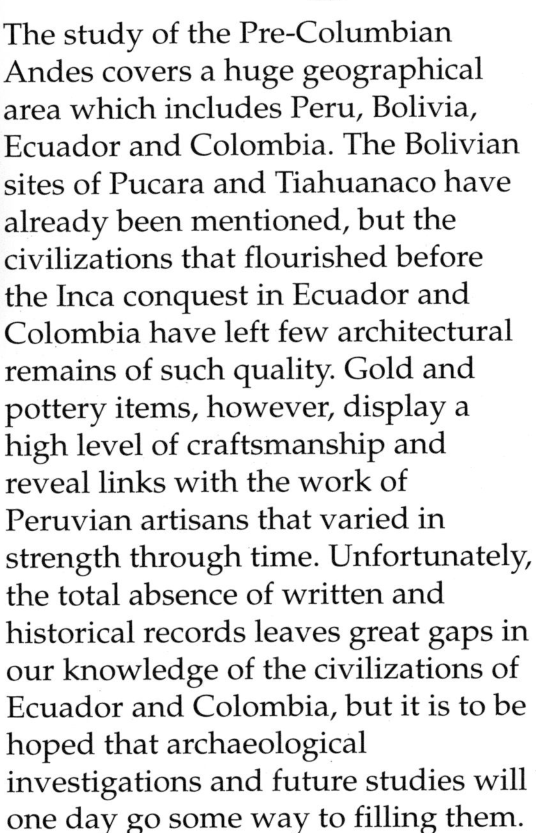

The study of the Pre-Columbian Andes covers a huge geographical area which includes Peru, Bolivia, Ecuador and Colombia. The Bolivian sites of Pucara and Tiahuanaco have already been mentioned, but the civilizations that flourished before the Inca conquest in Ecuador and Colombia have left few architectural remains of such quality. Gold and pottery items, however, display a high level of craftsmanship and reveal links with the work of Peruvian artisans that varied in strength through time. Unfortunately, the total absence of written and historical records leaves great gaps in our knowledge of the civilizations of Ecuador and Colombia, but it is to be hoped that archaeological investigations and future studies will one day go some way to filling them.

The history of Pre-Columbian Ecuador has been divided into different periods on the basis of archaeological finds: the Paleo-Indio Period, the Archaic Period, the Formative Period, the Era of Regionalism, the Era of Integration and the Age of the Incas. The Formative Period (4000–200 BC) is further subdivided into three phases. The first phase (4000/3500–1500 BC) is linked to the culture of Valdivia, whose existence was noted in 1956 following research by the archaeologist Emilio Estrada. The most important finds from this ancient Ecuadorian civilization are the famous ceramic figurines, the 'Venuses of Valdivia'.

A few years after their discovery, Estrada and American archaeologists dated them to around 3200 BC. This was very significant as it meant that at the time these figurines represented the oldest pottery finds in the New World. However, at the beginning of the 1990s, archaeologist Anna Roosevelt discovered pottery fragments along the delta of the river Marajo in Brazil which have been dated to approximately 6000 BC.

On the basis of their discoveries, Estrada and his colleagues confirmed the existence of a 'formative' culture along the Ecuadorian coast which had not previously been suspected. Following extensive studies of the Valdivian pottery figures, Estrada and his colleague Betty Meggers published some controversial conclusions: they claimed that the oldest Ecuadorian pottery was not produced there but crossed the Pacific following contacts, perhaps by chance, between the peoples of Ecuador and navigators from Japan carrying pottery of the Jomon culture. Not surprisingly, many scholars did not agree with this startling interpretation. The famous archaeologist Donald Lathrap was one who did not share their opinions. He felt instead that they had identified an indigenous cultural trait linked with agriculture and dating from the origins of the Valdivian culture.

It is likely that Early Valdivian agriculture originated in the fertile

72 (opposite above) *These touching female figurines with their elaborate hairstyles, each hold a baby in their arms. The theme of maternity was quite common in the pottery of the Bahia culture.*

72 (opposite below) *This head is a beautiful example of La Tolita pottery; it is simple but refined and the face has been perfectly realized.*

73 *Representations of humans and divine beings occur frequently in La Tolita pottery. This seated figure is perhaps a guardian deity connected with snakes.*

valleys of the Guayas and other small rivers, even if there is currently no archaeological evidence to support this theory. Remains of huts and stake-holes have been found on the Valdivia site, indicating that the inhabited area had an oval plan. The houses were built entirely from perishable materials such as cane and mud, with roofs probably made from palm leaves, as are still found in the area today.

Remains of a village of the same culture have also been found at Reál Alto. The village comprises seven buildings, a square and two mounds probably intended for ceremonial use. The peoples of Valdivia and Reál Alto fished, gathered molluscs and hunted. Although dating from a later period, evidence of the cultivation of maize, squash, beans, cotton and yuca means that these villages can be described as the first examples of a farming society in Ecuador.

The Machalilla culture developed in Ecuador during the second phase of the Formative Period (1500–1200 BC). This culture produced fine pottery, such as vessels with a lip, unlike the simple Valdivian containers that were inspired by squashes and decorated with pyrographic techniques. Machalilla pottery includes the first Ecuadorian examples of vessels in the shapes of animals or plants, not dissimilar to those of the Moche. The origin of the Machalilla is a subject of controversy: although Machalilla pottery has been found in archaeological levels immediately above those containing Valdivian pottery, suggesting a chronological and stylistic evolution between the two, some think that Machalilla pottery was imported. Machalilla pottery styles continued to evolve during the third phase of the Formative Period (1200–200 BC) and were then taken up by the Chorrera culture.

74 A female figure, perhaps a priestess, sits at the top of a stepped structure, possibly a temple. The external surface of this Jama-Coaque vessel is covered in elegant relief decorations that were originally painted in bright colours.

The Chorrera people evolved in the coastal areas and spread into the Sierra. Theirs was a structured farming society with trading links reaching as far as Chavín de Huántar in Peru and the Calima culture in Colombia. One of the principal units of exchange was the Spondylus shell, called *mullu* in Quechua. It was considered the food of the gods and a symbol of fertility. The Chorrera people lived in villages on artificial mounds arranged around a vast open area used for gatherings and ceremonies. Chorrera potters adopted and developed the forms and types of Machalilla ceramics, expanding the range of symbolism and perfecting the representation of human beings.

In the Era of Regional Development (300 BC–AD 500), some of Ecuador's fundamental cultural traits emerged. Numerous small 'kingdoms' flourished, with members of an élite establishing their power. The period also saw the birth and development of institutional religion associated with rituals and ceremonies that became part of village life. Metalworking and jewelry making developed, both of which would become principal features of Ecuadorian art.

Larger inhabited centres and many burial sites have been discovered dating from this period. Grave goods show that society was stratified and craft production was specialized. The remains of an important ceremonial centre called La Tolita have been found on an island in the estuary of the river Santiago, and this has given its name to the culture that originated at the end of the Formative Period and the beginning of the Era of Regional Development. Finds have confirmed the huge area of influence of this site and its cultural centres, from the northern coast of Ecuador to the southern coast of Colombia, where this phase is known as Tumaco.

Other centres along the central coast of Ecuador were linked to different cultures though they had

75 (left) A Manteña vessel in the form of a realistic male figure with almond-shaped eyes and a pronounced nose: the right side of his body is completely covered with geometric motifs which suggest tattoos or ritual paintings.

75 (below) Archaeologists have found evidence of cultural and commercial contacts between Peru and Ecuador from the earliest times. This delightful tortoise-shaped container was made by the Chorrera but strongly resembles examples from the northern coast of Peru.

trading links with La Tolita. One of these was the Jama-Coaque culture which inherited features of the Valdivian and Chorreran cultures during the later phases of the Formative Period. Bahia was another culture, characterized by centres organized around large artificial platforms which probably supported temple buildings.

Cerro Narrío, one of the cultures in the Sierra, was strongly influenced by coastal styles. Its numerous ceremonial centres, linked by intensive trade, flourished during the Era of Regional Development and were the focus of artistic and commercial activity which also brought economic power. As trading links strengthened, organized political and socio-economic structures typical of the Era of Integration began to take shape.

The Era of Integration (AD 550–1480) owes its name to the political phenomenon that was its main feature: the many small coastal communities led by *caciques* or local lords united to form larger kingdoms, while those of the Sierra became complex, organized centres governed by a single overlord.

Another significant culture, the Milagro-Quevedo, developed inland from the coast. There is evidence of the use of the 'axe–money' as a means of exchange in trade. The small states of the Puruha and the Cañarí in the Sierra produced large stone constructions and had the unfortunate distinction of being the first to defend themselves in vain against the Inca army around 1490. Following several futile attempts by Tupac Inca to conquer these peoples, the Inca Huayna Capac succeeded in vanquishing them after a long and bloody siege; he then established a hegemony over them and neighbouring kingdoms that lasted roughly forty years.

During this period, several important centres and fortifications were built such as Tomebamba and the famous 'castle' of Inga Pirca in the region of Cañarí. Quito, Ecuador's present-day capital, assumed great importance but no significant remains have been found there. During the period when the Inca empire had two leaders, Atahualpa was based in Quito.

77 (left) This portly male figure is a Quimbaya poporo *(lime container). He wears a simple head-dress and jewelry, including a nose ornament. Most of the figures depicted as* poporos *are naked.*

77 (below) Only the nose ornament and the head-dress topped with a small jaguar remain of the jewelry and adornments that once decorated this gold Quimbaya 'mask', also a container. The lines engraved on the cheeks represent ritual scars.

76 The refinement of works produced by the Quimbaya goldsmiths of Colombia ensures that they are not weighed down by their complex symbolism. In this piece the shape of the tumi *knife is counterbalanced by the magnificent head-dress of a part-human, part-bird figure, flanked by other tiny hybrid figures.*

Some of the contemporary Spanish chronicles record this development. It was associated with three innovations: the custom of providing tribute to rulers in the form of labour or goods; the birth of a corporation of navigator-traders who travelled along the northern Pacific coast; and the construction of large earth platforms called *tolas*. Many scholars claim that these innovations represent the embryo of a true state that would probably have evolved if the Inca conquest had not affected Ecuadorian territory and halted its development.

The most significant culture of the Era of Integration was the Manteña, which spread along the coastal area and has left many examples of fine pottery, stone- and metal-working, and textiles.

DAILY LIFE, ART AND RELIGION OF THE ANDEAN PEOPLES

78–79 Goldsmiths of the Ecuadorian La Tolita peoples created powerfully stylized objects such as the mask seen here, made from an embossed sheet of gold. It was probably suspended in a ceremonial area dedicated to the sun god to signify his presence.

80 (left) The llama was one of the few domesticated animals in pre-Inca times, along with dogs and ducks, and was of great importance to the peoples of Peru. This Chimú pottery container depicts a figure holding a small llama.

80 (below) This attractive pottery vessel in the shape of a woman leading a llama by a rope was made by the Nazca.

The absence of contemporary written records relating to pre-Inca Peru means that we know very little about the social aspects of the lives of Andean peoples of the period. However, images on pottery do supply some information and illustrate certain features of their everyday life, their clothing and their housing. Our most informative sources are for the Nazca and Moche civilizations which developed on the south and north coasts during the period 200 BC to AD 700.

To a large extent, the figures and scenes shown on their vessels are linked to religious cults and rituals, but there are also images of men and women carrying out simple domestic and everyday chores.

80–81 Agricultural labour in the Inca period is graphically illustrated on this painted wooden kero *from the Lake Titicaca region.*

81 (centre) This vessel reproduces a boat made of bundles of reeds tied together, known as a caballito, with a figure seated on top with a paddle. Such boats are still in use today.

81 (bottom) The vessel tied to the back of this seated man is an aryballo, *a sort of Inca amphora; it was used to carry water or other liquids such as chicha. He is also holding a small container, perhaps for coca.*

Fishermen holding fish or nets are frequently depicted, for example, a recurrence that relates directly to the economic importance of this resource for the cultures living along the coast. There are also images of deer- and fox-hunters and llama herders. Also interesting are scenes depicting musicians, usually playing wind instruments. Such images, however, cannot offer more than hints about the knowledge and beliefs of ancient Andean societies and it is often difficult to separate religious aspects from those linked to material life.

This problem takes on a different perspective with the advent of the Inca civilization. Tahuantinsuyu was described in great detail by the Spanish chroniclers of the 16th century, including the life of the court and the ruling élite, as well as the society and customs of the ordinary people. To the modern reader of the texts, particularly those of Garcilaso de la Vega and Guaman Poma de Ayala, one surprising aspect is the rigidity of the structure of the empire from a social and economic point of view, and also the absolute power that the king, the law and the state held over every citizen. The private and working lives of the individual and his economic maintenance were strictly controlled by central government to the extent that some scholars have likened the Inca political system to a totalitarian 'socialist' state.

82 (below left) *An Inca family cultivates the land* (topo) *assigned to the head of the family. The digging was done with a simple foot hoe.*

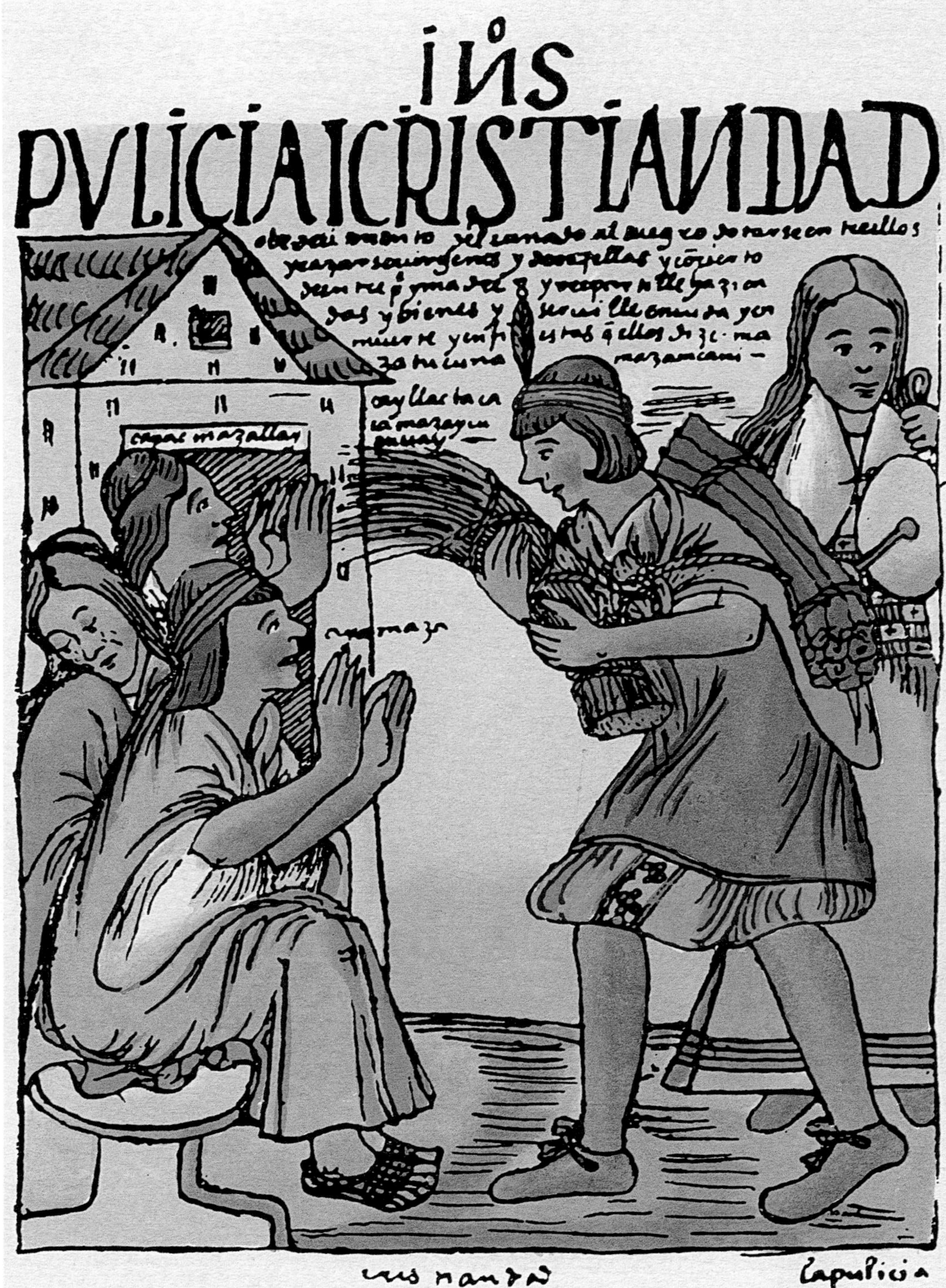

Society was based on the family but from an administrative point of view the *ayllu* was more important. The *ayllu* was a sort of clan formed by a group of families that were linked by a common ancestor and who worked and lived together.

Inca economy was based mainly on agriculture. No currency was used and goods circulated around the huge empire through barter and, more importantly, as a result of the tribute paid to the rulers and nobles. When he married, every adult male was given a parcel of land, called a *topo* in Quechua. The size of the plot varied, based on the fertility of the land and other conditions; according to Garcilaso it would be increased on the birth of each child. If he lived a long and healthy life, a man would remain in charge of his plot of land until he reached fifty years of age.

The head of the family would keep a portion of the crops the *topo* produced to support his family and relatives, while the Inca was the main beneficiary of the land's yield. The ruler received tribute not only in

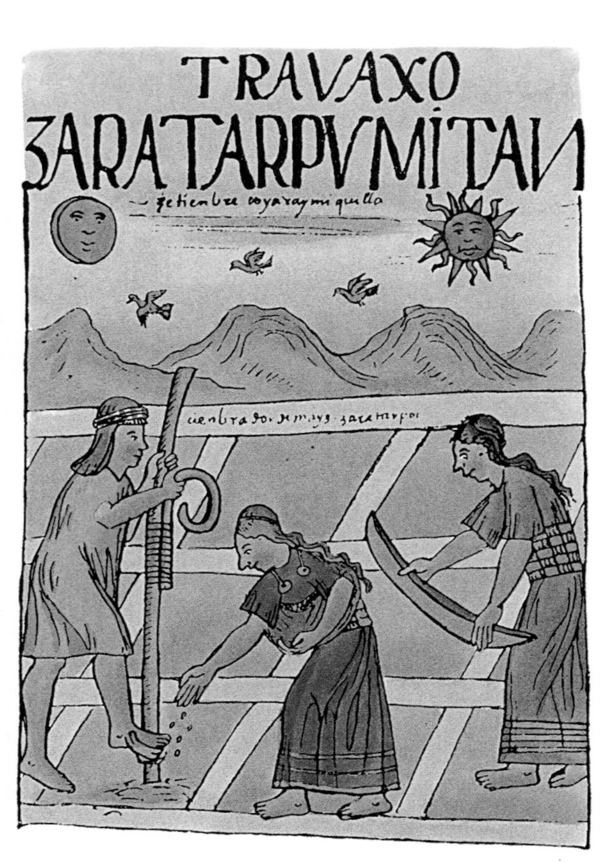

82 (above) *A young Inca man offers gifts to the family of his future wife.*

the form of crops but also, just as important, as labour.

A strong spirit of co-operation reigned in every *ayllu*: the men were obliged to build a house for everyone who got married and when anyone was called up to serve in the army or to perform public functions, other *ayllu* members had to replace him in the fields and to provide for his wife and children.

The men worked the fields using a very simple tool, a wooden hoe called a *chaki taclla*, and even after the Spanish Conquest, farmers continued to use it on slopes too steep for ploughs and oxen. It was

impossible not to work and it was practically impossible to escape the rigid and constant checks carried out by the central power. Only the sick and invalids could exempt themselves from agricultural work and receive help and subsidies.

Another category of worker was also obliged to pay a tribute to the Inca. This was the artisan – the goldsmiths, weavers and potters of the empire. Once these workers had contributed their labour obligation, they were exempt from any other dues to the ruler.

83 (above left) After harvesting in July, the agricultural produce that was the property of the state was taken to the storehouses, carried by llamas or by people.

83 (above right) Agriculture was the main economic resource for the Incas. Here a group of men carrying agricultural products to the state's storehouses as tribute are being watched by a special functionary in the centre.

TRAVAXOS
PAPA ALLAIMITAPA

Inca wealth was based on land and agriculture, labour and herds. It is amazing how productive Inca agriculture was given the huge but wholly unsuitable tracts of land available – the land was stony, set on steep slopes or desert, and difficult to irrigate. And yet the Incas managed to overcome the problems thanks to their rigid organization of labour and their ability to make use of terracing and water channels. These systems were often inherited from previous civilizations, such as the Moche and Huari, but the Incas adapted them to maximize the potential area of cultivatable land.

The crops most intensively cultivated, and which formed the basis of their diet, were the potato, corn (maize), quinoa, beans, squash and peppers. The potato, of which over 300 varieties have been identified, probably originated around Lake Titicaca. It can be grown up to an altitude of 3,960 m (13,000 ft). One of the most widely eaten foods in the Andes, not only in Inca times but also today, is *chuño*, the freeze-dried potato.

84 (opposite) The women of the ayllu *also took part in the work in the fields, even the heavier tasks, as seen here. Part of the harvest was used to feed the families while the rest was sent to the state storehouses as tribute paid to the emperor.*

85 (top left) A section of the account of Poma de Ayala is dedicated to farmwork and he describes each month of the year. This page represents January, and shows two farmers working with short hoes that are still in use in parts of rural Peru.

85 (centre left) This drawing from Poma de Ayala's 'almanac' is for the month of October. It shows a figure armed with a sling trying to scare the birds out of the maize fields.

85 (centre right) A reconstruction of the system used by the Incas to terrace slopes for agricultural use, utilizing rainwater run-off for irrigating the crops.

85 (right) A farmer irrigates his land: the water flows from a tank via a conduit.

86 (above) A warrior pours a libation to the sun god, Inti, in accordance with Tahuantinsuyu tradition, before he goes into battle.

86 (below) This shallow dish with a handle was used in special ceremonies, probably associated with the fertility of the land. It still contains corn-cobs from the age of the Incas.

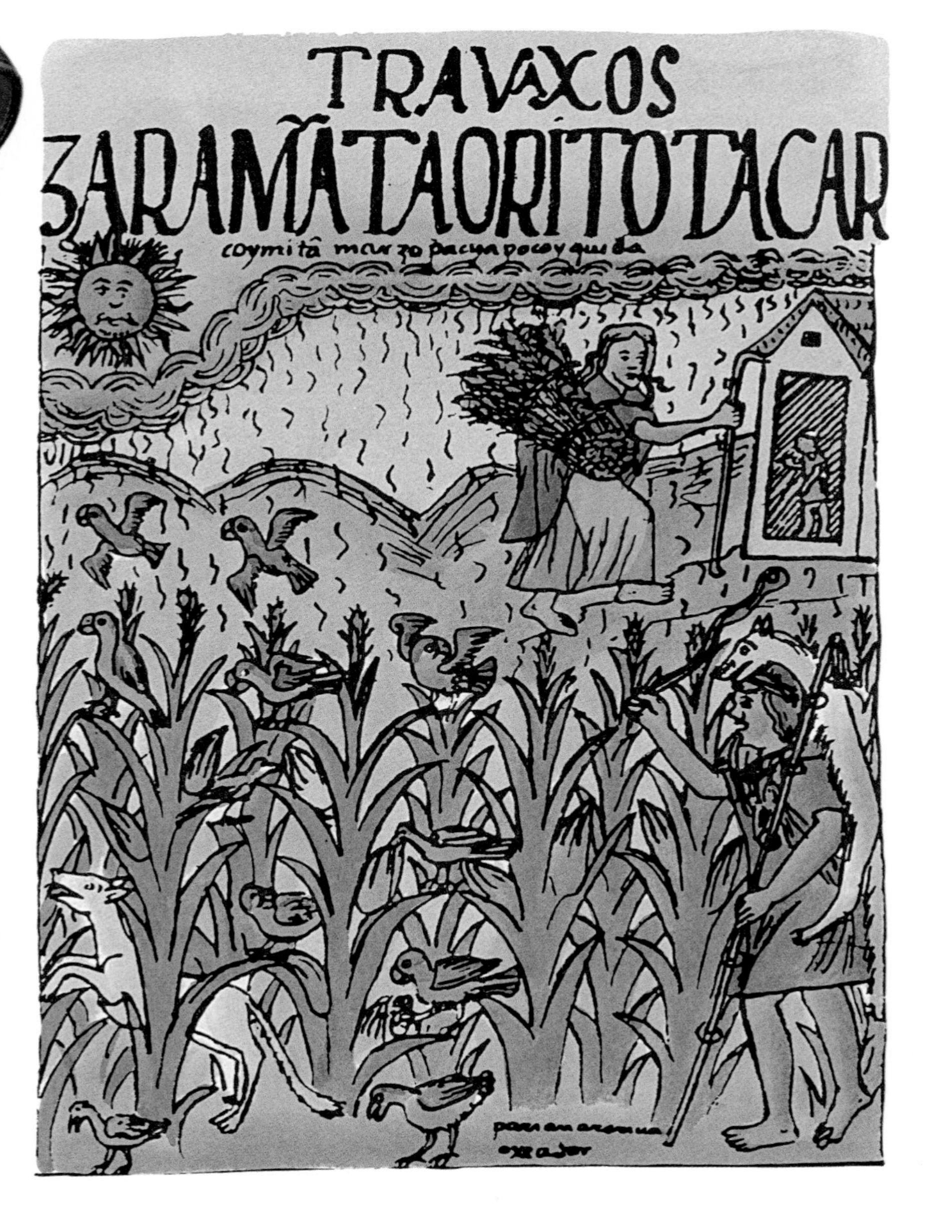

86 (above right) Chicha was an alcoholic drink made from young grains of corn. It was drunk at the end of a meal and at important rituals. This Sicán pottery vessel depicts two people making chicha.

Maize cannot withstand the freezing temperatures of the highlands and is grown in the warmer valleys below. Like the peoples of Mesoamerica, the Peruvians also ascribed this grain with a significance that went far beyond its nutritional value, and it was linked to ancient myths and sacred rituals. They also made a sort of beer from maize, called chicha, which was usually consumed at the end of a meal.

87 (right) A shallow dish with incised decoration made by either the Tiahuanaco or Huari peoples: it was used to contain a hallucinogenic powder that would have been inhaled through a straw or thin tube.

87 (below) In this drawing by Guaman Poma de Ayala a man of high rank (shown by his clothes) is obtaining coca leaves from a merchant. The consumption of coca was governed by certain rules.

86 (opposite, below right) Corn (maize), seen here being harvested, was one of the most widely cultivated crops in the Andes. It was also used as the basis of chicha, an alcoholic drink which was consumed in large quantities at festivals.

87 (above left) This small, richly decorated woollen bag was used to hold coca leaves. When chewed, the leaves were mixed with lime or potash to release the alkaloids.

In their first encounters with the indigenous peoples the Spaniards learned of a special plant, coca, which had magical powers. It had been grown in hot, humid areas for many centuries before the Inca civilization and its properties were much appreciated. When leaves of the coca plant are chewed and mixed with lime or potash, narcotic substances are released which suppress hunger, thirst and fatigue.

The antiquity of the use of coca is demonstrated by many archaeological finds. Images on Moche pottery show people with one cheek extended and their eyes dilated, probably shamans preparing to enter into a trance, a ritual use which was continued up until the Late Horizon.

Once the Inca dynasty collapsed and Spanish dominion replaced it, the use of coca leaves was (to use a modern term) 'liberalized' among the ordinary people, creating a market that quickly enriched the Conquistadors.

88 (left) A hunter armed with a sling is attempting to catch birds. The scarcity of domesticated animals meant that hunting was of major importance to provide meat for the diet.

88 (above) Animals familiar in Europe, such as cattle, horses, pigs and sheep, were unknown in America before the Conquest. Llamas were raised primarily for their wool and as beasts of burden, but also for their meat.

In addition to growing crops, Andean peoples also bred llamas and alpacas, especially in the highlands. Although the meat of these 'Peruvian sheep' (the name given to them by the Spaniards) was prized, they were mainly raised for their wool. They were also used as pack animals but they were not physically strong and did not have the resistance of mules or donkeys.

In the coastal regions and on the shores of Lake Titicaca, protein was mostly provided by fish. Elsewhere, guinea-pigs and ducks were bred for consumption. Guinea-pigs were unknown in Europe until their introduction after the Conquest in the 16th century.

Plants and animals were not only essential sources of food but were also imbued with magical and religious meanings that varied from people to people. From the earliest times, pottery objects frequently depicted plants and animals, either portrayed realistically or as religious symbols. Some plants, maize in particular, were associated with anthropomorphic beings with monstrous features that were

probably guardian deities of the plant. Symbolic images of squash were often assimilated with those of Pacha Mama, the Earth Mother of the Peruvians, an ancestral goddess linked to nature and fertility.

Although theories on the subject are controversial, it is probable that women had equal status and that wives were not relegated to being simply the custodians of the house and children. Instead, it is thought they performed the same tasks as their husbands, in particular in the fields, as well as weaving and performing other craft activities. Pregnant women were exempted from the more demanding tasks only during the last few weeks of pregnancy, but even then they were not allowed to sit around idle.

The birth of a child was considered a great event in Inca society as every baby represented another future labourer for the king. The father would sometimes be present at the birth, fasting and praying, but usually the mother gave birth alone in an isolated spot and went to purify herself and her baby immediately after the birth in a stream or river.

Once the child was weaned, a celebration was held by the family during which the nails and hair of the baby were cut. Presents were given by family and friends to wish the child a happy life as an adult and citizen of the king. Puberty was also an important event; this occurred for boys on their fourteenth birthday and was celebrated with a public ceremony. Girls' puberty was celebrated with a ceremony at home, with family and friends, at the onset of menstruation.

The children of the poor did not have the right to public education, unlike in Aztec society, and only children of Tahuantinsuyu's élite went to schools. The others simply had to learn from their parents how to work in the fields or to perform craft activities.

There were other differences between the ordinary people and the nobles: for instance the former had to be content with monogamy while polygamy was accepted only for the Inca emperor.

Marriage was considered a highly desirable state because every adult male was assigned a *topo*, a plot of land to cultivate, after the ceremony. It was rare that a young man stayed single after the age of 25 while girls married between the ages of 15 and 20. Living together was allowed in some parts of the empire as a sort of 'trial marriage'. If the experiment failed, the couple separated without problems and any resulting children were looked after by the mother and her family.

Contrary to modern mentality, virginity was not considered a state to be valued, on the contrary, unmarried mothers were highly appreciated as all babies were thought of as an extra hand for the lands of the Inca. Parents had the task of choosing a husband or bride for their children but, if they were undecided, the *curaca* would make the choice for them.

88 (opposite below) In this complex scene on a Moche vessel – in part depicted in relief – the god Ai Apaec seems to be hunting or fishing marine animals with monstrous features.

89 (above left) One of the buildings typical of the Inca world was the Aclla Huasi *or 'House of the Chosen Women'. Here the woman in charge stands in the centre, surrounded by young women.*

89 (above centre) The third historical-mythical period in Andean history, according to Guaman Poma de Ayala, was that 'in which the men learned to build solid houses, to weave and to spin'.

89 (above right) Guaman Poma de Ayala's drawings provide us with much information about life in the Inca world. This drawing shows two newly-weds.

ARCHITECTURE

90 (left) *A pottery vessel in the form of a U-shaped house: it has four rectangular windows and is painted with geometric patterns.*

90 (left) *Two identical houses with an overhanging roof form this Inca double container. They probably represent typical houses of the mountain regions.*

90 (above right) *No remains of ordinary houses have survived as they were built of wood or other perishable materials. However, pottery offers a wide range of models illustrating the structure of houses, such as this Cupisnique example.*

Archaeological research has uncovered a large number of temples of pre-Inca Peruvian civilizations. The most important are the Moche temples of 'the Sun' and 'the Moon', and the Chimú 'Huaca del Dragón' at Chan Chan. There are also buildings at Tiahuanaco, Cerro Purgatorio and Pachacamac.

Following traditional building types found in the oldest ceremonial centres of the Preceramic and the Formative periods, temples at these sites had a stepped design consisting of several superimposed terraced levels. As in Mesoamerica, temples had a particular significance: they were built in the form of a mountain so that humans could come as close as possible to the gods. The material used to build even the largest pyramids was adobe – simple sun-dried mud bricks.

It is thought that the shrine proper was situated on the uppermost terrace and that only the priests could enter it. The shrine was probably made of wood or other perishable materials and today our only clues to the original appearance of such structures are small pottery models. Some temples were decorated with wall paintings, for example the Moche temple called 'El Brujo' in the Chicama valley.

Adobe was used for many centuries in the coastal regions where the absence of rain meant it lasted well. The best preserved site is Chan Chan, the capital of the Chimú kingdom and the largest pre-Inca urban centre to have survived to the present day. The solid adobe walls that enclosed the various compounds are at least 4 m (13 ft) thick at the bottom and 1.5 m (5 ft)

91 (left) This Chimú-Inca vessel is a model of a house with an overhanging roof. The animal motifs in relief on the roof are typical of the Chimú culture.

91 (above) An Ica-Chincha model of a house with three floors and verandahs: human figures have been added and a dog at the entrance, possibly a guard dog.

thick at the top. It has been shown that two different methods were used to create the splendid reliefs that decorate the walls of the palaces. The first was to model wet clay directly on to the wall, while the second used large moulds. In many cases the reliefs were covered with plaster and painted in bright colours, traces of which can still be seen today. The iconographic motifs are always symmetrical and stylized, with geometric patterns alternating with animal figures. Marine creatures were particularly popular, and are similar to those found on textiles, which may have been the inspiration for the wall reliefs.

Both the Conquistadors and modern scholars were amazed at the complexity and precision of the techniques used in Inca stoneworking and at the sheer size of the buildings. It should be remembered, however, that the Incas were not the first to erect megalithic constructions. Impressive examples of stone architecture are found at Tiahuanaco on the shores of Lake Titicaca which date from many centuries earlier. Moreover, the system of Inca town-planning that divided the city into residential areas was of Huari origin. The Incas did add new ideas and techniques to those inherited from earlier cultures, however, and produced excellent constructions that would last for centuries. One of the great Inca skills

92 (opposite below) The Incas probably inherited the designs for their cities and fortresses from the Huari empire that dominated Peru during the Middle Horizon. This is a circular Inca structure at a fortress near the village of Camar.

92–93 The circular tower in this drawing from a 19th-century atlas is characteristic of Inca architecture and resembles the famous example at Machu Picchu.

93 (above) The Incas built monumental structures using enormous blocks of stone. The techniques used to transport and life the blocks, and to fit them together so precisely, are still not fully understood.

was to integrate walls and structures perfectly into the Andean landscape, often with the help of artificial terracing, as can be seen today at Machu Picchu and Ollantaytambo. Although few remains survive of the small houses of ordinary people, parts of palaces and administrative and religious buildings demonstrate the extraordinary precision achieved by the Incas in working stone.

On the coast, the lack of rain meant that the flat-roofs and adobe walls of traditional buildings continued to be used, but Inca innovations include the repeated windows and trapezoidal niches.

Although some stone Inca buildings were cemented together using a type of mud-mortar in the *pirka* technique, the majority of their huge constructions used no binding agent. The few surviving remains at Cuzco are marvellous examples of Inca ability: enormous blocks of irregular shape are fitted together like pieces of a jigsaw so perfectly that the blade of a knife cannot pass between them. The stoneworkers carved the rock using bronze and stone tools but the question remains of how the Inca builders moved the huge blocks of stone without wheeled transport or pulleys.

94 (left) This strange pottery figure was made by the Jama-Coaque of Ecuador. It may depict a shaman during a trance or perhaps a snake deity. Despite the early date of the figure, possibly 500 BC*, the elaborate forms and evolved style show great technical understanding and a mastery of pottery production.*

94 (opposite right) A very distinct style identifies this female figurine as belonging to the Ecuadorian Bahia culture. The large head-dress, the nose ornament and other jewelry suggest that she is a high-ranking woman or priestess.

95 (right) Paracas pottery is often decorated in many colours, which were applied after firing.

The oldest pottery fragments so far found in Peru have been dated to approximately 1800 BC, which is quite recent compared to the date when pottery was first used in Ecuador. The earliest shapes found are plates, bottles and jars, which were decorated.

There were two major types of pottery produced in Peru: one, simple and unrefined, was for everyday use, while the other, elegant and well-finished, was for use in ritual ceremonies. Almost all finds either displayed in museums or published fall into the second category. These were mainly found in burial chambers or temples, places which have favoured their preservation. Such vessels were probably containers intended to contain votive offerings or libations, or alternatively they simply accompanied the deceased on his or her final voyage.

Among the range of pottery shapes are 'tripod pots' which were quite common in Mesoamerica but are relatively unknown in Peru. A few examples have been found in the Virú valley and the area of Cajamarca, dating to the Early Intermediate Period.

A characteristic feature of many vessels is a stirrup-spout or handle. This innovation seems to have been inspired by examples from Ecuador, perhaps made by the Machalilla culture, whose influence would have spread south to Peru. The most

95 (above) Made with great simplicity and stylization, this female figurine from Curayacu in the Lima region dates to the Early Horizon.

96 (right) Cylindrical vessels in the shape of a human head are typical of Nazca pottery production. It is thought that their symbolism was linked to the cult of the trophy-head.

96 (below) Nazca pottery is painted with a wider range of colours than is found elsewhere. This example is a tripod pot with a double spout and bridge handle.

sophisticated and numerous examples of vessels with stirrup-shaped handles were produced by the Chavín, Moche, Sicán and Chimú civilizations.

Excavations at Kotosh have identified two types of pottery there: the older had incised figures that were coloured after firing; the more recent type has incised decoration.

It must be remembered that these civilizations produced such complicated shapes without the use of the potter's wheel, which was unknown in America until the

96 (above) Marine imagery recurs frequently in the art of both the Moche and Nazca peoples as they derived a major part of their resources from the sea. This fine Nazca container is in the shape of a sea bird and is decorated with painted fish.

arrival of the Europeans. Peruvian pottery was produced by two fundamental techniques: one was the coil method, and the other, particularly widespread along the northern coast, used moulds. Vessels have also been found that were produced using both techniques. There were also various methods of decoration: painting, which could be applied before or after firing; incision; modelling in relief; and three-dimensional decoration. Peruvian potters had the choice of a wide range of colours.

The most surprising aspect of pottery produced by the ancient Peruvian civilizations is without

97 (below) Chavín pottery was usually monochrome and decorated with stylized incised motifs. These were mostly associated with religious symbolism and are similar to designs found on stone sculptures. The stirrup-shape handle, adopted during the Early Horizon, was also used by later cultures, especially on the northern coast.

97 (above) Sicán pottery vessels often reproduce shapes made in gold or silver. In this example a bridge handle connects two slender spouts. The surface is decorated with reliefs and attachments in the form of lobsters and a head, probably of the god Nylamp.

doubt the variety of motifs found. Jars, bottles, beakers and all types of container were modelled in the shape of animal and human figures, including demons and gods, and decorated with a huge range of designs and details which are an important source of information in the absence of written records.

Although all Peruvian peoples have left us remarkable and varied examples of their pottery production, the richest and most interesting are the creations of the two civilizations that dominated the Early Intermediate Period both culturally and politically: the Moche and Nazca.

98 (left) Vessels produced by peoples of the northern coast of Peru were often globular in shape. Form took pre-eminence over the use of colour, which was usually limited. This fine Vicús container is in the form of the head of an owl and has a slim handle joined to the slender spout.

98 (above) Vicús and Moche potters often made vessels in the shape of parts of the body, such as this one in the form of a hand. Such objects were probably made as votive offerings.

99 (above left) A Huari vessel in the shape of a human head: the face is decorated with a pattern resembling the spotted coat of a jaguar. A cylindrical head-dress forms the neck of the vessel, which is painted with squares, a typical motif of the Middle Horizon.

99 (left) Nazca bottles are recognizable by their wide variety of colours. This example is in the form of a young woman with long hair worn in braids.

99 (above) The iconography of this Chimú vessel may be religious, in which case the building is perhaps a temple.

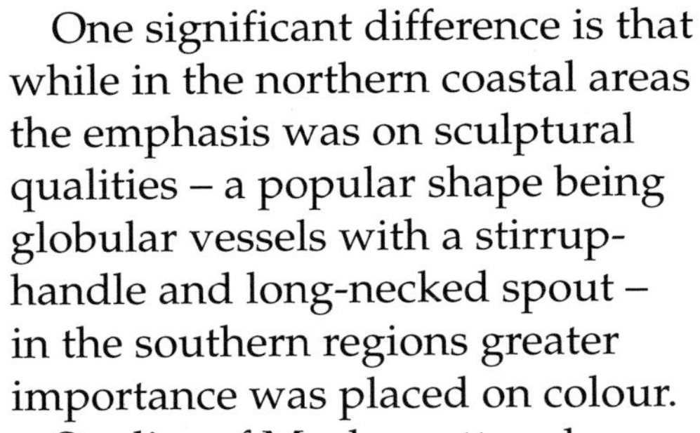

One significant difference is that while in the northern coastal areas the emphasis was on sculptural qualities – a popular shape being globular vessels with a stirrup-handle and long-necked spout – in the southern regions greater importance was placed on colour.

Studies of Moche pottery have identified the techniques used to create the vessels. Many were modelled by hand but most were produced using moulds, sometimes in two halves that were then fitted together. These potters were not interested in colour and they mostly painted their wares in red or white.

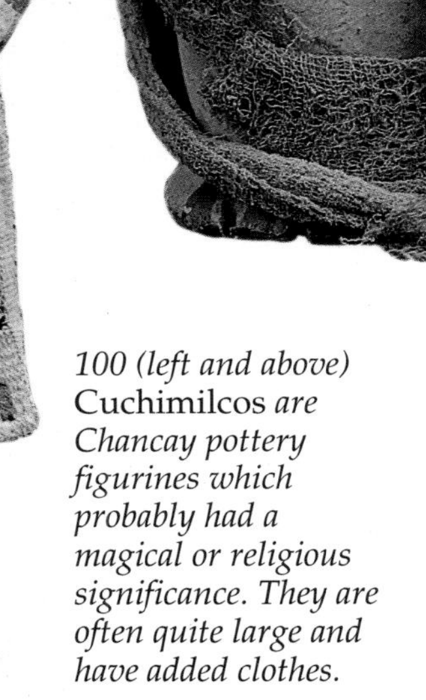

100 (left and above) Cuchimilcos *are Chancay pottery figurines which probably had a magical or religious significance. They are often quite large and have added clothes.*

The figurines are usually female but the one above has male genitals. Smaller versions have holes in them so that they could be suspended to ward off evil spirits from the home.

101 (opposite) The geometrical motifs of Chancay textiles also appear on their pottery. This flask is decorated with the symbol of the sun with a cross in the centre. Two small monkeys, considered sacred by Andean peoples, have been added on either side of the spout.

102 This marvellous Moche portrait vessel depicts a person with an austere expression, wearing a head-dress decorated with marine motifs. It is probable that such vessels depicted members of the political or priestly élite.

Firing was usually carried out in an oxidizing atmosphere which coloured the clay beige or reddish-brown. Black was also a result of firing techniques.

The Moche range of shapes and images was so great that an entire book could be devoted to it. One typical form is the 'portrait vessel'. All the faces depicted on these bottle-shaped vessels are different and are therefore considered to be actual portraits. Warriors, prisoners, anthropo-zoomorphic hybrids, gods, demons, priests in ceremonial dress, animals, plants, musical instruments and small pyramidal temples are all frequent images on Moche pottery.

Another type of decoration depicts complex scenes that unfold around the body of the container, such as people running (perhaps the *chasqui*, the messengers of the Inca period), fishing scenes, ritual hunts, ceremonies and episodes from war in which prisoners are captured and sacrificed.

103 Moche 'portrait vessels', like the expressive example seen here, were containers with stirrup-shape handles. They depict different male faces with such realism that scholars think they are actual portraits.

104 (right) The puzzling symbolism of this Moche vessel has been variously interpreted. A figure with feline fangs is seated inside a structure, possibly a temple, and twists its head around while pulling its hair. Another small figure seems to be watching the scene, which may depict a god engaged in some ritual.

104 (left) In contrast with the enigmatic decorations that characterize many Moche vessels, some are quiet and gentle – such as this container showing a person sleeping.

105 (opposite) Moche vessels are decorated with a rich variety of symbolic images which are often difficult to interpret. The figure in this example, wearing a large head-dress and an animal-like mask, appears to be blowing on a type of trumpet in the shape of a two-headed fish. It perhaps portrays a shaman during a ceremony.

106 (above left) The frog was considered a guardian deity of rain and aquatic fertility. The geometric motifs on this vessel, painted in red on a cream background, are linked to the sun.

106 (left) The condor was associated with the gods because of its strength and huge wingspan. This Moche bottle depicts the great bird very naturalistically.

106–107 Another important bird, the duck was probably domesticated by the coastal populations of ancient Peru.

107 (left) The demon-crab was one of the monstrous hybrids in the Moche religious pantheon. Its terrifying appearance results from the combination of the body and shell of the crab, with a human face and feline fangs.

107 (above) Animals appear very frequently in Moche pottery. This charming example shows a snail in minute detail. Moche paintings depict elegantly dressed figures collecting snails.

108 (left) Examples of Moche 'erotic' pottery include many scenes of fellatio. The precise meaning and purpose of such explicit representations are not fully understood, but they may be associated with magical ceremonies.

Several peoples of the northern coastal regions in Pre-Columbian Peru depicted sexual activity on their pottery vessels, including the Vicús, Recuay and Chimú cultures. The most interesting 'erotic' pottery vessels, however, are those produced by the Moche.

Simple symbolic images of female and male genitalia, connected with fertility cults as in other civilizations on other continents, date back to the earliest periods. 'Erotic' images from later ages, however, are not always associated with a cult or an ancestral concept of fertility.

Among the many scenes of sexual activity, there are examples of masturbation, fellatio and sodomy. Sodomy was commonly practised during the Inca period, as we learn from the many disapproving accounts of the chroniclers. There are also numerous figurines which show human features on a phallic shape, and others that depict humans with very large phalluses.

Much has been written by archaeologists on the possible interpretations of this erotic pottery. Some argue that these objects have a magico-religious meaning; others have identified examples of erotic scenes where one of those involved is clearly depicted as ill. This, they believe, shows that the vessel had the purpose of warding off venereal disease. In the light of current knowledge and with our modern mentality, however, it is difficult to find conclusive answers to the many questions surrounding the erotic art of Moche pots.

109 (below) A Nazca vessel of a crouching male figure perhaps depicts a member of the élite: his short tunic, loin-cloth and head-dress – a sort of net held in place by a band – are shown in great detail. On the face and lips are signs of ritual painting.

108 (opposite below) Another example of Moche erotic pottery showing sexual activity. Moche pottery also frequently depicted childbirth.

109 (above) This Nazca vessel takes the form of a strange figure wearing a mask and holding objects in each hand. He may be a shaman wearing ceremonial dress.

Nazca pottery is very different from that of the northern cultures, with an emphasis on colour rather than sculptural qualities or variety of shape. Nazca bottles, bowls and other pots inherited the Paracas feature of the double spout joined by a flat bridge handle. The refined forms and thin walls of these items were not created with moulds but using simple manual techniques. The most common method was the coil technique, which built up the pot by coiling strings of clay on top of one another. The potter would then turn the base and work the clay to create a smooth surface. This method is not to be confused with throwing on the wheel, which only arrived with the Spaniards. It is still used in many parts of Peru today, particularly in the region of Nazca.

When the body of the pot had been shaped, the surface was painted with water and mineral pigments using the slip technique. Red was obtained with iron oxide, black with manganese, and these were added to white clay or ochre to create fine, coloured slips. Using this

110 (above) So-called 'salt-cellar' vessels, such as those seen here, are typical of the Chimú-Inca style. Small twin containers joined by a flat handle, they were made during the Inca period but incorporated decorative themes that are similar to those of the northern coast. The small monkey on top of one spout was unique to the Chimú.

110–111 The Chimú inherited many of their techniques and motifs from Moche pottery, especially animal images. This vessel depicts a toucan pecking at a fruit.

method and firing at low temperatures, the Nazca craftsmen had available a choice of thirteen rich colours, which included burgundy red, violet and blue-green. Once firing was completed and the slip was baked, the surface of the pots was burnished until it shone.

It is thought that the Nazca preference for brightly coloured pottery was not coincidental, but was linked to the tradition of the splendid multicoloured woven textiles of Paracas.

111 (right) The aryballo *was widely produced throughout the Andes after the advent of the Inca empire. It is a type of amphora with a pointed bottom that was used to hold water or other liquids and was carried on the back tied by a cord around the head.*

112 (left) *A fine example of an Inca* kero, *this beaker takes the form of a feline head. The cult of the jaguar and its imagery survived until the Spanish Conquest.*

112 (below) *The vast range of symbolic images found on* keros *provides us with a great deal of information about the daily life, warfare and clothing of the Inca people. This* kero *has a stylized human face in relief on one side and a painted scene on the other.*

The Incas introduced few stylistic innovations into their ceramic production compared with the numerous variations that had characterized the pottery of earlier civilizations. One particular type of vessel, which became widespread during the Late Horizon and which perhaps had originated in the Tiahuanaco area, was so unusual and aesthetically elegant that it continued to be produced during the Colonial era – the *kero*.

This is a Quechua word denoting a cylindrical wooden pot with an incised or painted surface that was used only for special ceremonial libations. The wood was from a particular tree, the Chachacomo, or *Escallonia resinosa*. There were two basic types of *kero*: one was a simple cylindrical beaker flaring towards the top, while the other was carved in a particular form, usually a human or feline head. *Keros* made before the Spanish Conquest had simple incised geometric decorations, while those made

during the Colonial period were painted in bright colours with scenes of daily life in Tahuantinsuyu. This second type of *kero* is a rich source of information. It is thought that the period of the greatest diffusion of the *kero* was the 16th century, linked to the formation of a new society of Inca nobles who had taken refuge in Vilcabamba, in the Amazonian forests of the Andes.

Many painted scenes depict Inca warriors, armed and magnificently dressed, engaged in combat with the warlike forest peoples. Other images are of hunting, animal raising and agriculture, and there are also many models of Inca dwellings. Although these *keros* come from a later age, the images are very representative of Inca subjects and styles.

The technique used to paint Colonial period *keros* was generally one introduced by the Europeans, which consisted of applying a special paste formed of mineral oxides, beeswax and colours on to the surface of the wood. This technique, coupled with the many colours used, gave the *keros* an extremely bright and shiny surface.

113 (left) Vertical bands with paintings of small houses, people, animals and geometric patterns decorate the surface of this large kero. *Two stylized jaguars form the handles.*

113 (right) Wooden keros *produced by the Incas were cylindrical beakers decorated with painted scenes used for libations. This brightly coloured* kero *has the repeated motif of a jaguar in relief.*

114 (above) The civilizations that flourished along the southern coast of Peru produced the highest quality weaving. This detail is from a Nazca textile decorated with stylized zoomorphic motifs.

114 (left) This Inca female figurine made of gold is wrapped in brightly coloured woollen material, tied with a belt and also fastened by a large pin called a tupu.

115 (opposite left) Inca men wore an unku *– a sleeveless, rectangular tunic in bright colours, often decorated with a horizontal band of geometrical motifs called* tocapu.

WEAVING AND THE ART OF FEATHER-WORKING

115 (right) In this drawing by Guaman Poma de Ayala an Inca weaver is working on a typical Andean backstrap loom that is still used today. Weaving was a fundamental means of artistic expression in Pre-Columbian Peru.

The Spanish chroniclers described and illustrated in detail the types of clothing worn in the Inca world. Ordinary people wore a simple tunic made of coarsely woven cotton or alpaca wool. The material was called *awasca*. The *cumbi* was a finer cloth which was reserved exclusively for members of royalty or those who enjoyed special privileges. *Cumbi* was made with delicate fibres that were dyed in bright colours and woven to form regular geometric patterns. The Spaniards compared the texture of the *cumbi* with silk.

In the Inca world in general and in Cuzco in particular, people displayed their membership of a high caste by the quality of the materials and the richness of the patterns of their clothes. Some scholars believe that these patterns were actually part of a graphic system with pictographic and phonetic values.

Peruvian clothing was on the whole rather simple. Men wore a short, sleeveless tunic called an *unku*. Women wore an *acsu*, a tunic that was similar to the *unku* but longer. A cloak might be worn over the top of these simple clothes that was called a *llacolla* for men and a *lliclla* for women.

People of high rank also wore jewelry, sandals, coloured bags and head-dresses adorned with feathers. Textiles were regarded as a form of tribute and each family was required to weave for the Inca as well as perform agricultural obligations.

116 (above) Fardos *or mummy bundles (mummies wrapped in many layers of textiles) have been found at many Pre-Columbian burial sites. This Huari mummy bundle is wrapped in a coloured tunic decorated with complex motifs; it also has a long necklace and a false head.*

Textiles were also used as votive offerings, a means of exchange and gifts to seal a promise of marriage or a diplomatic alliance. They also represented spoils of war.

Weaving was a fundamental activity for all Pre-Columbian civilizations, as clothes and textiles had a value in the eyes of Andean peoples that was not much less than that of jewels and precious metals. The art of weaving vegetal fibres was also the first means of artistic expression in Pre-Columbian Peru and predated pottery making and metalworking. Traces of woven vegetal fibre material have been found in the Guitarrero cave that have been dated to approximately 5780 BC (the Preceramic Period). The first fragments of textiles made from cotton have been found at the site of Huaca Prieta in the Chicama valley and date to around 2500 BC.

In addition to vegetal fibres and cotton, the domestication of the llama and alpaca added an important new material to weaving. The tools used were simple. Wool was spun using a spindle and a distaff; the spindle was made from a rod of hard wood, generally *chonta* (*Guilielma chiliata*), tapered at the end where it was inserted into a stone or bone whorl. The most common device for weaving cotton was the backstrap loom, still used by Andean women today. This simply consists of two wooden bars; one was tied to a pole and the other was held behind

116 (opposite below) The iconographic motifs of Paracas and Nazca textiles are generally linked with the religious sphere and share elements common to other Peruvian cultures. This detail from a woven textile shows the Staff God, whose cult is thought to have been handed down from the ancient civilization of Chavín.

116–117 A very fine example of Paracas weaving, this manto, *a sleeveless tunic with a V-neck, was found in a tomb. The hybrid figure with the snakes resembles the Staff God found at Chavín and Tiahuanaco.*

117 (above) Tiny stylized figures decorate this textile of the Paracas-Nazca culture. Some scholars think that the motifs are graphic symbols that have not yet been deciphered.

the back of the weaver, tied by a belt. Images on pottery and in the chronicles illustrate the use of a vertical loom, but no example has yet been discovered.

However simple the equipment may have been, there were many different techniques used to weave cotton. The most frequent was the crossed-weft technique which gave the basic structure for the cloth. Another was the gauze method, utilized to great effect by the Chancay culture, in which the crossed-warp system was employed. The most exquisite *mantos* and tapestries were produced by the Nazca and Paracas cultures using a sort of satin stitch. Mineral and vegetal dyes were used to colour the cloth. There were specialized artisans in Inca culture whose task it was to prepare and dye fabrics. They collected indigo (*Indigofera suffruticosa*) to create blues, greens, black and violet; chilca (*Baccharis polyanta*) for yellows and greys; and achiota (*Bixa orellana*) for orange. Red was extracted either from the roots of plants or from the cochineal insect (*Coccus cacti*) which was a parasite of the *Opuntia cactus*. To obtain the desired colour, the insect was dried in the sun and then boiled, though this use of the insect has not been documented before the Huari period. Purple was also obtained from an animal source, but this time from two molluscs: *Murex brandaris* and *Murex truncullus*.

118 (opposite) The motif on this Paracas manto *is related to imagery of the southern coastal cultures of the First Intermediate Period, derived from Huari art. The strange creature holds snakes in its hands and also seems to be spitting them out of its mouth.*

119 (below left) Paracas weaving is characterized by patterns of squares containing repeated motifs. This mantle from the Paracas peninsula glows with a wonderful range of rich colours.

119 (above) The motif of the mythical hero in a crescent-shaped hat appears in this detail of a Chimú textile. Chimú weavers often also decorated their textiles with feathers and metal ornaments.

120–121 Brightly coloured feathers of tropical birds were sewn on to textiles to create magnificent decorations. The Ica-Chincha piece seen here is decorated with three figures in yellow and red feathers on a blue background.

121 (opposite right) Strange creatures in red and green appear on this Chimú feather textile. It is thought that the Chimú civilization inherited the traditions of feather-working from their predecessors, the Moche.

120 (above) Feathers were often combined with other materials to create elaborate clothes and head-dresses. This Chancay crown on a wooden support is decorated with yellow and turquoise feathers from the Blue and Yellow Macaw. It is further decorated with attached pendants, bells, gold discs and small model birds.

120 (right) Another Chancay cylindrical crown: in this example different coloured feathers have been attached to a frame made of wood and vegetal fibres. Feather head-dresses had a ceremonial function and were common during the Late Intermediate Period.

deities and religious rituals, similar to those found on pottery.

Excavations at Huari sites have uncovered large quantities of elegant tunics, probably intended for members of the political and military élite. Production of such items required time, skill and large quantities of raw materials. It has been estimated that each tunic required between 9.5 and 14.5 km (6 and 9 miles) of yarn.

The most frequent imagery found on Huari tunics consists of stylized figures linked to the Gateway God and other human-animal figures found on the Gateway of the Sun at the site of Tiahuanaco. The standardization of decorative motifs, number of threads and size of the Huari tunics leads us to suppose that there was some kind of imperial control over the textile industry, and therefore probably also over other means of artistic expression.

It has not yet been established what type of mordant was used to fix the dyes to the material. Clothes and textiles were also often decorated with metal ornaments and coloured feathers from tropical birds which were sewn on to the fabric using complex techniques.

If the Andean civilizations on the northern coast excelled in the production of gold artifacts, those in the south were responsible for creating true textile works of art. The finest examples, brightly coloured and of excellent quality, mostly come from the burial sites of the Paracas, Nazca and Chancay cultures, with some also from Huari sites. The particularly dry climate of these regions means that organic and fragile materials, such as cotton, wool and feathers, are well preserved. The Paracas mummies were wrapped in many layers of brightly coloured and embroidered textiles called *mantos*, which were symbols of wealth or rank. Most of the materials found in burials have rich decorations consisting of geometric patterns or stylized figures of fish, birds and insects, achieved with great delicacy.

Nazca artisans created tapestries with complex scenes of monsters,

Many textiles also been found in the centres of the northern coast, in particular Sicán and Chimú, though on the whole they are not so accomplished. The geometric and zoomorphic motifs on the Chimú tapestries and tunics have strong similarities to plaster reliefs decorating the adobe walls of the capital, Chan Chan.

122 (below) Tumbaga, *an alloy of gold and copper, was widely used in the Andes. This pendant in the form of a figure with the jaws of a crocodile and an elaborate head-dress was produced by the Tairona of Colombia.*

122 (right) Also from Colombia, this pectoral in the form of a divine figure is made from tumbaga.

The central Andes from Ecuador to Bolivia was the home of one of the most important metalworking traditions in the world. The earliest evidence of the working of gold in Peru comes from the small village of Huayhuaca in the form of thin gold sheet dating to around 1900 BC. At Mina Perdida copper foil has been found that dates to 1250 BC. These two isolated cases are proof of the antiquity of metalworking in Pre-Columbian Peru. It is probable that it was from these regions that the goldsmith's art spread to the remaining areas of the American continent. In Colombia, where it reached very high levels of skill, goldworking appeared around the beginning of the 6th century BC.

Three technical innovations were crucial to the development of the working of gold from the beginning of the Early Horizon. The first was the use of different metals to create alloys that were useful both in lowering the temperature needed during fusion and for ensuring that the soft metal held its shape. The second was the technique of soldering, by which pieces of metal were fused together with drops of molten metal. Soldering gave volume to foil sheets so that they could be transformed into objects. The third discovery was the technique of beating gold on hard wooden or metal surfaces using a type of hammer. This allowed large sheets to be created which could then be cut and hammered further to create objects in relief.

Gold artifacts produced in Chavín style often take the form of cylindrical crowns made of gold sheet, which were decorated with images of the Staff God.

123 (left) The striking appearance of this Calima pendant is accentuated by the repetition of the crescent-shaped plates that decorate it. Colombian goldsmiths often added these mobile attachments to create a shimmering appearance.

123 (below) This Calima gold figure is decorated with such imposing regalia that its features are hidden. It is a pendant to be hung from a necklace and shows a person holding a staff of power and a shield of animal hide.

Current research shows that gold was the first metal to be worked and appreciated. It was probably relatively easy to find in its pure state in the form of nuggets in stream beds. Other metals that were mined and worked were silver, copper and tin (tin was discovered in the 6th century AD). Iron was not known in the Andean world until the arrival of the Europeans. Metals were usually worked in the form of alloys, such as bronze, made from a mixture of copper and tin, and *tumbaga*, a mixture of gold and copper.

Hammering was the most widespread technique used in metalworking from the earliest times. Splendid items such as masks and crowns were created, but also elegant containers, small ornaments, jewels and figurines, which might then be decorated by incision or using a punch.

Tools such as axes, hammer heads and scalpels were made by casting metal in a simple mould. In Peru, only Moche craftsmen mastered the technique of casting gold that was widely used in Colombia – the 'lost-wax' method. A small model of the object to be produced was made in wax and covered with a thick layer of clay, leaving a hole in the bottom. Once the clay hardened, the mould was heated and the molten wax ran out of the hole. This was then replaced with metal and left to cool, at which point the clay mould was broken to reveal the desired object. Using this technique Moche craftsmen produced figurines and magnificent sceptre heads.

Later, in the Inca period, solid gold and silver figurines were made in two-part moulds rather than by the lost-wax method. A speciality of Peruvian goldsmiths was the transformation of the external surface of an object by gilding. One method was simply to apply a thin layer of gold to the surface of a silver or copper object. Another allowed the gold held in a silver-copper alloy to emerge: a sheet of metal was heated and beaten so that a layer of copper oxide formed on the surface; this was removed with a weak acid, leaving a silvered layer containing a small percentage of gold. The object was then placed in acid which dissolved the silver to create a magnificent gilded surface.

The use of alloys, particularly *tumbaga*, to produce enormous quantities of objects was a cause of great anger and disappointment for the Conquistadors. When they melted down their precious booty received from Atahualpa they realized that the quantity of pure gold was almost negligible.

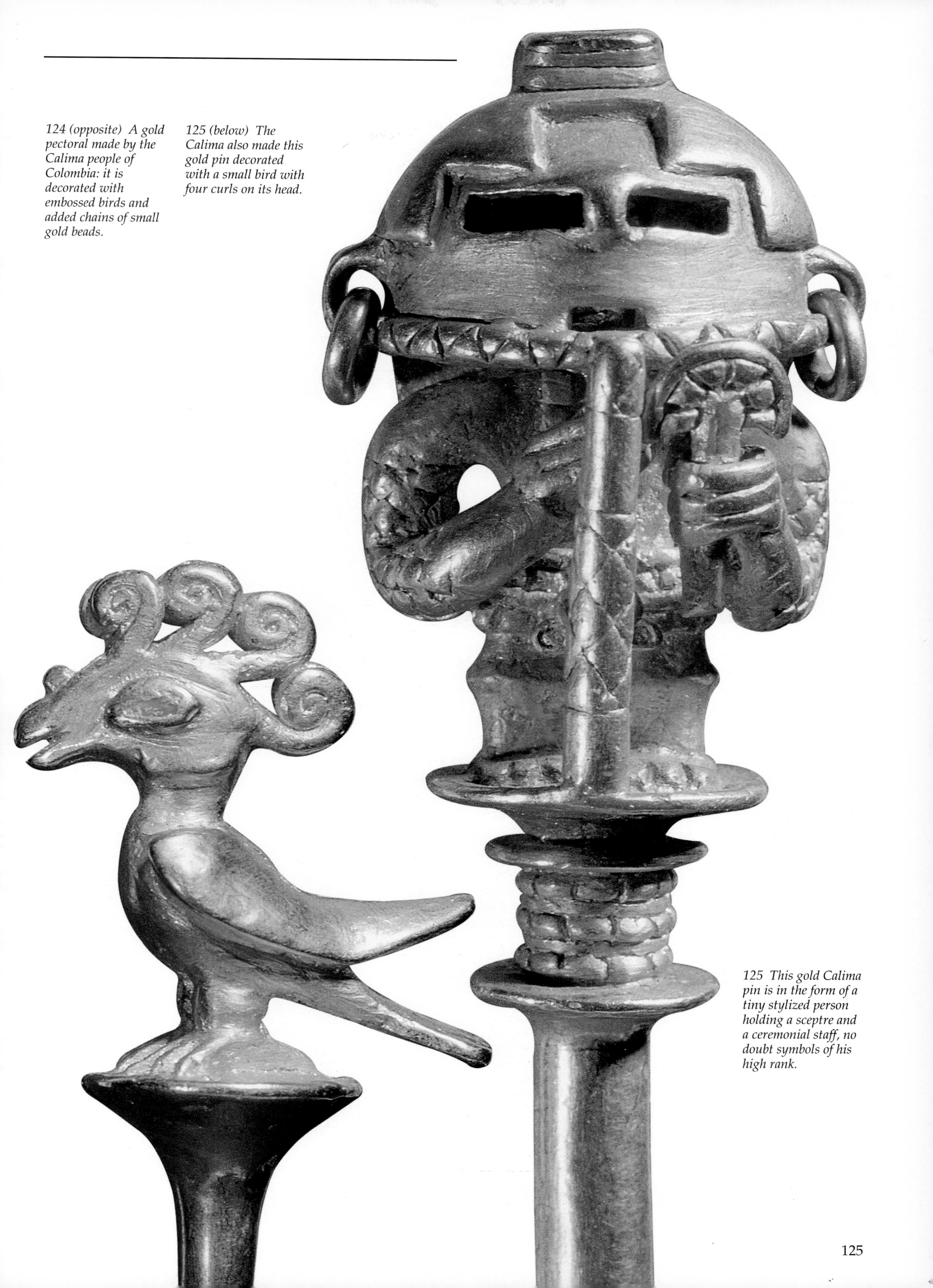

124 (opposite) A gold pectoral made by the Calima people of Colombia: it is decorated with embossed birds and added chains of small gold beads.

125 (below) The Calima also made this gold pin decorated with a small bird with four curls on its head.

125 This gold Calima pin is in the form of a tiny stylized person holding a sceptre and a ceremonial staff, no doubt symbols of his high rank.

126 Poporos *are containers for lime, which was mixed with coca to increase its effect. They are found in very varied shapes. These small, quite plain examples were made by Quimbaya craftsmen, who produced the finest Colombian goldwork.*

126 (below) This Quimbaya pendant is made from tumbaga, *an alloy of copper and a fairly low percentage of gold. Colombian craftsmen used it to create objects that appeared to be made of solid gold.*

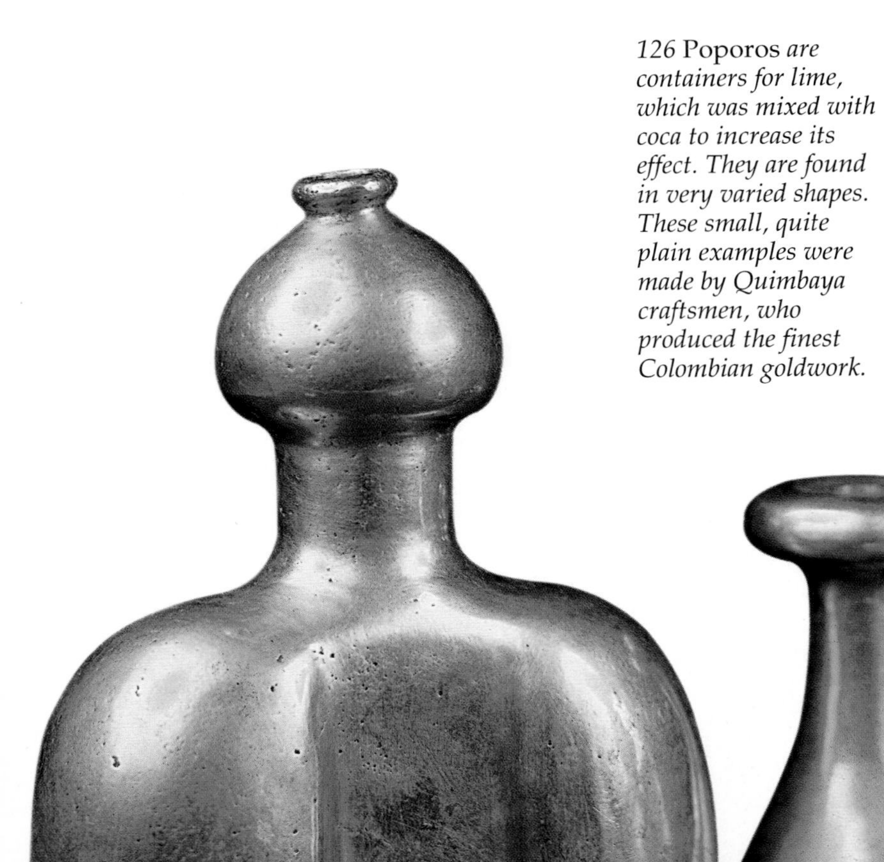

In Tahuantinsuyu, gold was regarded as the 'Sweat of the Sun' and silver the 'Tears of the Moon'. As lovers of jewels, jewelry and other precious objects, the Inca rulers surrounded themselves with the most expert and renowned metalworkers, frequently from Chimor, to satisfy their desires. The civilizations of the northern coast inherited Chavín traditions of metalworking, which they carried on until the arrival of the Spaniards.

Not only the Moche but also the Vicús, Sicán and the Chimú created marvellous gold and silver ornaments. The range of Sicán objects discovered so far includes large burial masks, ceremonial knives called *tumi*, beakers, pectorals and discs to be worn on the ears. Pottery vessels with a double spout and flat bridge handle were also reproduced in gold and silver, probably for the exclusive use of the élite. Decorative motifs were often added in relief and inlaid with mosaics of turquoise and shell.

Chimú metalworkers continued the Sicán traditions and maintained the quality of work. Tunics and tapestries were decorated with gold and silver plaques and coloured feathers, transforming them into 'textile treasures'. It was probably Chimú smiths who created the 'Coricancha', the Golden Enclosure and Sun Temple of Cuzco – a house of all the gods, where walls were lined with gold and the gardens were studded with miniature golden plants. This architectural marvel was sacked and destroyed by the Spaniards.

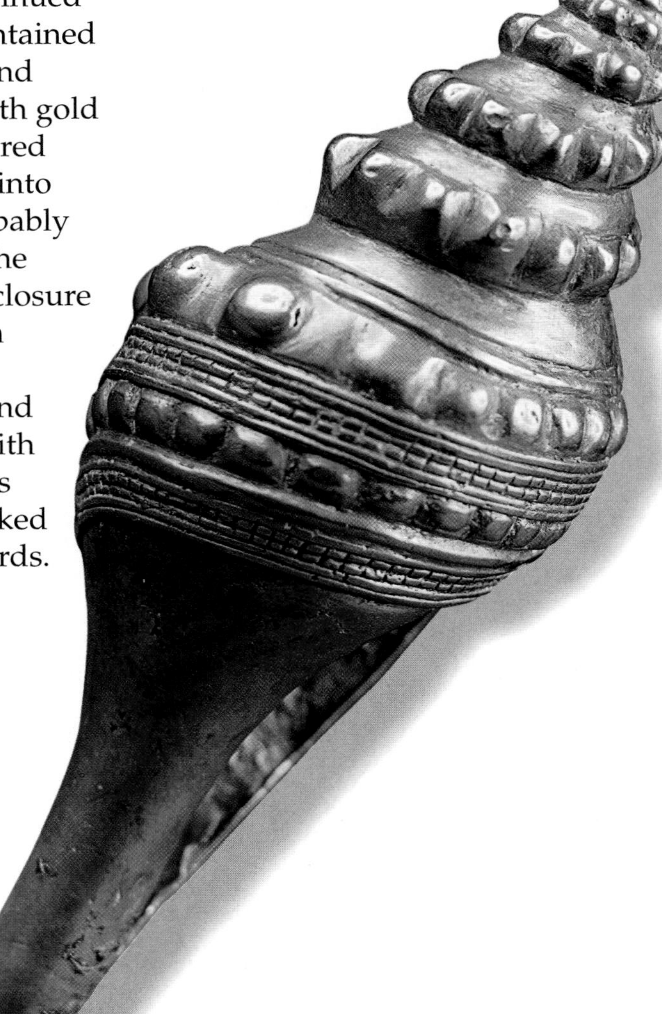

127 (opposite) Another splendid product of the Quimbaya goldsmiths, this poporo *has the added figure of a* cacique *or tribal chief. Only members of the highest castes owned these objects.*

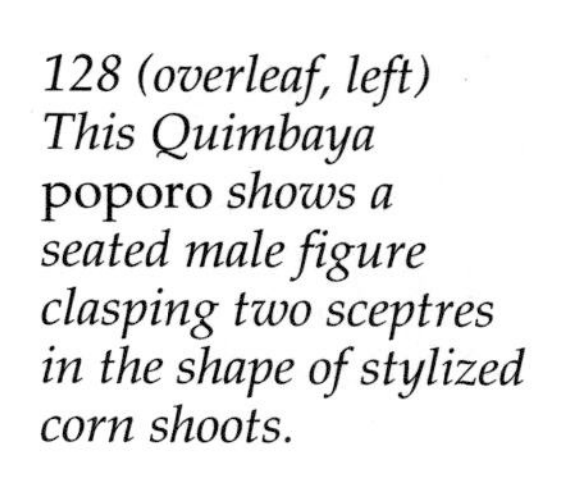

128 (overleaf, left) This Quimbaya poporo *shows a seated male figure clasping two sceptres in the shape of stylized corn shoots.*

128 (overleaf, right) A typical poporo *produced by the Quimbaya of Colombia: these elegant containers were only used by members of the élite at rituals linked to the use of the drug coca.*

129 These are further examples of poporos: *two depict naked men, one slim, muscular and standing, the other rather portly and seated.*

130 (below) The Incas greatly appreciated the metalworking skills and products of the people they conquered, in particular the Chimú. These skilful craftsmen were brought to the court at Cuzco to continue making jewelry and other objects. This female figurine wearing large earrings dates from the Inca period.

130 (right) In the centre of this fine silver pectoral is the realistic image of an owl. The Spanish chroniclers relate that owls were worshipped as divine beings associated with ritual sacrifices and death, and the kingdom beyond the grave.

130 (above) This tiny model of a feline has been dated to 700–500 BC and is therefore contemporary with the Chavín period. It demonstrates the high quality achieved in metalworking during the Early Horizon. The first evidence of gold working in Peru has been dated to the 2nd millennium BC.

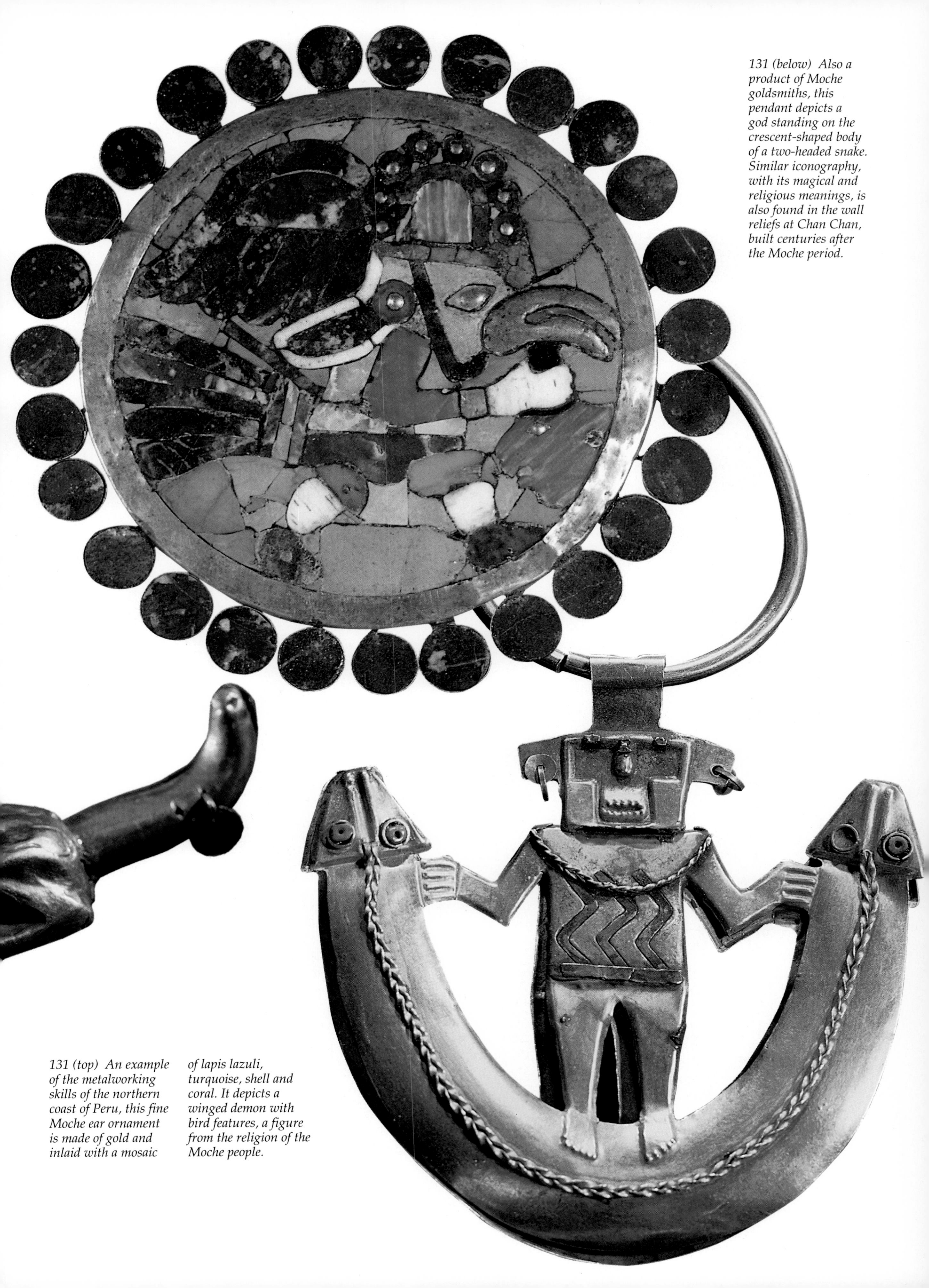

131 (below) Also a product of Moche goldsmiths, this pendant depicts a god standing on the crescent-shaped body of a two-headed snake. Similar iconography, with its magical and religious meanings, is also found in the wall reliefs at Chan Chan, built centuries after the Moche period.

131 (top) An example of the metalworking skills of the northern coast of Peru, this fine Moche ear ornament is made of gold and inlaid with a mosaic of lapis lazuli, turquoise, shell and coral. It depicts a winged demon with bird features, a figure from the religion of the Moche people.

132 (left) The surface of this cylindrical gold Sicán beaker is covered in embossed decoration. Around the neck are images of Nylamp wearing his characteristic crescent-shaped head-dress.

132 (below) This embossed gold plaque depicts a jaguar with a prominent tongue and a crested back. It was made by a Sicán goldsmith and was perhaps attached to material or clothing.

132–133 The skill of the Sicán goldsmiths is demonstrated by a series of vessels made from metal, such as the one seen here with a bridge handle connecting two slender and tapering spouts. The figures are connected with the cult of Nylamp. Objects like this were not for everyday use but were made for ceremonial occasions.

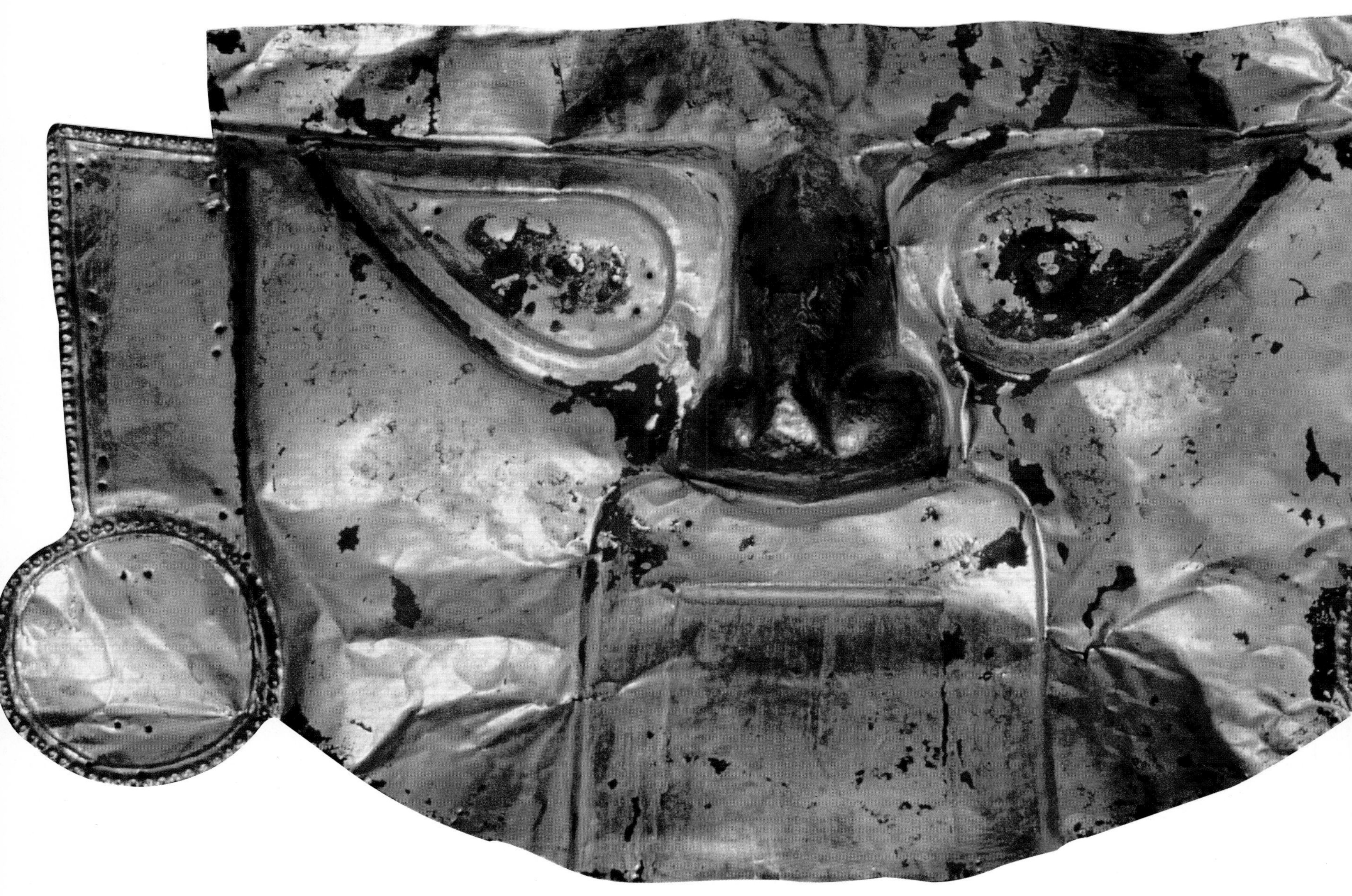

134 (above) On the northern coast of Peru, people of high rank were buried with objects of great beauty, and a gold or silver burial mask was placed over their faces. This example in embossed gold comes from a Sicán tomb.

134 (right) Also a Sicán piece, this elegant gold beaker is decorated with pieces of turquoise around the rim and has a figure in the centre. The iconography is once again that of the god-hero Nylamp who, according to tradition, founded the Sicán civilization after arriving from the sea on a raft.

135 (opposite above) This funerary mask retains traces of its original red and blue colouring and is decorated with a nose ornament and numerous earrings.

135 (opposite below) Sicán burials found on the northern coast of Peru have yielded marvellous gold, silver and tumbaga *burial masks. The narrowed, bird-like eyes are once more a reference to Nylamp. The original red colouring is still quite bright.*

136 This is a fine example of a Sicán tumi *– a crescent-shaped ceremonial knife used by the peoples of the northern coast in the Late Intermediate Period. This* tumi *is topped with the figure of Nylamp, with his characteristic bird-like eyes, crescent-shaped head-dress and bird pendants, inlaid with turquoise. The back of the knife is also richly decorated and the quality of the object means it almost certainly belonged to a noble or a ruler of the Sicán dynasty who, according to tradition, were the descendants of the god Nylamp.*

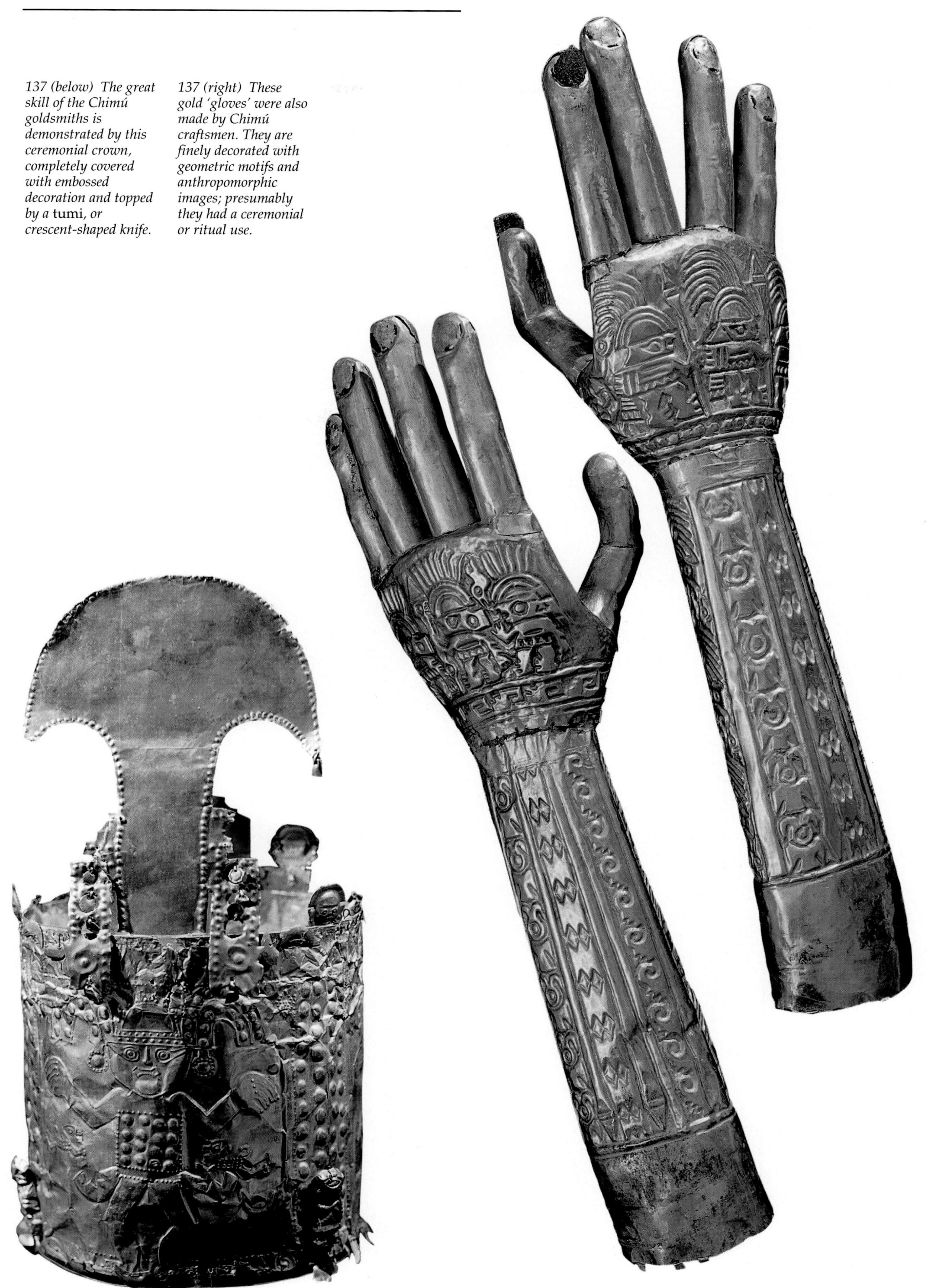

137 (below) The great skill of the Chimú goldsmiths is demonstrated by this ceremonial crown, completely covered with embossed decoration and topped by a tumi, *or crescent-shaped knife.*

137 (right) These gold 'gloves' were also made by Chimú craftsmen. They are finely decorated with geometric motifs and anthropomorphic images; presumably they had a ceremonial or ritual use.

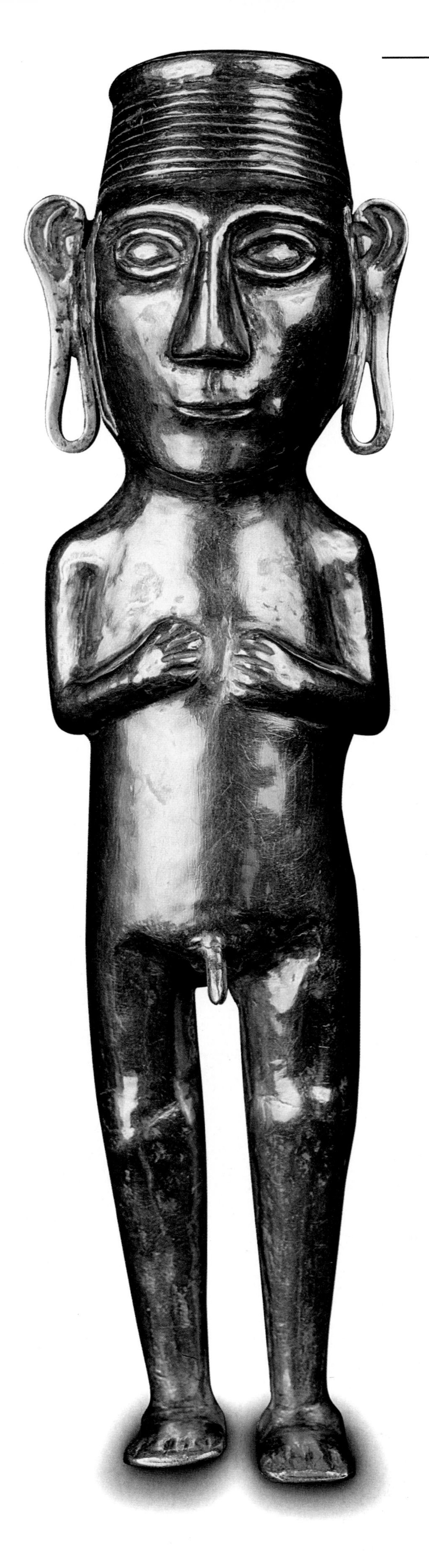

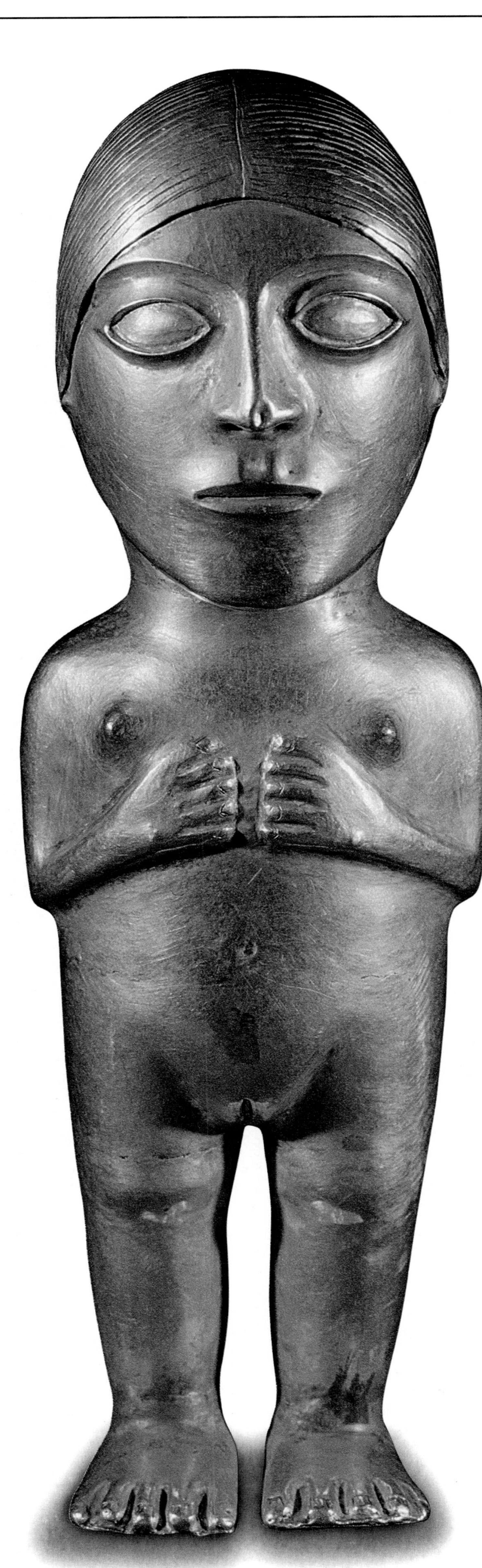

138 (far left) For the Incas elongated ear lobes – represented very realistically on this male figurine – were a mark of high rank. For this reason the Spaniards referred to Inca nobles and rulers as orejones*, or 'big ears'.*

138 Inca female figurines were usually depicted with arms crossed and their long hair tied back.

139 (left) This tunic made from camelid wool is a wonderful example of gold decoration applied to textiles. It was found in an Inca tomb on the southern coast.

139 (below) In addition to human figurines in gold and silver, Inca craftsmen also produced animals, such as this llama.

ENTERTAINMENT, MUSIC AND DANCE

140 (below) This Moche pottery vessel depicts a seated figure playing a wind instrument that is similar to the panpipes of the Old World. His closed eyes indicate that he is blind.

140 (right) A Nazca artist created this musician, who is also playing the panpipes, as well as other instruments.

Our information about the musical instruments of pre-Inca peoples comes from a range of objects made from pottery and other materials. Music accompanied the dances and singing that were performed at religious ceremonies as well as seasonal and agricultural festivals. Many Moche, Nazca and Huari funerary assemblages included pottery musical instruments painted in various colours. The instruments, especially flutes and drums, were the same design as those used many centuries later by the Incas. Some vessels depict people playing drums, while others show animal herders playing a small version of a panpipe.

The oldest images of dancers are found in rock art and graffiti dating from the early periods of the hunter-gatherers. An example showing a war dance between two combatants has been dated to the Chavín period, but, once again, most of our information relates to Inca times. We have the accounts by chroniclers of the festivals and ceremonies that they witnessed, many of which have survived to the present day despite colonization.

According to the chroniclers, festivals only began after the priests had performed rites and sacrifices to propitiate the gods. These ceremonies were followed by collective drinking of chicha, the alcoholic drink made from maize. Pedro de Cieza de León describes in detail the famous festival of Inti Raimi that took place at the winter solstice. 'After eating and drinking, everyone was intoxicated, including

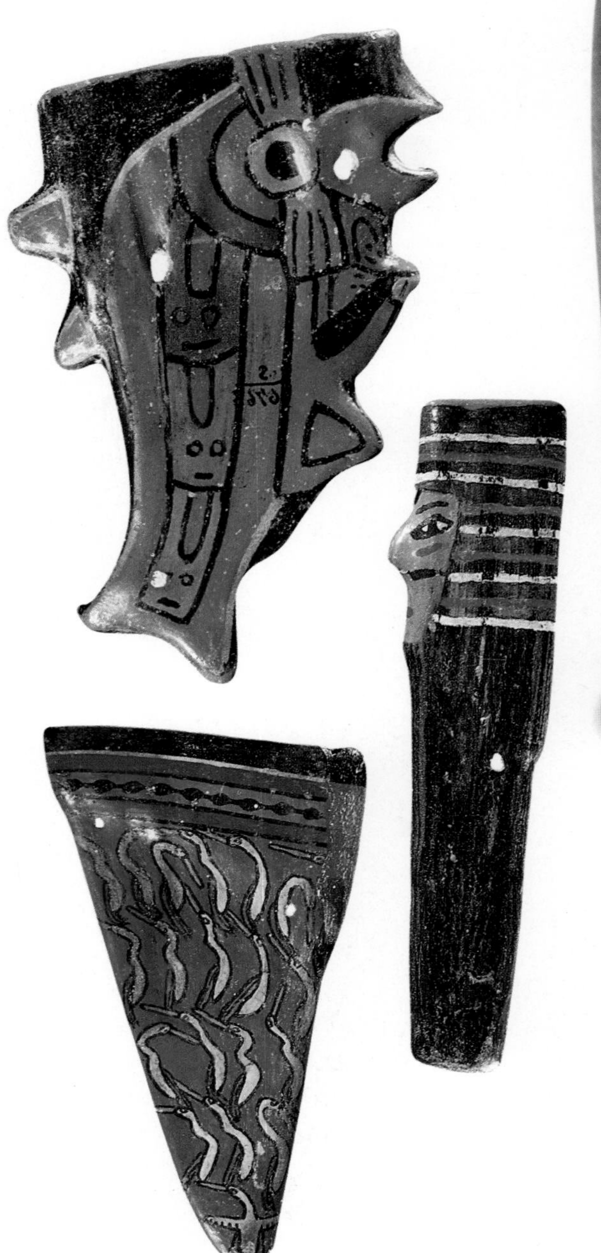

141 (left) These three small, exquisitely made pottery flutes painted in bright colours are examples of Nazca instruments. One is in the form of a fish, another has a human head and the third is completely covered with painted birds.

141 (above) This curious Vicús vessel takes the form of a figure playing the panpipes, still one of the most common wind instruments in South America today.

142 Two elaborate Moche ceramic trumpets: one ends in an animal-head and the other has an added figurine, perhaps a god, wearing a crescent-shaped hat. Their curled shape is reminiscent of the European hunting horn.

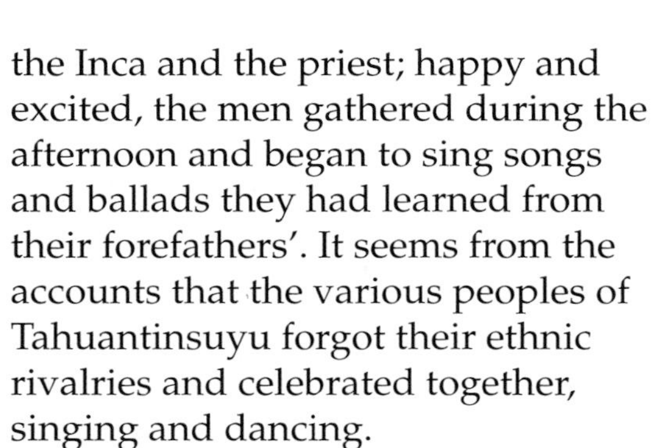

the Inca and the priest; happy and excited, the men gathered during the afternoon and began to sing songs and ballads they had learned from their forefathers'. It seems from the accounts that the various peoples of Tahuantinsuyu forgot their ethnic rivalries and celebrated together, singing and dancing.

Each province of the empire had its own traditional ritual dances that were usually preceded by melodies so mournful that they were capable of hypnotizing their listeners. The province of Collao was famous for the number of dances that accompanied its festivals. In one, the dancers wore animal masks and skins; in another, the men and women dancers had their faces painted and wore gold and silver bands in their noses and ears.

The Incas used wind and percussion instruments of various kinds to accompany their songs and dances. There were different types of drums, called *huancar* in Quechua; the smaller ones were played by women. Guaman Poma de Ayala writes of a certain type of drum made with skin from the scalps of enemy warriors. Several examples of another instrument that was used from ancient times have been found

143 (far left) *This graceful figurine comes from the region of Ica in southern Peru. The musician is wearing a tall cylindrical hat and is playing a flute, an instrument found throughout the Andes.*

143 (left) *Poma de Ayala's drawing illustrates a solemn festival celebrated by the people of Contisuyu, one of the four regions of the Inca empire. While the men dance, wearing bird masks and feathers, the women play tambourines and sing.*

143 (below) *A Moche vessel depicting a curious musician playing a drum: his face, with its pointed nose and narrow eyes, resembles that of a bird. The seated figure may be a shaman participating in a musical ceremony.*

at Chavín. This was the *pututu*, a sort of trumpet or bugle made from a type of marine shell, the *Strombus galeatus*, found along the coasts of northern Peru and Ecuador. The deep tone of this shell created the rhythm for collective work and sacred ceremonies. *Pututus* were also made from clay, and several Moche objects have been found illustrating people playing this instrument. Flutes were also popular and there were many different types. They were made from wood, bone, bamboo and clay. One of the best-known took the form of a panpipe that had at least five sections joined together. The *quena* was made from a single reed or bamboo and had eight holes. Stories and epic poems accompanied by traditional ballads were also popular during festivals. These had been handed down from generation to generation from ancient times.

144 (below left) Rows of bells hang from the roof of the temple reproduced in this Chancay silver model.

144 (right) Moche ceramics are our main source of information for the different architectural styles of religious buildings. This stepped model has a circular base and a small shrine on the top. It is probable that only priests could enter the shrine.

Studies of the spiritual world and religious beliefs of the peoples of the Pre-Columbian Andes have been carried out alongside investigations of their material world. Most of the available information once more relates to the Inca period because of the detailed accounts given by the Spanish chroniclers. For earlier periods, the modern scholar has to rely on the sometimes mysterious scenes reproduced on pottery, textiles, jewelry and sculptures.

As already mentioned, there are some remains of temples from pre-Inca times. The Moche temples of 'the Sun' and 'the Moon', and the Huaca del Dragón at Chan Chan from the Chimú era are the most complete and informative. There are also buildings at Tiahuanaco, Cerro Purgatorio and Pachacamac.

On the coast the most common building material was sun-dried mud bricks – adobe – which were used to build temples in a series of stepped terraces. The shrine proper was on the topmost level and could probably only be entered by the priests of the cult. These shrines were made from wood or some other perishable material and so our only clues today to their appearance are small pottery models.

145 (left) Although only a few temple buildings have survived in Peru, many pottery models have been found. This Sicán vessel takes the form of a well-proportioned building covered with relief decorations. Two tiny figures, probably temple guards, stand beside the entrance.

145 (below) Steps terminating in a spiral form the stylized symbol of a stepped temple in this Moche vessel. The stepped pyramid was perhaps itself a model of a mountain, the sacred place where humans could come closest to the gods.

The wall paintings surviving in some temples, such as the Moche temple called 'El Brujo' in the Chicama valley, provide important iconographical information.

There are links between Inca religion and cults and those of other Andean civilizations, but they are too imprecise to be able to discover their origins and establish their provenance with certainty. While in Mesoamerica many deities have been identified whose cults continued over the centuries until Aztec times, in Peru only a few images of supernatural beings have survived. Some of these recur with great frequency and are linked to three animals: the jaguar, the snake and the bird of prey. One of the oldest such representations is that

146 (left) A terrifying grimace and large fangs are the striking features of this wooden face, added as a decoration to a Moche mirror. It has been identified as Ai Apaec, the principal god in the Moche religious pantheon, perhaps inherited from the ancient cult of Chavín.

on a textile fragment found at Huaca Prieta dating from the Preceramic Period. It is possible to distinguish a bird with a hooked beak – a condor or an eagle – holding a snake.

Fanged monsters with numerous legs and strange probosces appear in the famous plaster reliefs at the temple of Garagay of the Early Ceramic Period. No one knows the meaning of these images, which have been found in the oldest buildings in the coastal regions of Pre-Columbian Peru, but they must represent the cults worshipped by the first settled communities of farmers and fishermen.

One of the most important sites for the study of Andean religions is Chavín de Huántar. Construction at the site, at an altitude of 3,150 m (10,335ft) above sea level, began around 900 BC. Despite intensive study, Chavín is still full of mystery,

146 (right) Images of the supernatural being known as the Staff God entirely cover the surface of the monolith at Chavín called the Raimondi Stela. His strange iconography is a mixture of human, feline and snake-like features and is found throughout the Andes, notably on the Gateway of the Sun at Tiahuanaco.

146 (above) Complex, hybrid images also appear on the Tello Obelisk at Chavín. Elements from the Amazon forest are mixed others from the coast. Scholars have identified the caiman in the symbolism of the main deity of this iconographic puzzle. Like the Lanzón and the Raimondi Stela, this obelisk embodies the main themes of the cult venerated at Chavín de Huántar.

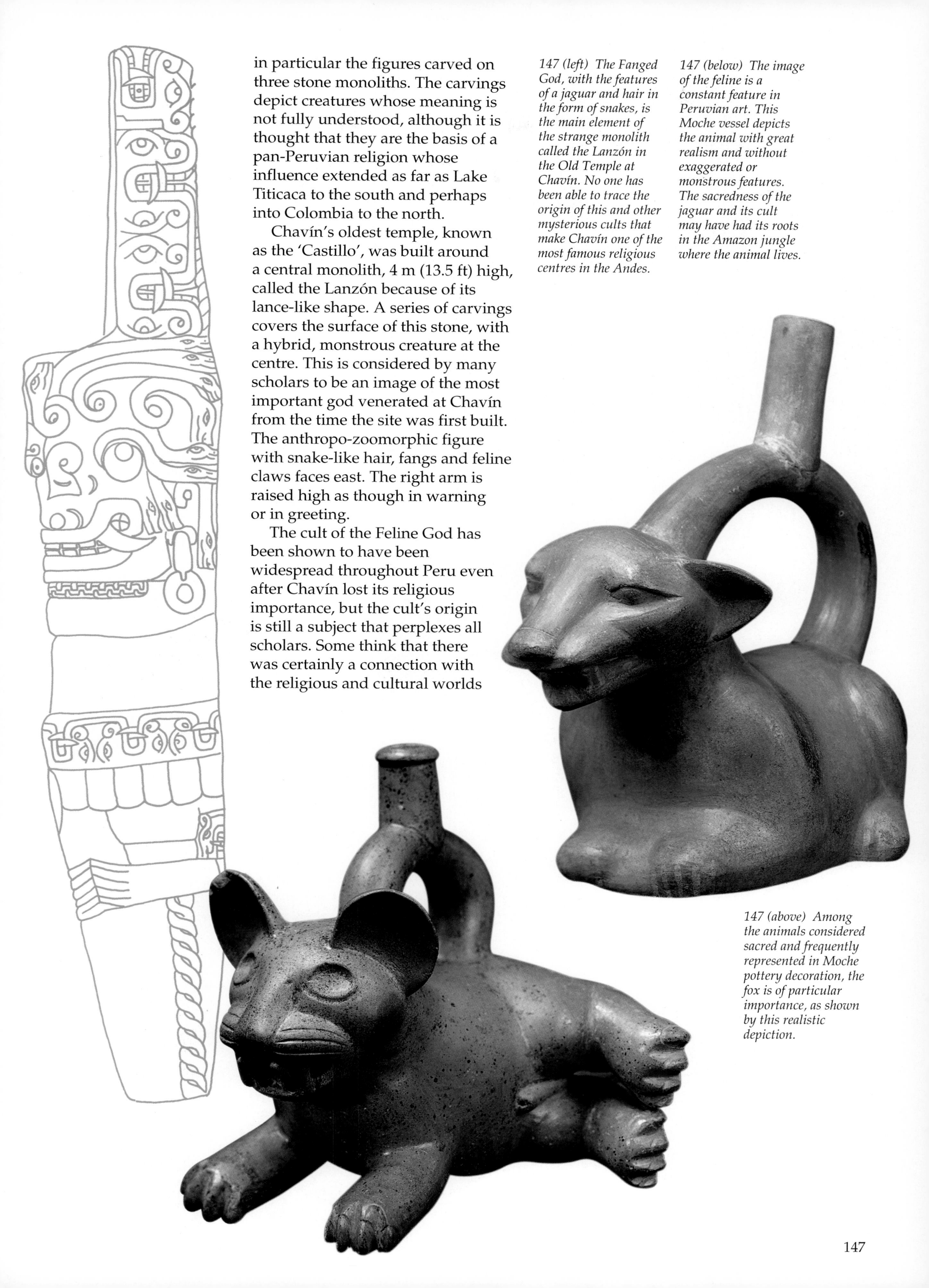

in particular the figures carved on three stone monoliths. The carvings depict creatures whose meaning is not fully understood, although it is thought that they are the basis of a pan-Peruvian religion whose influence extended as far as Lake Titicaca to the south and perhaps into Colombia to the north.

Chavín's oldest temple, known as the 'Castillo', was built around a central monolith, 4 m (13.5 ft) high, called the Lanzón because of its lance-like shape. A series of carvings covers the surface of this stone, with a hybrid, monstrous creature at the centre. This is considered by many scholars to be an image of the most important god venerated at Chavín from the time the site was first built. The anthropo-zoomorphic figure with snake-like hair, fangs and feline claws faces east. The right arm is raised high as though in warning or in greeting.

The cult of the Feline God has been shown to have been widespread throughout Peru even after Chavín lost its religious importance, but the cult's origin is still a subject that perplexes all scholars. Some think that there was certainly a connection with the religious and cultural worlds

147 (left) The Fanged God, with the features of a jaguar and hair in the form of snakes, is the main element of the strange monolith called the Lanzón in the Old Temple at Chavín. No one has been able to trace the origin of this and other mysterious cults that make Chavín one of the most famous religious centres in the Andes.

147 (below) The image of the feline is a constant feature in Peruvian art. This Moche vessel depicts the animal with great realism and without exaggerated or monstrous features. The sacredness of the jaguar and its cult may have had its roots in the Amazon jungle where the animal lives.

147 (above) Among the animals considered sacred and frequently represented in Moche pottery decoration, the fox is of particular importance, as shown by this realistic depiction.

148 (left) Priests and shamans are often represented in Pre-Columbian art. This Moche vessel shows a figure of high rank (demonstrated by the headband, cloak and hood) with his hands joined, perhaps in meditation.

148 (below) This enigmatic Salinar vessel is of a tattooed figure with facial paintings, who seems to have cut his throat with a knife.

of Mesoamerica and that the Feline or Jaguar God was perhaps passed on from the Olmec civilization through trade links. Others consider that both civilizations were influenced by a religious cult that had its origins in the Amazon.

At an unknown date, another monolith was erected at Chavín with even more complex iconography; this is the Tello Obelisk, named after the archaeologist who first studied its images and tried to understand their meaning. The set of carved motifs is so elaborate and intricate that it could almost be called baroque; it includes a pair of caimans, snakes, jaguars and birds, all with hideous features, but also plants from the tropical forest such as peanuts and manioc. These images are clearly typical of the Amazon, so distant from the Andean highlands. But the iconography also includes images of two shells from the coastal regions of Ecuador, the Strombus and the Spondylus. Tello suggested that the religious cult at Chavín had its roots in the geographical and cultural area of the Amazon forest, but, basing their hypothesis on the shells and on the architectural style of the temples, other archaeologists have recently suggested that it originated on the coast. It is possible that diverse currents of belief from distant areas came together at Chavín, creating new ideological beliefs and iconographic symbolism.

In a later phase contemporary with the construction of the 'New Temple' at Chavín, the Raimondi Stela was erected, named after a famous traveller. This stela stands about 2 m (7 ft) tall and has the double incised image, one upright and one upside down, of the Staff God. This deity is part man, part animal; he has fangs and feline claws and holds two snake-like sceptres in his hands. As with the other two monuments, the symbolism is a rich and complicated mixture of elements, from which the jaguar and snake emerge. But what are the origins of the figure in the

149 This object, related to fertility rites, was called a paicha. The bowl has an opening which is connected to the mouth of the bird; liquid poured into the bowl flows from it into the drinking trough below and then runs along the channel in the handle until it reaches the end.

double image on the Raimondi Stela? What is his precise connection with the people of Chavín and with many other peoples of Peru and neighbouring regions? These questions are without clear answers and consequently many hypotheses surround this enigmatic deity, whose cult spread throughout the ancient Andes before the rise of the Inca empire.

After the collapse of Chavín as an important religious centre, this cult was continued by subsequent peoples in the following centuries. Archaeological evidence of the Moche, Nazca and other peoples reveals the same symbolic imagery of a hybrid deity with feline and snake-like features. Despite stylistic differences in some of the details, which are blended with elements of local cultures, this deity can clearly be identified as a direct derivation of the one worshipped at Chavín. Another recurring and important deity is Ai Apaec, the monster demon of the Moche culture, whose name was handed down to the Incas.

The site that reveals the Chavín legacy most clearly is Tiahuanaco, whose ruins stand on the shores of Lake Titicaca. Most scholars believe that Tiahuanaco was founded as a religious centre once Chavín had fallen into ruins. The purpose of Tiahuanaco was perhaps to perpetuate the cult of the Staff God and it became a powerful religious centre. The emblem of the cult worshipped at Tiahuanaco was carved on the Gateway of the Sun and, despite some differences, it clearly resembles the Staff God. Oral tradition handed down over the years names this god as Viracocha, 'He that arrived on the spray of the sea'. The figure on the gateway is surrounded by a host of

149 (below) An Inca ceramic figurine depicts a man, perhaps a priest of the cult of water and springs, holding a container.

other winged figures (demons or servants?), each of which also has human and animal features.

Viracocha, or whatever name was given to the Staff God, was not only worshipped at Tiahuanaco. This deity also had an important role throughout the Huari region, as demonstrated by the images found on many items of pottery and textiles. This cult, diffused by the peoples of Tiahuanaco, became widespread and prevailed over local deities. The Incas worshipped the sun god Inti, but they always tolerated the veneration of the mysterious Viracocha who was considered the supreme Creator God and who was linked to water and fertility.

Images of the Feline God and the Staff God are found everywhere in the Andean world before the advent of the Inca empire, but it should also be remembered that in Peru, as in Mesoamerica, all natural elements – plants and living creatures – were worshipped alongside the deities. *Huacas* existed everywhere; this Quechua word expresses the concept of 'sacred' and was used to indicate places where the supernatural was present, such as water, mountains, tombs and temples but also the homes of the spirits of the woods and springs.

The Moche, Nazca and Chimú civilizations often depicted fish, birds, shells, foxes and deer with human or monstrous features. Equally, plants important for subsistence, such as the bean, maize and squash appear in human form as guardians of fertility. The cult of Pacha Mama was also still strong at the time of the Incas; Pacha Mama was a sort of Earth-Mother figure who had human female features.

Chroniclers tell us that the Inca rulers imposed the cult of the sun god on their subject peoples, to whom they dedicated temples like the famous Coricancha at Cuzco, the 'Golden Enclosure', with walls lined with gold and silver. The Inca himself was also worshipped as an incarnation of the Sun, together with his wife-sister, who was the incarnation of the Moon.

Unfortunately, however, the lack of written information means that our knowledge of so many of the gods and beliefs of ancient Peru is still fragmentary and based on an interpretation of the iconography of pottery, wall paintings and textiles.

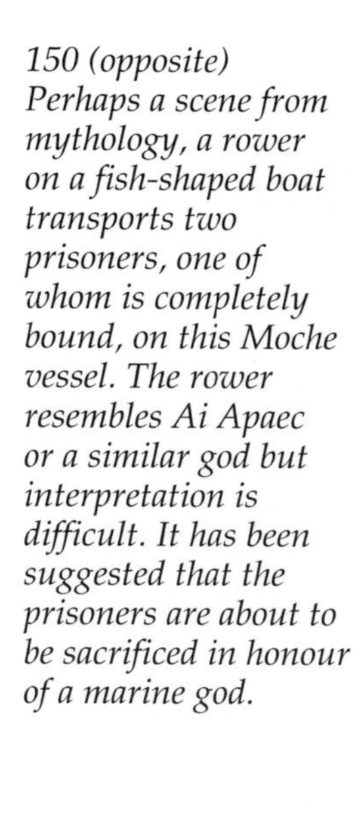

150 (opposite) Perhaps a scene from mythology, a rower on a fish-shaped boat transports two prisoners, one of whom is completely bound, on this Moche vessel. The rower resembles Ai Apaec or a similar god but interpretation is difficult. It has been suggested that the prisoners are about to be sacrificed in honour of a marine god.

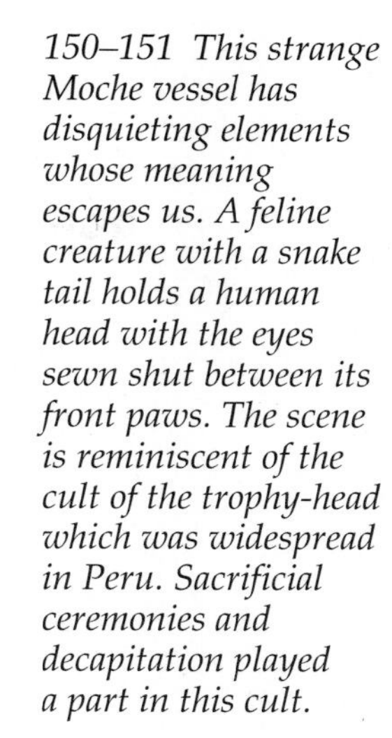

150–151 This strange Moche vessel has disquieting elements whose meaning escapes us. A feline creature with a snake tail holds a human head with the eyes sewn shut between its front paws. The scene is reminiscent of the cult of the trophy-head which was widespread in Peru. Sacrificial ceremonies and decapitation played a part in this cult.

151 (right) The bird of prey is a common Andean image. This ceramic bottle depicts a bird, probably an eagle, devouring a snake. Both creatures were important in Andean cosmogony and were linked with the celestial world.

151 (below right) Another important bird for many Andean peoples was the owl, represented very realistically in this Moche pottery vessel.

152 (above left) In this funerary scene on a Sicán pottery vessel four people carry the deceased on a sort of stretcher. Their expressions of grief and lamentation are touchingly depicted.

152 (right) As with all ancient peoples, in the Andes death was represented as a skeleton. This Moche vessel probably depicts a priest wearing a ceremonial mask.

152–153 A funeral procession of small wooden figurines accompanies a coffin in this Chimú model. This type of image is found frequently in the art of the northern coast, demonstrating the importance of the cult of the dead.

153 (right) For the Incas too the traditions and ceremonies associated with the cult of the dead were very important. In this drawing by Guaman Poma de Ayala a ritual connected with death is being enacted.

The greatest number of finds from Pre-Columbian Peru come from the funeral assemblages found in tombs. The dry climate, particularly along the coast, has contributed to the exceptional preservation of pottery, jewels and organic materials such as textiles, feathers and food and human and animal remains. Almost all Andean civilizations practised burial, as shown by the oldest collective tombs dating from the Preceramic Period.

As with so many other ancient peoples, the inhabitants of the Andes believed strongly in the afterlife and venerated their ancestors. A dignified burial was thought necessary so that the dead might be able to continue to enjoy the privileges and happiness of earthly life in the afterworld. Both cultural traditions and religious beliefs led Pre-Columbian Peruvian civilizations to practise the cult of the dead, not only to preserve their spirits but also to safeguard the bodily remains from destruction.

Naturally, nobles and members of the ruling élite received special treatment; this is demonstrated by several tombs, of which the most famous is that of the Moche 'Lord of Sipán'. In addition to the jewels, weapons and other precious objects found in the tomb beside this high-status individual, there were also the bodies of companions sacrificed to accompany him on his final journey to the afterlife.

The largest and most interesting collection of tombs is found in the two cemeteries at Paracas. These vary from the modest to the sumptuous, depending on the social rank of the deceased. Archaeologists have discovered that ordinary people were buried in fairly shallow graves after being wrapped in a rough cotton cloak called a *manto*, and were accompanied by simple pottery objects.

Members of the élite and wealthy individuals were recognizable from the numerous layers of high quality textiles that were wrapped around their mummified bodies, creating a large mummy bundle known as a *fardo*.

Mummy bundles were typical of the coastal cultures of southern Peru and were prepared by placing the body in the seated position inside a basket and then wrapping layers of material around it, which were then sewn together. Often the mummy bundle was adorned with a tunic of coloured feathers, a cloak or a funeral mask and sceptre. Some scholars have suggested that the number of layers of material was not random but was linked to magical and religious rituals.

The funerary assemblage that accompanied the mummy bundle could be quite magnificent, including jewels, feathers, shells, pottery and animal skins.

The tombs of the oldest cemetery at Paracas were bottle-shaped, while more recent ones took the form of underground rooms. Both types served as multiple tombs with as many as forty mummy bundles being found together, sometimes heaped one on top of another.

153 This mummy bundle of a high-ranking individual, covered with a fine woollen cloak, was found at Paracas. The status of the deceased is shown by the ceremonial sceptre topped by a human skull, probably a trophy-head.

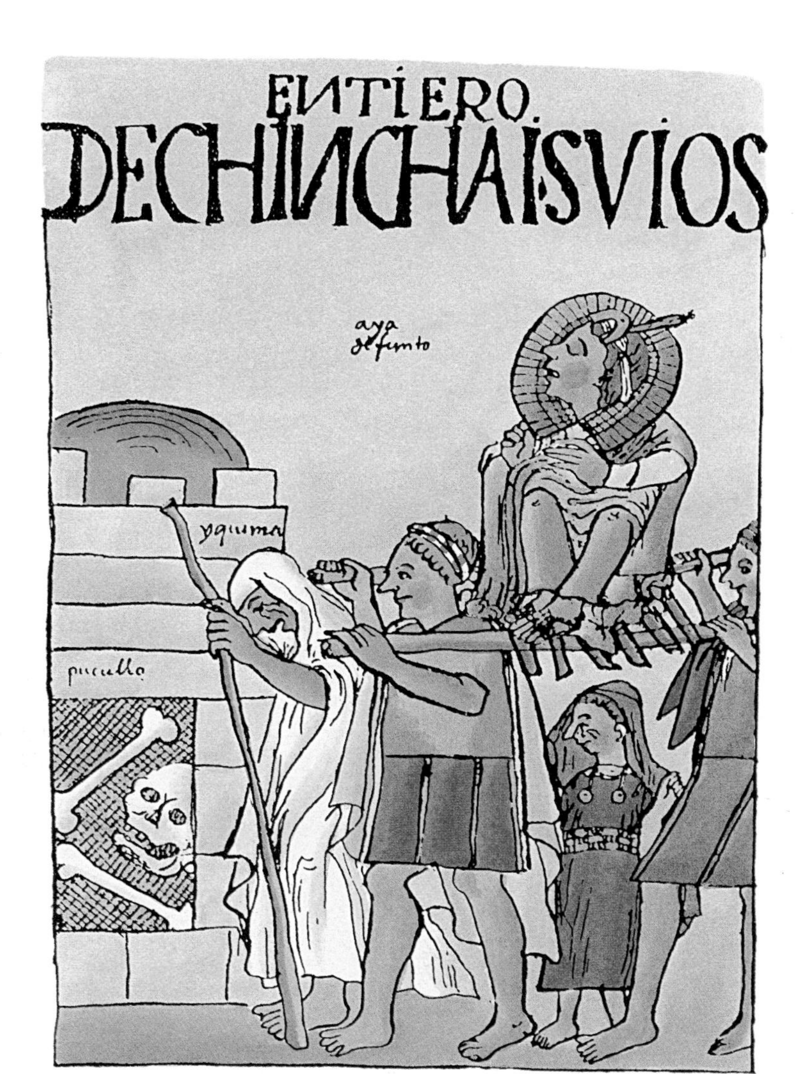

154 (left and below left) Two wooden Chancay masks: burial masks such as these were placed over the face of the dead person.

154 (left) In this drawing of a festival that took place each November, the body of a dead person is carried in a procession to receive offerings from the living.

Large mummy bundles were less frequent than the more modest versions, as they contained the bodies of the members of the ruling élite. Analysis has shown that the bodies were of men. As mentioned above, the dry coastal climate of the desert means that the contents of the tombs are wonderfully preserved, as long as the *huaqueros* (tomb-robbers) have not already removed all objects of value, thus destroying an enormous amount of cultural history.

One interesting aspect of the tombs at Paracas and elsewhere is the state of preservation of the bodies. In 1896, the German archaeologist Max Uhle found a mummy bundle in his excavations at Pachacamac near Lima. Inside was the mummified body of a 12-year old girl wrapped inside a basket and still perfectly preserved after 500 years. The body had not been embalmed but simply left in the extremely dry soil. This discovery, and many others, demonstrated that bodies, simply wrapped in lengths of magnificent textiles, had undergone a natural process of mummification.

154 (opposite, right) The mummy bundles of the Paracas, Nazca and Chancay cultures often had 'false heads'. This one is made of cotton, with eyes, nose and mouth applied. It also has a gold and copper head-covering.

155 (below) Found in a Chimú burial site, this wooden figurine is carved in a stylized but elegant style and doubtless had a religious meaning.

155 (right) These two small dolls are typical of the Chancay culture. They were made from wool, cotton and vegetal fibres and were not toys but were images used in magical or ceremonial rituals.

It has been shown that the practice of mummification in Peru began around 4000 BC and was adopted by every culture until the Inca empire. The majority of the mummies found, both Inca and pre-Inca, were dried by natural processes and only certain groups used artificial embalming. Modern scholars have not yet discovered the secret of these embalming techniques.

For natural desiccation, burial sites where the climate and soil were completely dry were chosen. To facilitate the process, corpses could be placed to dry near a fire. More sophisticated methods involved removing the entrails from the body and replacing them with plants which acted as preservatives, then sprinkling the body with special resins and unguents.

After mummification, the rulers of Tahuantinsuyu, nobles and the founding fathers of *ayllu* virtually assumed the role of *huacas*, that is sacred idols, and were carried around Cuzco in processions during religious festivals, dressed up and masked, just like the living. These mummies were never buried but were preserved inside cool caves where they received offerings and sacrifices during the year. Garcilaso and Guaman Poma de Ayala give interesting accounts of this custom and describe their amazement at the exceptional condition of preservation of the Inca mummies.

Modern laboratory analyses carried out on Andean mummies from different periods have revealed fascinating information about the state of health of the individuals at the time of death, their illnesses, the type of food they ate and even whether they took coca or other drugs during their lifetime.

Chroniclers have left us accounts, often confused and contradictory, of human sacrifices ordered by the Inca leaders to propitiate the sun god Inti. However, recent discoveries of the mummies of children and adolescents who had suffered violent deaths during rituals and whose bodies were preserved by the freezing temperatures of Andean glaciers have confirmed once again the accuracy of the historical sources.

The power of the Inca rulers was closely linked to the army. A rigidly organized war-machine was an essential foundation for their far-reaching imperial ambitions. There were two basic types of soldier: those in permanent service and the adult men who could be called up at any moment to serve their 'state'.

When they were needed, the part-time soldiers were forced to leave their fields, which must have resulted in economic disadvantage. The full-time soldiers were generally officers from the higher castes from the different provinces of the empire. Their families could only follow their movements from afar: women were never involved in fighting.

The troops were well trained and well armed. As the empire grew, so the army increased in size, both to keep up with the expansionist policy of the Inca and also to be able to put down the continual revolts by different ethnic groups who did not accept the authority of the emperor.

Inca armies had wide range of weapons, but all were similar to those used by other Andean peoples.

156 (left) In this drawing by Guaman Poma de Ayala of an Inca war scene the emperor Huayna Capac, standing on a litter, is preparing to hurl missiles against an enemy with his sling. This type of weapon, called a huaraca *in Quechua, was common in the Late Horizon.*

156 (opposite above) Moche iconography provides valuable information about the war equipment of the peoples of the northern coast. This vessel depicts a warrior wearing an elaborate head-dress and holding a club.

157 (below) Armed warriors are often depicted on Peruvian pottery. This kneeling warrior armed with a shield and club was made by the Vicús culture. His head-dress is a symbol of social rank.

157 (right) Armed with a shield and a lance, this pottery Moche warrior has a very threatening appearance.

Without a doubt, however, the Inca army was the best armed and most effective of all Pre-Columbian forces in the Americas up to the time of the Spanish Conquest.

The Inca army also benefited from an efficient infrastructure of communications and provisioning. Supplies of food and weapons were moved along the many roads of the empire, thousands of miles long and provided with rest points.

The officers wore distinctive clothing: the *unku*, a sleeveless tunic that was a symbol of nobility, a *huara* which was a sort of loincloth, and *ojotas*, or sandals. A wooden helmet decorated with feathers and fringed knee-caps were symbols of status.

Battles took place in the open and the most common form of fighting was hand-to-hand. It seems that the Incas knew how to use a bow and arrow but looked down on this weapon as being typical of the Chunchos, the 'savages' of the forest.

The first weapon to be used in battle was generally the *huaraca*, or sling, when the troops were still at a distance from one another. Close quarter fighting saw the use of a sort of javelin which had a metal or wooden tip, whereas the weapons used in hand-to-hand fighting were clubs designed to crack the skull of an opponent. One type had a head in the form of a spiked copper ball tied on with cord, while others were in the shape of a star made of stone or copper, attached to a shaft. Often a T-shaped axe blade was fixed to the handle instead of a club-head. For defence, the Inca soldier had a small shield and a wooden helmet. Clothing was sometimes padded with cotton for protection. After a victory, survivors from the defeated army were taken to Cuzco to be submitted to humiliation there.

158 (opposite below) This colourful scene painted on wood shows three women dressed in simple skirts walking in procession towards the Inca emperor seated on his throne. The women have their wrists tied as prisoners and may be destined for the Aclla Huasi, *the 'House of the Chosen Women'.*

158–159 A warrior, possibly Inca, grips a prisoner by the hair and brandishes an axe at him, in this scene painted on a wooden kero *of the Colonial era. Holding a prisoner by the hair is a common motif in the iconography of the Andean world.*

159 These are examples of Inca weapons, although such stone star-shaped club-heads and T-shaped axes are also found in much earlier periods. The club-heads had wooden shafts inserted and the axe-heads were attached to long wooden handles.

159 (top right) Details of warfare are carefully depicted in this painted scene in which Inca warriors confront a European on horseback. The Incas wear plumed helmets, carry rectangular shields and brandish stone axes fixed to long wooden handles.

159 (centre) These are two typical Andean weapons: a bronze, T-shaped axe with a wooden handle, and a stone club set on a shaft. Iron was not used in the Andes until the arrival of the Europeans.

159 (below left) An Inca warrior is depicted on this kero. *He is armed with a lance and shield and wears a feather head-dress and a cloak over a tunic. The feather ornaments were emblems of power and status.*

160 (right) Many images from different Andean cultures graphically depict the fate of prisoners of war. This horrifying scene shows the punishment of a noble, probably accused of betraying the Inca.

160 (below) A naked prisoner is tied to a framework of posts that end in animal heads in this Moche pottery vessel. Scholars believe that many prisoners of the Moche were sacrificed.

The Inca had the power to have prisoners sacrificed.

When the Spaniards began their conquest of the Andes, they found their horses, sabres and firearms gave them a huge advantage: even the sight of them frightened the indigenous peoples. During battle, the local peoples tried to defend themselves using an ancient weapon called a *boleadora*, formed by three stones tied together with twisted llama tendons. The weapon was whirled and thrown at the legs of the horse or soldier. If successful, the cords would wrap themselves around the target and trip the enemy.

Images of warriors and their weapons are also known from civilizations before the Late Horizon. Many Moche vessels show warriors wearing helmets and armed with clubs and shields of different shapes. An equal number show naked and bound figures, certainly defeated troops destined for sacrifice.

Nazca art depicts a particular ritual that was also linked to war – that of preserving the heads of the enemy. The cult of the 'trophy-head' is also seen in some burials, in which mummified heads are placed next to the mummy of the warrior.

161 Images of prisoners were frequently depicted on Moche pottery. This vessel shows a prisoner sitting cross-legged; he has a rope around his the neck and his hands are bound behind his back.

AN ARCHAEOLOGICAL JOURNEY THROUGH SOUTH AMERICA

162–163 A detail of a relief from the Huaca del Dragón near Chan Chan. The scene includes numerous part-animal, part-human figures surrounded by the two-headed snake, an image which occurs very frequently in Chimú art.

SEARCHING FOR LOST WORLDS

When the Spanish Conquistadors visited the majestic Inca cities and were amazed by their architectural perfection, they learned that other cities had been built many centuries earlier by different peoples, about whom the Incas knew little or nothing. Even at that time, only the ruins of these ancient cities remained, some of which were described in the accounts of the Spanish chroniclers.

The route we follow here winds through the highlands and along the coast of Peru, stopping to admire the ruins of the most famous and important sites. Some, perhaps well preserved or still visited over the centuries, such as the sanctuary of Pachacamac, were never forgotten. Others have only recently been cleared of sand or vegetation and brought to light

We begin our journey high up in the mountains with the most important religious site of the Early Horizon: Chavín de Huántar. On its walls, menacing images of the Jaguar and other monstrous beings represent the fundamental symbols of Andean religion. Another very ancient site is Cerro Sechín, where the strange reliefs have also been intensively studied by scholars.

Descending from the highlands towards the northern coast, we come to huge temples in the form of terraced platforms. This is the site of Moche where the Pyramids of the Sun and of the Moon are the architectural evidence of a rich and advanced civilization that developed during the first centuries AD, named Moche after the site. The valleys of this coastal region are now desert but were once made fertile by the peoples who lived in them and they became the sites of two important cities: Chan Chan and Paramonga. The first was decorated with lovely adobe reliefs that were plastered and painted. Its importance made it the capital of the Chimú kingdom, one of the most powerful in Pre-Columbian Peru, and it is still possible to make out the huge urban centre, though unfortunately, it is not well preserved. Paramonga looks like a fortress and though it may have been a Chimú foundation it was perhaps remodelled by the Incas and its precise historical importance and chronology are still a puzzle.

Moving south along the coast, we reach Tambo Colorado, an Inca administrative centre. This site is a perfect fusion of architectural

164 (above left) The imposing ruins of Chavín de Huántar are located in a mountainous area that is difficult to reach; the temple site is one of the oldest and most mysterious complexes in Pre-Columbian Peru.

164 (below left) The Nazca people transformed an arid, desert-like terrain into cultivatable land and supplied their towns with fresh water by using water channelling systems like the underground aqueduct, or puquio, *seen here.*

164–165 Tiahuanaco is the most impressive example of Pre-Inca megalithic architecture in the Andes. This is a detail of the Semi-Subterranean Temple, with the large gateway of the Kalasasaya in the background.

165 (right) Tambo Colorado was built as a coastal outpost of Tahuantinsuyu. Today it is the best preserved example of an Inca site blended with a more ancient coastal tradition.

166 (below) *The system of terracing the sides of mountains for agriculture was a typical Inca practice.*

166 (above right) *The Incas probably inherited their knowledge of building terrace irrigation and drainage systems from the Huari and other, older, civilizations. These devices formed the basis of their agricultural economy.*

features typical of the Late Horizon with coastal styles and traditions. Farther south, our journey reaches one of the most mysterious and debated areas of the world: the Pampa, where the surface of the land is marked by the huge designs, or geoglyphs, ascribed to the peoples of Nazca. The enigmatic figures they have left are so large that some can only be recognized from above.

Leaving the coast, our route takes us up into the mountains on the border between Peru and Bolivia. The region of Lake Titicaca is the location of the richly decorated and ancient site of Tiahuanaco; this has been identified by some experts as the centre of a powerful theocratic empire which spread the cult of the Gateway God throughout the Andean world during the Middle Horizon. In the same area are the *chullpas* of Sillustani, curious tombs in the shape of towers which were built by the Colla people and were reused by the Incas.

Tombs of a different sort are represented by the clay coffins modelled to resemble humans that are found on the rocks of Ulasa in the Amazonian forest. These cemeteries have only recently been discovered and were probably the work of one of the most bitter enemies of the Incas, the warring Chachapoyas.

The final stops on the journey are at the sites where the rulers of Tahuantinsuyu built their palaces and temples, leaving impressive and massive works of construction that some chroniclers thought must have been 'raised by the gods'. We first visit sites on the islands in Lake Titicaca and then Cuzco, the 'centre of the world' and capital of the Inca empire. Cuzco was a rich city endowed with palaces and roads and systems that provided its inhabitants with running water. Today, it is only possible to appreciate the scale of the Inca city by the ruins of walls that have been incorporated into the colonial city. Near Cuzco is the megalithic 'fortress' of Sacsahuaman which may have been dedicated to the sun.

The Inca passion for working and carving rock and stone is evident at Kenko and Tambo Machay, sites of great ritual significance that were centred on the cult of water. Of all the places imbued with a sacred presence, the most famous in Pre-Columbian Peru was without doubt the sanctuary of Pachacamac, the seat of the ancient cult dedicated to the god Pachacamac and a place of pilgrimage. The temples at this site were visited for many centuries before the rise to power of the Incas

166–167 These ruins are at the site of Sillustani, near the modern town of Puno. They are the remains of a chullpa*, one of the many burial towers built by peoples living on the shores of Lake Titicaca who were incorporated into the Inca empire.*

167 (left) The valley of the Urubamba was regarded as sacred by the Incas. Large stone ruins still crown the mountains that line the river.

and pilgrims continued to visit the site into the 16th century.

Our journey continues with the cyclopean walls, steep flights of steps and solar monoliths of Ollantaytambo and Pisac, built among the narrow valleys and bare mountains of the region of Cuzco. Although experts have attributed many functions to these sites, their real meaning is still unknown.

After a stop at Raqchi to visit the ruins of a gigantic temple thought to have been dedicated to the supreme god Viracocha, our journey reaches the luxuriant forests covering the peaks where the most inaccessible city in the New World was built: Machu Picchu. No visitor to this city, whether scholar or layman, can fail to be amazed by this site. Wandering around the walls, houses, towers and terraces of this ghost city, perhaps abandoned on the eve of the arrival of the Europeans in Peru, it is easy to understand why so much has been written about the extraordinary art and culture of the Incas and other Andean peoples.

Our final site is Sipán where, in the last few years, splendid tombs have been brought to light. The story of the site and its treasures is told by the person who discovered them, Walter Alva.

168 (top) One of the most impressive Inca monuments carved from rock is the famous Sayhuite Stone, which stands at 3,500 m (11,500 ft) above sea level near Curahuasi. This monolith measures 4 m (13 ft) in diameter and 2.5 m (8 ft) high. Two hundred figures of animals and plants carved on the upper surface may be connected to the cult of water and Pacha Mama, the Earth-Mother figure.

168 (below) The site of Pisac provides one of the best examples of Inca architecture. Its ruins dominate the Urubamba valley from the top of slopes covered with terraces.

168–169 The massive walls of Sacsahuaman, the mysterious site near Cuzco, give it the appearance of a fortress, but it was probably a religious centre linked to worship of the sun.

169 (opposite, below left) These are the ruins of a complex Inca structure known as the Red Fortress at Puca Pucara, not far from Cuzco. The structure contains rooms, terraces and flights of steps.

169 (opposite, below right) The walls of Ollantaytambo rise steeply up a mountainside. They are all that remains of what was once perhaps a temple and observatory dedicated to the cult of the sun.

CHAVÍN DE HUÁNTAR: GODS IN STONE

170–171 The Old Temple, or Castillo, was the first building constructed in the ceremonial centre at Chavín, between 900 and 700 BC. The large temple is U-shaped, a form typical of early coastal structures.

171 (opposite above) This stone head comes from the New Temple. Characterized by feline fangs, it is similar to heads that have been found on the walls of the Semi-Subterranean Temple at Tiahuanaco.

171 (opposite right, above) A view of the ancient religious centre of Chavín de Huántar. Although in a deep valley in Callejón de Conchucos, the site lies at an altitude of 3,150 m (10,335 ft).

171 (opposite right, below) The relief on an architrave of the New Temple depicts one of the mythical creatures connected with the cult at Chavín de Huántar, a bird of prey with monstrous features and feline fangs.

The site of Chavín de Huántar is located at 3,150 m (10,335 ft) above sea level in Callejón de Cochucos on the eastern slopes of the Cordillera Blanca. The main centre of the site, spread over a sloping and terraced expanse that covers around 4.5 ha (11 acres), is formed of a number of ceremonial, U-shaped pyramidal buildings with sunken plazas, arranged on terracing. One of the most important features of the site is the puzzling and monstrous nature of the stone sculptures that represent, at least in part, a synthesis of pan-Peruvian religious beliefs.

A Gallery of the Double Cantilever
B Gallery of the Captives
C Gallery of the Carved Stones
D Chamber of the Ornamental Beams
E Los Murciélagos
F Las Alacenas
G Las Escalinatas
H Los Laberintos
I The Lanzón
J El Loco
K Los Laberintos
L El Campamento
M Las Caracolas
N Rocas Canal

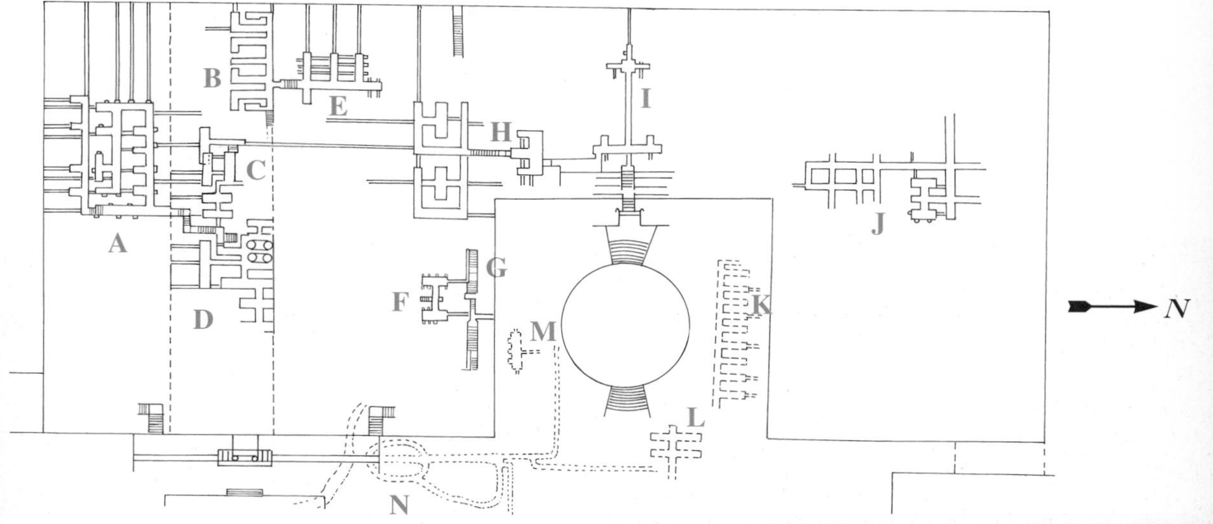

Chavín art and architecture can be divided into two chronological phases: the first is between 900 and 500 BC (in the Early Horizon); and the second is around 500 to 200 BC. At Chavín we find stylistic and cultural elements that are typical of coastal sites blended with influences from the Amazonian *selva* and the highlands. The result is a baroque imagery that is linked to mysterious cults.

Chavín de Huántar became a large religious centre, a place of pilgrimage and the seat of an oracle from about 900 BC; it was equal in importance to the coastal site of Pachacamac. At the time of the European Conquest, the local people told the Spaniards of the existence of this ancient shrine that was abandoned and in ruins.

One of the oldest buildings at the site is the Old Temple, incorrectly called the 'Castillo' because of its huge size. It consisted of a large U-shaped platform, with a small, sunken circular plaza. The rear side was originally 100 m (330 ft) in length and it was 15.25 m (50 ft) high overall. The entrance faced the river Mosna where the sun rose. Behind the temple were a road and some civil structures. The circular plaza, sunk 2.4 m (8 ft) below ground

level, could hold 500 people and was lined with stone slabs decorated with reliefs. The images were of human and feline figures marching or dancing in a procession, probably reflecting the rituals that took place in the temple. Two enclosure walls around the platform were made of carved and polished stones, of which only traces remain.

Inside the temple were galleries and passages that were part of the sacred route. This labyrinthine route led to a large sculpture in the centre of the temple, around which it seems the whole structure was built. The so-called 'Lanzón' is one of the three key monuments at Chavín de Huántar. The monstrous anthropo-zoomorphic creature carved on the huge, pointed monolith was the oldest cult object in the sanctuary – the image of the oracle itself.

Around 500 BC, the Old Temple underwent partial modification that coincided with a new cultural influx, as shown by a different type of pottery. A structure called the 'New Temple' replaced the previous one. The priests, or whoever held power at Chavín, modified the old U-shaped structure which was now an obsolete architectural model. New squares were cleared, stretching from the river to the entrance of the New Temple. The temple had an entrance of imposing size made from white and black stone blocks. The squares could hold a huge number of people, a clear sign of the increase in the flow of worshippers to the shrine. The main façade of the building was adorned with about forty sculpted tenoned heads and numerous carved panels. The ancient cults were not abandoned, despite the architectural changes, however – there is no evidence at Chavín to suggest that there were changes in ideology or sacred images. Although the Tello Obelisk and Raimondi Stela were created later than the Lanzón, they share similar elements. The fusion of a man-jaguar image with symbols such as the bird of prey, the caiman, the snake, tropical plants and sea-shells, however, makes interpretation difficult.

After 700 years of continuous use, Chavín began to lose its power around 200 BC. The causes are not known but archaeological studies show a slow and constant decline. The temples and squares of the first great unifying force in Peru were abandoned. Chavín de Huántar became a ghost city but its deities remained 'immortal', absorbed into the succeeding Andean religions.

173 (above) Two carved stone heads in the 'labyrinth', a long ceremonial corridor inside the Old Temple.

173 (below) This pottery vessel from a tomb at Chavín de Huántar also relates to the iconography of the Jaguar God.

172–173 A view of the Old Temple at Chavín de Huántar: the rear façade of the building was originally over 100 m (325 ft) long.

172 (opposite, below left) The long west wall of the Old Temple is decorated with carved stone heads of monsters. They recall the cult of the trophy-head found throughout Peru.

172 (opposite, below right) Strange reliefs decorate the walls of the Old Temple at Chavín. The west wall, seen here, is carved with a monster created from volute motifs.

173 (above) This huge monolith, measuring nearly 4.5 m (15 ft) high stands in the heart of the Old Temple. It is known as the Lanzón as its shape resembles a long, pointed lance.

173 (top right) A view along one of the corridors inside the Old Temple known as the 'Gallery of the Double Cantilever'.

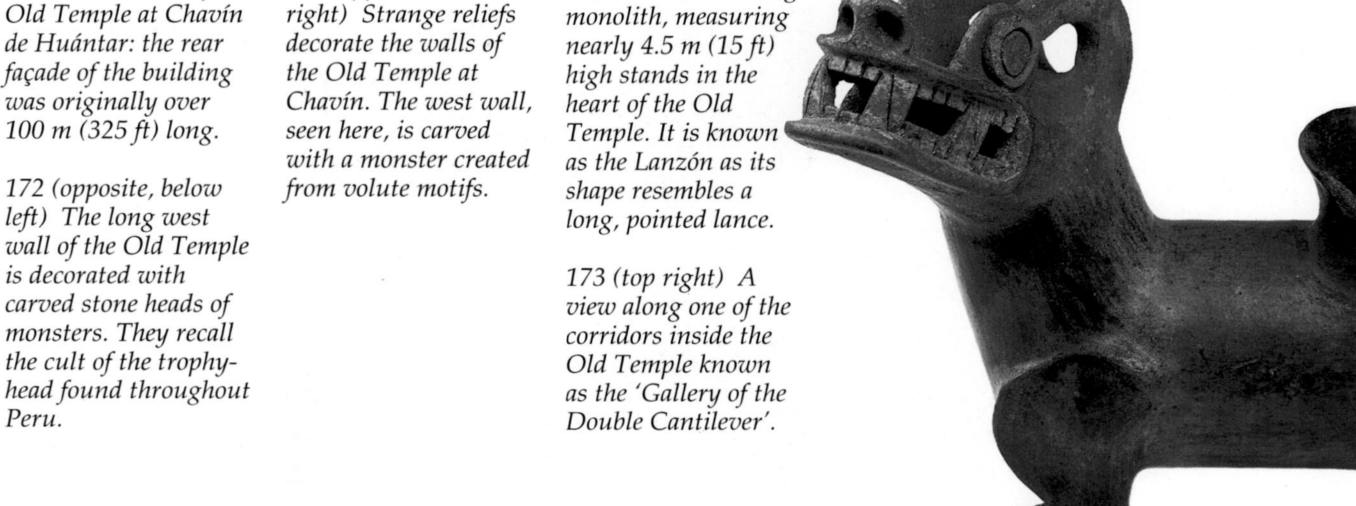

174–175 One of the carved stone slabs that cover the external walls of the temple at Cerro Sechín. Each of the over 400 slabs is decorated with a large, incised figure whose imagery seems linked either to war or human sacrifice.

174 (right) A view of the adobe temple at Cerro Sechín. It is not known exactly when this ceremonial platform complex was built though some scholars believe it may have been founded as early as 1700 BC.

CERRO SECHÍN: THE SACRIFICIAL PLATFORM

Cerro Sechín stands in the Casma valley and covers an area of some 5 ha (12 acres). The date of its foundation is still the subject of debate, with some scholars arguing that the oldest buildings were constructed as early as 1700 BC, while the most recent may be 500 BC.

The main structure at this site is a three-tiered pyramidal platform, with smaller buildings to either side and possibly a sunken circular plaza. The walls of the building were made from plastered adobe and were partially decorated. The pyramidal platform was around 50 m (165 ft) square and around its outer wall was a remarkable frieze of stone slabs decorated in low relief with strange figures – some of the earliest stone sculptures found in the Andes.

Julio C. Tello, the archaeologist who explored the site in 1937 together with other colleagues, felt that this was the oldest building on the site. More recently it has been possible to date it to around 1500 BC.

The carved stone slabs that adorn the walls of the structure are somewhat reminiscent of the 'dancers' at Monte Albán in Mexico, though there is a huge geographical gap between the two sites. The large figures depicted on the slabs are mostly armed warriors, mutilated human heads and dismembered and disembowelled bodies. This macabre and horrifying imagery has been interpreted in different ways.

One suggestion is that the human figures, usually armed and carrying sceptres, represent dignitaries, warriors or shamans. It is not clear, however, whether the scenes relate to battle or to sacrificial rites that were linked to the cult of the trophy-head, which was quite widespread

175 (right) Two of the mysterious figures on the carved stone slabs at Cerro Sechín, on the 'Gateway of the Warriors'.

175 (top right) Dismembered bodies, decapitated heads and mutilated figures with closed eyes are some of the macabre images incised on the monoliths of the large temple platform at Cerro Sechín. It has been suggested that it was a ceremonial centre dedicated to human sacrifice.

175 (centre right) One of the oldest Peruvian images linked to the cult of decapitation and the trophy-head, this carving depicts a warrior holding human heads.

throughout the Andes. The armed figures are always whole and not only carry weapons and sceptres, but also wear a pillbox hat and a sort of loin-cloth. Although these images are very particular to this site, comparable sculptures are known from Sechín Alto. Depictions of dismembered humans can be found on Moche pottery and Chimú textiles, while images of the trophy-head are more frequently found in Nazca art.

Scholars are still divided over the interpretation of the figures on the slabs at Cerro Sechín: some regard them simply as warriors engaged in a bloody battle, while others are convinced they are participants in a sacrificial ritual. Indeed, there are those who think that Cerro Sechín was a ceremonial centre where human sacrifices were made to propitiate supernatural forces and to gain their favour in solving problems created by overpopulation.

176–177 The temple of Cerro Sechín reconstructed at the time of its greatest splendour: the reliefs may have been painted in bright colours to increase their visual impact.

THE PYRAMIDS OF THE SUN AND THE MOON

178 (left, below) A mysterious deity with feline features and snake-like hair is depicted in relief on the walls of the Huaca de la Luna.

178 (below) Repeated reliefs painted in red yellow and black decorate the Huaca de la Luna.

179 (opposite) A detail of a painted wall relief from the Huaca de la Luna, depicting the mask of a deity with feline fangs.

178 The huge Huaca del Sol, or 'Pyramid of the Sun', rises above the site of Moche. This imposing structure was begun in the 1st century AD and is made from millions of adobe bricks.

178 (centre below) Motifs such as this stylized two-headed snake are similar to decorative elements in Moche textiles.

Archaeological research has shown that the Huaca del Sol and the Huaca de la Luna, two temple complexes in the form of vast pyramids, were the political, religious and perhaps administrative centre of the southern area of the 'kingdom' of the Moche.

The Huaca del Sol is one of the largest Pre-Columbian buildings in the Americas and is made from millions of adobe bricks. It stands almost 40 m (130 ft) high, although it has been badly damaged, and its base measures 345 by 160 m (1,130 by 525 ft).

The structure is formed of four superimposed terraces, with the summit originally reached by a ramp on the northern side. Scholars have ascertained that what remains today is the result of eight separate building phases carried out over a long period. Construction began around AD 100 and was completed before AD 450. Traces of the paint that once decorated the external walls of the pyramid are still visible. The temple proper probably stood on the summit of the highest terrace, but has since disappeared.

Remains of decorated tombs and houses at the foot of the pyramid suggest that the temple was also a residence and burial site for the ruling élite. It was probably enlarged and embellished by each succeeding dynastic generation.

The name Huaca del Sol (Pyramid of the Sun) was assigned to it rather arbitrarily by the Spaniards, and in fact we do not know the identity of the god in whose honour the Moche people built it.

The same is true of the Huaca de la Luna (Pyramid of the Moon), which was also the temple of a deity whose identity is unknown. This *huaca* was built in six phases at the

foot of a large hill called Cerro Blanco. It is also a terraced structure made from adobe, measuring 290 by 210 m (950 by 690 ft) and consists of three asymmetrical, communicating platforms and four plazas, which have a certain harmony and elegance and give the building the air of a palace. Houses and workshops originally formed part of the ceremonial complex and surrounded the *huaca*.

A special feature of the Huaca de la Luna are its brightly coloured relief murals that decorate many of its courtyards. These were painted in white and red and yellow ochre, and depict a Moche decapitator god. Each image hides layers below. The symbolic themes are reminiscent of those also found on Moche pottery but scholars are still far from being able to interpret their meaning accurately.

PARAMONGA: TEMPLE OR FORTRESS?

180 (opposite, above left) Archaeologists disagree on the date of the construction of the site of Paramonga. Some think it is an Inca foundation (as claimed by the Spanish chroniclers), while others believe that it is a Chimú site.

181 (top) Various Spanish chroniclers refer to the site of 'Paramunca', and attribute its construction to one or another Inca emperor. It is possible, however, that the curious ruins date back much earlier than the Incas.

The Chimú people who lived in the Moche valley from about AD 1000 used the ancient systems of water channelling built by their predecessors, the Moche. Thanks to their skill in land management, it is thought that the Chimú succeeded in doubling the area available for agriculture by reclaiming land that had been desert for centuries. Consequently, numerous urban centres sprang up in oases. Examples include Pacatnamú and Túcume, where not only residential buildings have been found but also structures that were used for political and religious purposes.

It is more difficult to understand the precise role of a different type of site. Paramonga, like similar sites, has the appearance of a defensive fort on the boundary of the kingdom. It stands on a rise overlooking the coastal plain of Pativilca and comprises four superimposed artificial terraces. Although it does not prove that Paramonga or similar sites were indeed forts, its quadrangular design, with a diamond-shaped bastion at each corner made from adobe bricks, certainly recalls medieval European strongholds.

Some scholars believe that Paramonga was simply a 'reception' centre used by the reigning power, or perhaps a temple that had nothing to do with military or strategic functions. Others doubt that it was even built by the Chimú and that it may instead be related to the Late Horizon and the Incas.

More probably it was a complex dating from the Late Intermediate Period, and therefore a Chimú

180 (opposite, above right) The site of Paramonga dominates the flat coastland of Pativilca. Seen from afar, this strange complex certainly resembles a fortress.

180–181 Paramonga is laid out on four terraces. This ground plan and the corner bastions do give the site the appearance of a fortress, but Paramonga may simply have been a temple complex.

181 (bottom) These two tower-like structures flank the entrance to the site of Paramonga.

182 (top) *A stone stairway flanked by adobe brick walls leads to the top of the terraced platforms where Paramonga's main building, perhaps an ancient temple, stands.*

182 (bottom) *This adobe structure on the top of Paramonga's terraced platform is divided into rooms and corridors. The fact that so little remains of the site makes it difficult to understand its original function.*

construction, which was later modified by the Incas. It is certain that the Incas built a temple on the top, with brightly coloured walls. A section of a wall decorated with red and white squares survived until a few years ago, but has since collapsed.

It is thought that the structures were rebuilt and adapted to the king's needs, as happened at many other Inca sites. To add confusion to the matter, chroniclers have done much to cloud the question of Paramonga's origin: Pedro de Cieza de León recounts that it was a monumental work built by the Incas soon after subjecting the kingdom of Chimú and its ruler. Garcilaso also agrees with this opinion as shown by this excerpt from his account, although its accuracy may be doubted: 'In particular, as far as the valley of Paramunca was concerned, the Prince commanded that a fort be built there to commemorate the victory over the Chimú king … and the fort was built strong and it was splendid for its paintings and the other lovely things placed there. But the foreigners did not respect either the one or the other, nor did they abstain from razing it to the ground; and so only some reliquaries remained to show the uncivilizedness of those that destroyed it and to show what it had been'.

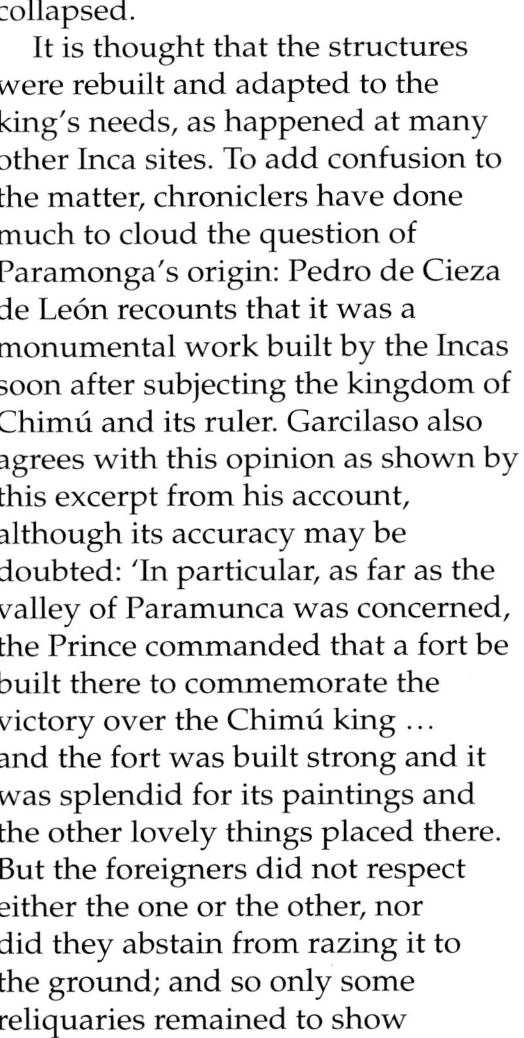

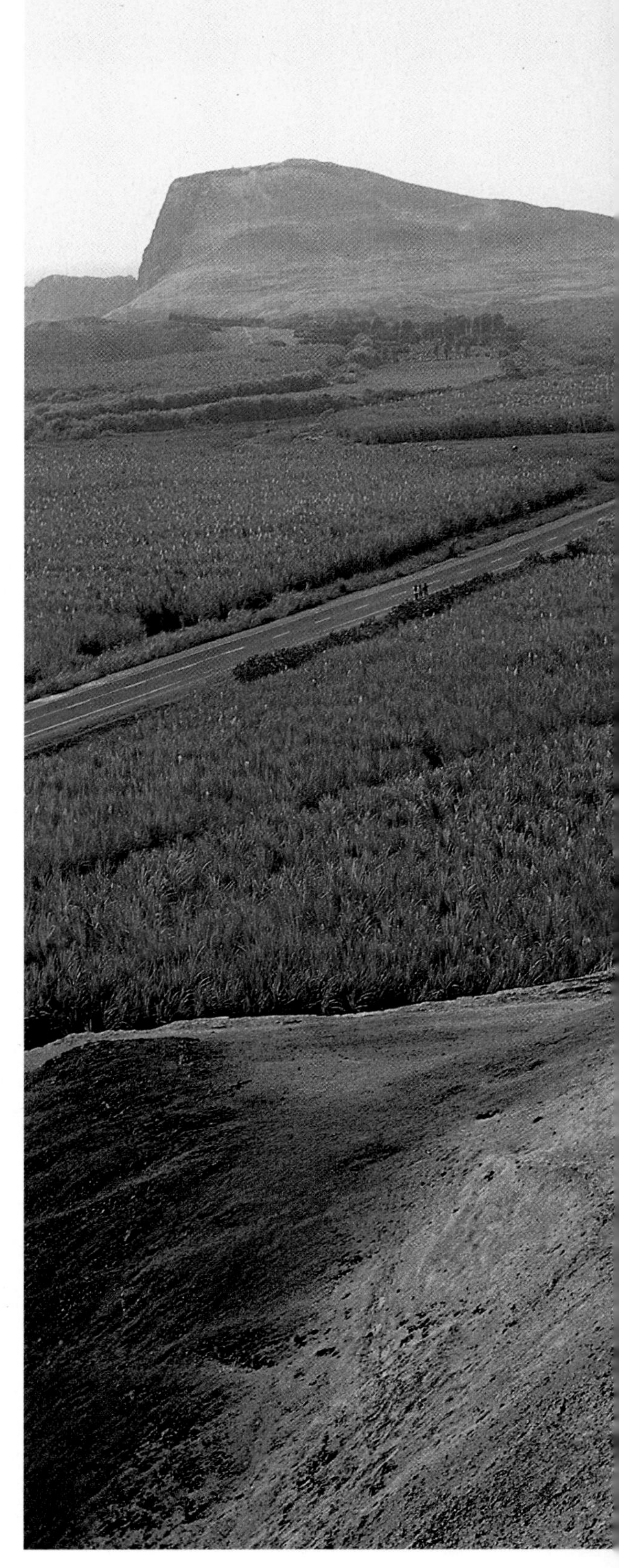

182–183 *Paramonga has four diamond-shaped bastions, one of which is seen here. These give the site the appearance of a fortress from the Old World.*

183 (right) *These remains of a massive structure with large entrance portals stand at the top of Paramonga complex.*

184–185 (overleaf) Enigmatic and imposing, the 'fortress' of Paramonga stands on the coastal plain of Pativilca. Although some chroniclers say it was built by the Incas, it was probably constructed during the Late Intermediate Period. Despite its fortified appearance, it may originally have been a temple.

CHAN CHAN: FRIEZES AND CITADELS

A Squier
B Gran Chimú
C Velarde
D Bandelier
E Laberinto
F Tello
G Uhle
H Rivero
I Tschudi
L Chayhuac

186 (above left) A view of Tschudi, showing the entrance to the Main Square via the South Gate. The reliefs at the base of the adobe walls were originally plastered and painted.

186 (below left) This magnificent relief combines a ladder motif with a line of small fish. Marine creatures were popular images in the wall decorations and are also found on Chimú textiles and pottery.

186–187 (above) This imposing gateway gives access to the north side of Tschudi citadel. Again the decoration includes the ladder motif, a symbol that is linked to the cult of mountains and to temple buildings.

187 (right) The ruins of Chan Chan are not well preserved, but the reliefs, with motifs reminiscent of patterns on textiles, still decorate the walls of many buildings, such as here on the Tschudi citadel.

By AD 1300, the rulers of the Chimú dynasty had selected the site of Chan Chan as the capital of their kingdom. It was an existing centre in the Moche valley not far from the coast, on the edge of land that was unsuitable for irrigation and agriculture. During their political and economic peak, the Chimú people transformed the desert into a true 'metropolis' that still holds many secrets. The centre of the city covers some 6 sq. km (2.3 sq. miles) while the city as a whole covers 20 sq. km (8 sq. miles), making Chan Chan the largest city in the Andes.

The layout of the centre was complex and original: it was made up of several enclosed areas, each surrounded by walls up to 7 m (23 ft) high and only slightly under 1,005 m (3,300 ft) long. The term 'citadel' is not accepted by certain scholars, who instead prefer 'palace',

187 (above right) In addition to marine creatures, the friezes at Chan Chan also depict birds with elaborate plumage, as seen in this detail.

understood in its widest meaning, including that of a medieval court. Each of these architectural units contained alleyways, dwellings, walk-in wells, adobe pyramids, a cemetery, tanks and storage areas. Irrigation canals brought water to the city from the river. Such a system would have produced enough food to support the population of 30,000.

One of the outstanding aspects of Chan Chan is the elegance of its architecture. The enclosures and the

188 (right) A detail of a frieze at Huaca del Dragón. This motif of an anthropo-zoomorphic hybrid creature is frequently found in Chimú art, but its precise significance is still not understood.

188 (far right) Strange animals and hybrid creatures appear repeatedly as decorative motifs in reliefs at Chan Chan and neighbouring ceremonial centres. This small bird adorns a wall of the Huaca del Dragón.

walls of the buildings were made of adobe bricks and were decorated with reliefs that were plastered and painted. The motifs include fish, birds, hybrid marine creatures and geometric patterns. Perhaps the artists who created the Chan Chan reliefs found their inspiration in textiles.

Despite the poor state of Chan Chan's ruins, the result of centuries of theft, looting and torrential rains, the visitor is still struck by the originality of the architectural style and the quality of the arabesque relief decorations. It seems probable that not all the areas of the site were inhabited at the same time: its expansion was gradual and reached its peak around AD 1300.

An account in a chronicle of 1604 known as the *Anonymous History of Trujillo* has aided archaeologists in reconstructing the history and expansion of the Chimú kingdom and its capital. The account, which probably contains a core of historical truth, states that the founding father of the Chimú line, Tacaynamo, reached the region from the north in a balsa boat. He laid the foundations of the future kingdom at Chan Chan and then his sons subdued the inhabitants of the Moche valley and the neighbouring regions.

Seven kings then succeeded to the throne, until Minchançaman, a historical figure who ruled until Chan Chan was conquered by the Incas in 1470, was captured and taken to Cuzco as a prisoner of war. This account in the *Anonymous History* finds some archaeological support. Scholars suggest that the

188–189 Archaeologists believe that the massive adobe construction known as the Huaca del Dragón was one of the most important Chimú cult buildings. Complex decorations cover its external walls, including the repeated motif of the two-headed snake – the symbol of the sky and the rainbow.

189 (above) Images found in the relief decorations, such as this human figure and monster, are also depicted on Chimú metal and pottery vessels and textiles.

number of citadels may represent the number of rulers mentioned in the historical tradition, but it is difficult to establish the dividing line between fact and fiction. There is still a debate among archaeologists about the number of citadels: some identify nine, while others claim there are twelve. There are also problems with the chronological order of their construction and their function. It is possible that these impressive structures were built as residences for successive kings or officials of Chimú as power was handed on. Some citadels were perhaps not designed as residences but as centres of administration.

Recent research has shown that, later in the Chimú dynasty, the dead king may have been buried in the citadel, where his family continued to live and administer his estate, so transforming it into a sort of mausoleum. Another theory suggests that the way the citadels were designed – detached and isolated from each other – supports the idea that each was used by the members of a certain social class so that they would not mix and could concentrate on their own duties.

With regards to dating, many archaeologists consider the citadel called Chayuac in the south of the city to be the oldest. It has high solid walls made in sections, a single entrance on the northern side and funerary platforms that face south. Some rectangular mounds that were built slightly later, as well as a T-shaped tomb and other burial places are considered to be the tombs of kings or officials which have been completely despoiled. Deposits of votive offerings, probably dedicated on the death of a king, have been identified around the burial platforms. The small number of these deposits in comparison with those of the more recent citadels shows that Chayuac was built when the kingdom was still early in its development. If we relate the evidence to the account in the *Anonymous History*, it was perhaps the palace of the first king, Taycanamo.

The Uhle and Tello citadels may date to a later or contemporary phase, but several of their architectural and structural features suggest they were built for other purposes. The citadels called Laberinto and Gran Chimú belong to a later phase in the life of Chan Chan, and many elements such as the numerous storehouses and so-called 'audiencias' are evidence of a period of economic success and

190 (below left) Gold and silver burial masks produced by Sicán and Chimú goldsmiths are often decorated with the image of the god Nylamp, with his characteristic narrow bird-like eyes.

190–191 Many fine examples of the metalworking skills of the Chimú people have survived to this day. This is the wooden side panel of a litter covered with gold and silver plates and pieces of turquoise and shell. The upper part of the panel is decorated with groups of people and crescent-shaped motifs. The litter was doubtless used on ceremonial occasions to carry high-ranking people.

rapid expansion of the city. Gran Chimú is the largest of Chan Chan's citadels: it measures 402 by 595 m (1,320 by 1,950 ft) and it has all the signs of a being royal palace – a collection of buildings aimed at exalting a reigning élite.

At this time there was a large increase in the amount of residential housing built for members of a class of officials whose power was growing. Increasing numbers of small houses were also built for the craftsmen who produced items to satisfy the desires of this ruling class.

The later citadels, of which the one called Tschudi is the most famous, were built one after another at shorter and shorter intervals following the same plan that had been established earlier. The buildings, walls and roads formed a sort of maze, which meant that access to the administrative centres could be controlled and therefore the immense riches amassed by the rulers kept secure.

Other buildings typical of the Chimú civilization are the *huacas* (artificial platforms and places of worship) found near the city centre. The most celebrated are the Huaca Esmeralda and the Huaca del Dragón. The latter, restored in the 1960s, consists of a wall that encloses two platforms, one on top of the other. The name of this *huaca* comes from the imagery of the wall reliefs: in the centre is a two-headed snake, a symbol of water and fertility.

Many questions still surround the kingdom of Chimú, its opulent civilization, its hierarchies, its treasures and luxuries and the people that built the largest city in the Andes, turning an arid and inhospitable desert into fertile countryside. Historical sources tell us that, despite the Inca conquest and total subjection of the people, the Chimú dynasty was only finally extinguished in 1602 when Chan Chan was already a mass of ruined and abandoned palaces.

192–193 An artist's reconstruction of Huaca del Dragón around 1300, the period of maximum expansion of the Chimú civilization and its capital, Chan Chan. The decorative motifs that cover the external surfaces of its walls and platforms have also earned it the name the 'Temple of the Rainbow'.

193 (right) This interesting wooden model comes from a tomb and probably depicts a ceremony that took place inside one of the main palaces at Chan Chan. The figure in the centre seated on a platform is a mummy.

194–195 Although the buildings at Tambo Colorado were built with adobe bricks, the site is still in an excellent state of preservation. Tambo Colorado is a perfect example of the fusion of Inca architectural styles with coastal traditions.

194 (right) The impressive walls of Tambo Colorado: traces of the original ochre, yellow and red paint are still visible.

TAMBO COLORADO: AN INCA OUTPOST

195 (below) The adobe walls of this palace at Tambo Colorado face on to the central square. The trapezoidal shape of the door and windows is an Inca addition to the traditional coastal style. In the square stands an ushnu, *a ceremonial altar found at many Inca sites.*

195 (bottom) A coastal outpost of the Inca empire, Tambo Colorado was built to decentralize the administrative and political power of Cuzco. Archaeologists believe that the Inca town was built on the remains of a pre-existing centre. This is a view of Tambo Colorado's main square.

A major Inca road ran from Pampa de Sechas, crossing Huaytará, to the coast, where it reached Tambo Colorado. One of the most important of the Inca coastal centres, Tambo Colorado was founded around AD 1450 in the Pisco valley as an administrative and provisioning centre, though some scholars think that its origins date to before the Late Horizon.

The centres built by the Incas in coastal areas contain both masonry buildings in the style of Cuzco and others built using local traditions and materials such as tapia and adobe. They also incorporate the typical Inca elements of trapezoidal doors and window niches.

Tambo Colorado is one of the best preserved coastal centres and is a clear example of Inca town planning mixed with local architectural and building techniques. The layout of the town is based around *kanchas* (enclosed and independent quarters). Accommodation and store rooms were arranged around a huge trapezoidal square. The Inca road ran along the right edge of this

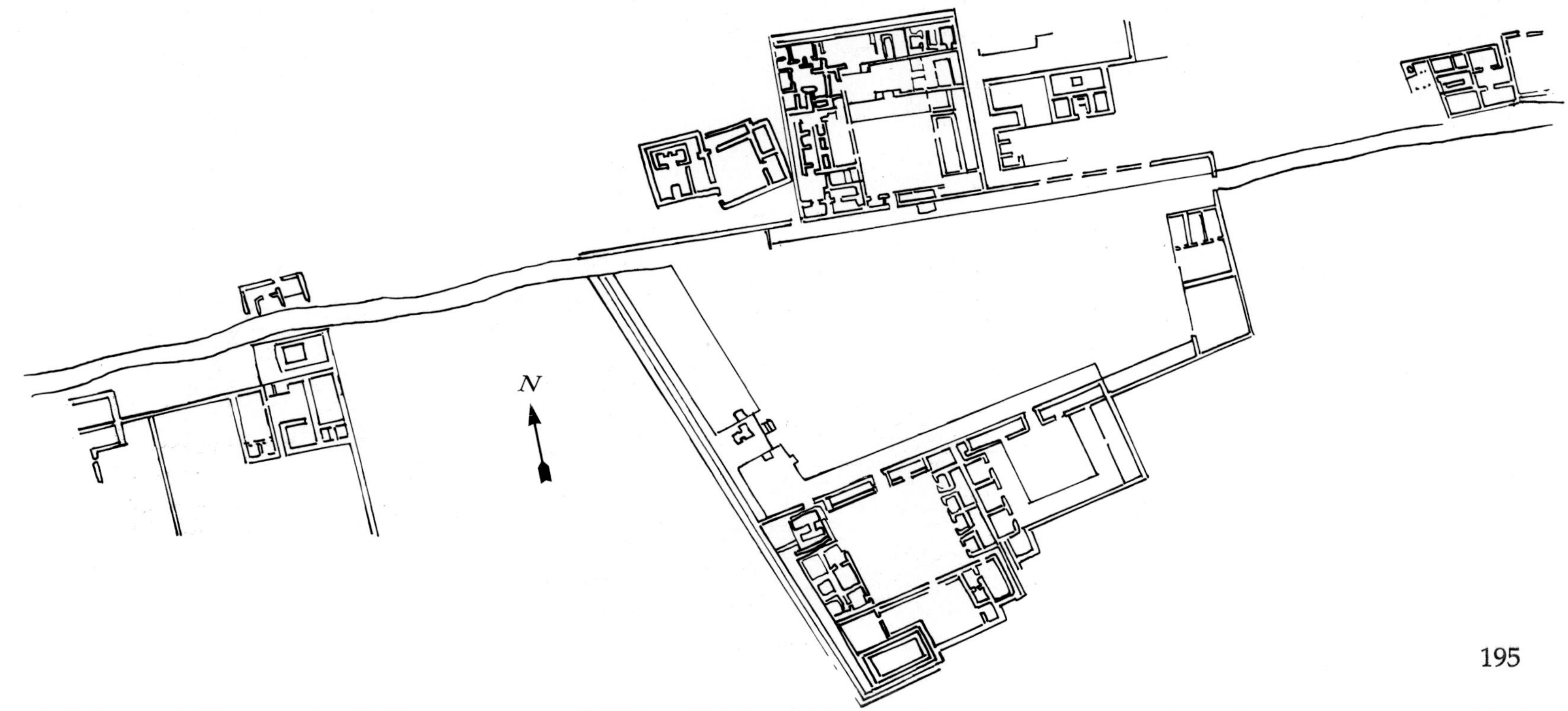

196–197 *A view of the magnificently preserved adobe buildings of Tambo Colorado, situated in the arid Pisco valley. The town stood on an important road that connected the Inca capital of Cuzco with the coastal territories of the empire.*

196 *(opposite below, left) Another example of the trapezoidal windows and doors of a building at Tambo Colorado. The plan of this administrative outpost, with different sectors arranged around a central square, resembles the layout of Huari sites.*

196 *(opposite below right) A detail of one of the most important buildings at Tambo Colorado, the so-called 'Fortress'. It was in fact probably a building used for administration and had rooms set aside for storage.*

square. Some quarters were used as residences by the high-ranking officials involved in administration; other areas were used as workshops where raw materials were processed into finished objects to be sent to the court at Cuzco. The walls of the buildings still retain traces of their original red and yellow ochre and white paint. A low platform near the west corner of the square was probably the *ushnu*, or sacred altar.

The presence of large walls at Tambo Colorado has led to the site erroneously being labelled a fortress. But Tambo Colorado, like Cajamarca and Huánuco Viejo, is one of a group of peripheral sites that were created by the Inca rulers to decentralize administrative power following the rapid expansion of the empire.

197 *(top) Excavations have revealed the existence of older towns below the foundations of many coastal centres, such as Chan Chan and Tambo Colorado. The buildings, roads, terraces and irrigation systems were first reused by the Chimú and then by the Incas.*

197 *(above) Windows at Tambo Colorado have the trapezoidal shape that is a typical feature of Inca architecture.*

NAZCA: ENIGMAS IN THE DESERT

● Nazca

1 Killer whale
2 Wing
3 Baby condor
4 Bird
5 Animal
6 Spiral
7 Lizard
8 Tree
9 Hands
10 Spiral
11 Spider
12 Flower
13 Dog
14 Astronaut
15 Triangle
16 Whale
17 Trapezoids
18 Star
19 Pelican
20 Bird
21 Trapezoid
22 Humming-bird
23 Trapezoid
24 Monkey
25 Llama
26 Trapezoids

The Pampa of Nazca is situated in the southern coastal region of Peru at the feet of the Andes. During the early part of the 20th century, the existence of one of the most extraordinary enigmas of the American continent was revealed here: the Nazca geoglyphs.

The Nazca civilization flourished in the Early Intermediate Period. At this time, the vast area covered by modern Peru saw numerous regional cultures flourish, each characterized by its own artistic expression, but all of them unified by the shared religion of the Feline God.

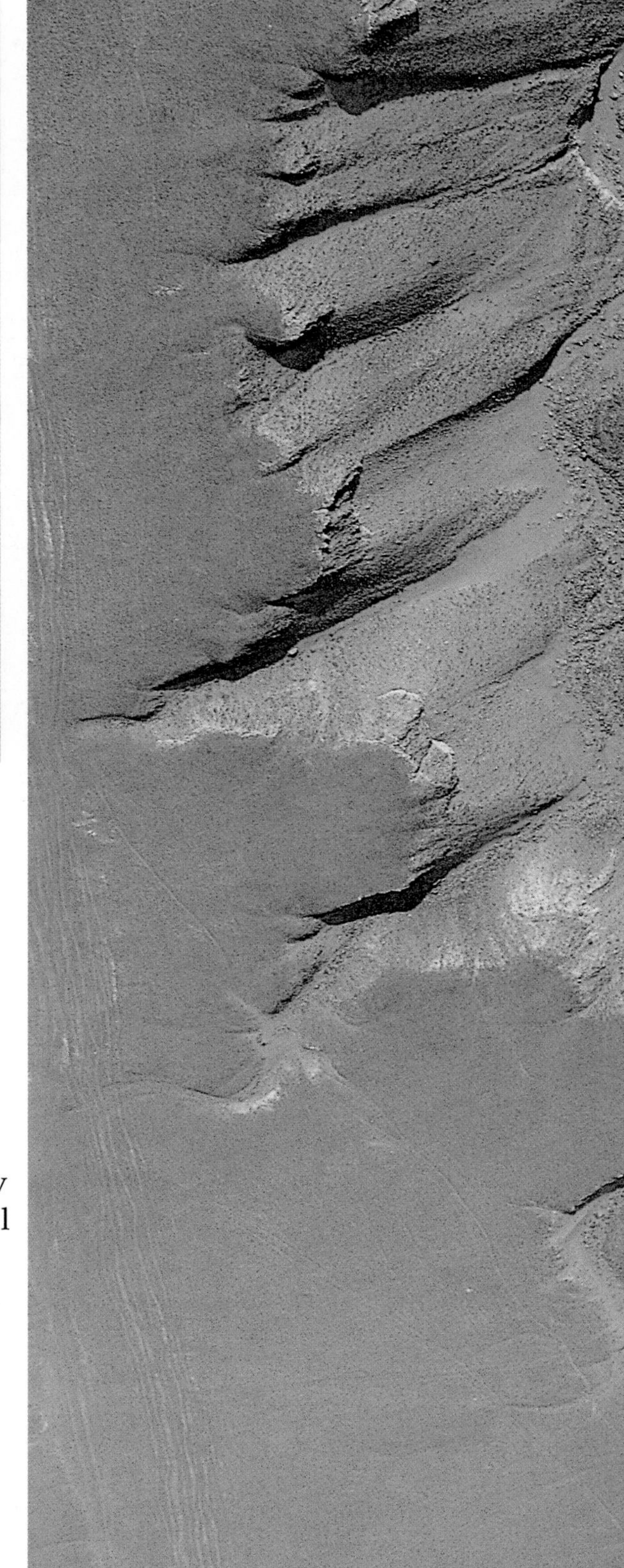

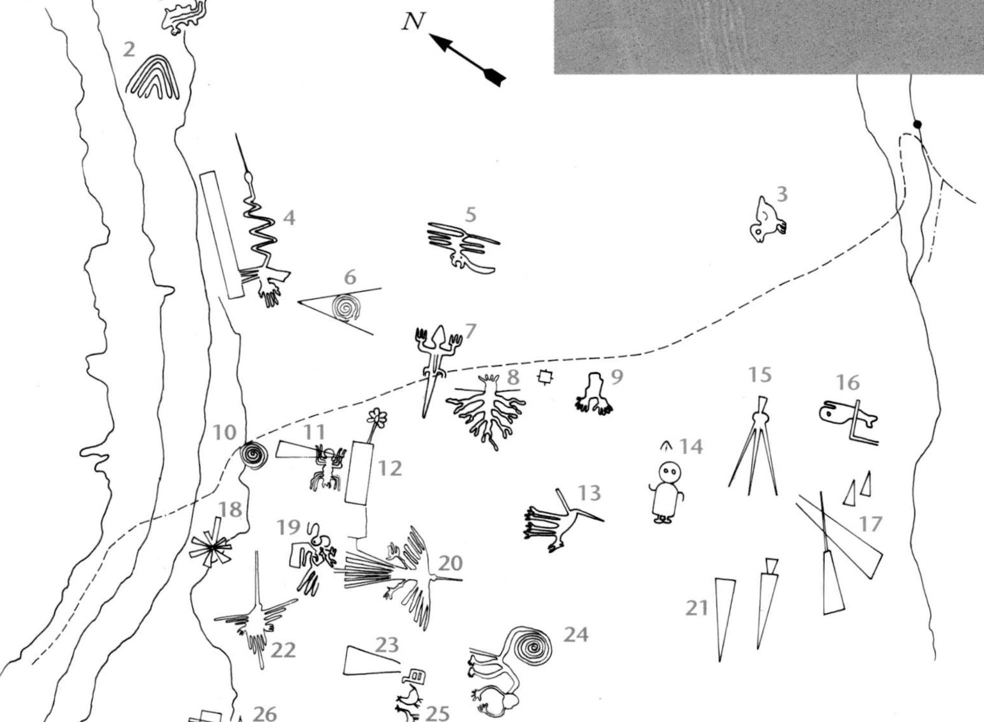

The geoglyphs left by the Nazca people vary in shape, from a large number of long embankments, similar to tracks, to geometric patterns such as triangles or rectangles, and more than a hundred spirals, as well as thirty animals and birds. The drawings were created by digging away the red, rocky surface layer of the desert to a depth of 30 to 38 cm (12 to 15 in), exposing a band of the paler coloured sand below. Their survival over the centuries is due to the dry climate and the absence of rain.

198 (opposite left, above) This aerial photograph shows the perfect outline of the spider, one of the most famous Nazca geoglyphs. No one has yet discovered the meaning of the gigantic designs traced out in the dry soil of the pampa, but one theory is that they marked celestial events or bodies.

198 (opposite, left centre) Many scholars from all over the world have joined in the search for the solution to the enigma of the geoglyphs ascribed to the Nazca civilization. Some consider the designs to be a large map of the heavens, in which each symbol is linked to a star. This is the geoglyph of the dog, which may represent the constellation of the same name.

198 (opposite, below left) A bird-like figure crossed by intersecting lines is another of the puzzling Nazca geoglyphs. Their enormous size means they are only visible from above.

198 (opposite, top right) Some geoglyphs seem to depict trees or hands. Comparison with the vehicle on the road gives a good idea of the scale of these drawings.

198–199 Another animal created by the Nazca people is this humming-bird, considered sacred by many Pre-Columbian peoples and sought after for its coloured plumage.

201 (opposite, above left) A monkey is also included in the range of animal figures etched in the surface of the pampa; its spiral tail makes it one of the most spectacular. Like the dog, the spider and the humming-bird, the monkey may also represent one of the symbols in a huge map of the stars or an astronomical calendar.

201 (opposite, above right) As well as animals and geometric symbols, supernatural and monstrous figures are found among the geoglyphs of the Peruvian pampa.

One surprising aspect of the figures is that they were designed on such a gigantic scale: the straight lines are up to 48 km (30 miles) long and the pictures of animals measure from 15 to 305 m (50 to 1,000 ft) in size. Consequently, many geoglyphs can only be seen from a certain height. But why did the Nazca people, of whom we know so little, create these gigantic figures in the sand of the desert? Why did they depict spirals, a spider, a monkey, a humming-bird, without being able to see them unless standing on surrounding hills?

In 1926, Toribio Mejia Xesspe was the first to explore the pampa around Nazca systematically. He formulated the hypothesis that the geoglyphs, especially the straight lines that resemble runways, were ancient ceremonial roads that the Nazcas travelled along dancing and singing in honour of their gods – possibly the Feline God, whose cult had reached the southern extremes, or the 'Mythical Beings', depicted almost obsessively on pottery.

Paul Kosok, who 'rediscovered' the figures after they had been forgotten, examined the various geometric forms and animal designs and produced a new theory that has never really been superseded: he proposed that the Pampa had been transformed into a giant astronomical calendar. According to him, the figures and lines had a precise meaning linked to the passing of time, and to the stars and constellations. This hypothesis was accepted by many scholars, including the mathematician Maria Reiche, who spent much of her life in scholarly research and detailed on-site examination in an attempt to reveal the secrets of the drawings.

Despite all the hypotheses, the meaning and purpose of the huge drawings are still a fascinating enigma. Certain images on Nazca pottery resemble the animal geoglyphs, and perhaps these were deified symbols of the natural world linked to the ancestral cults of the earliest inhabitants of Pre-Columbian Peru.

200 This 'candelabra', like a huge trident, was traced on the slopes of a desert hill facing the coast and is clearly visible from the sea. This geoglyph may date from the Colonial period.

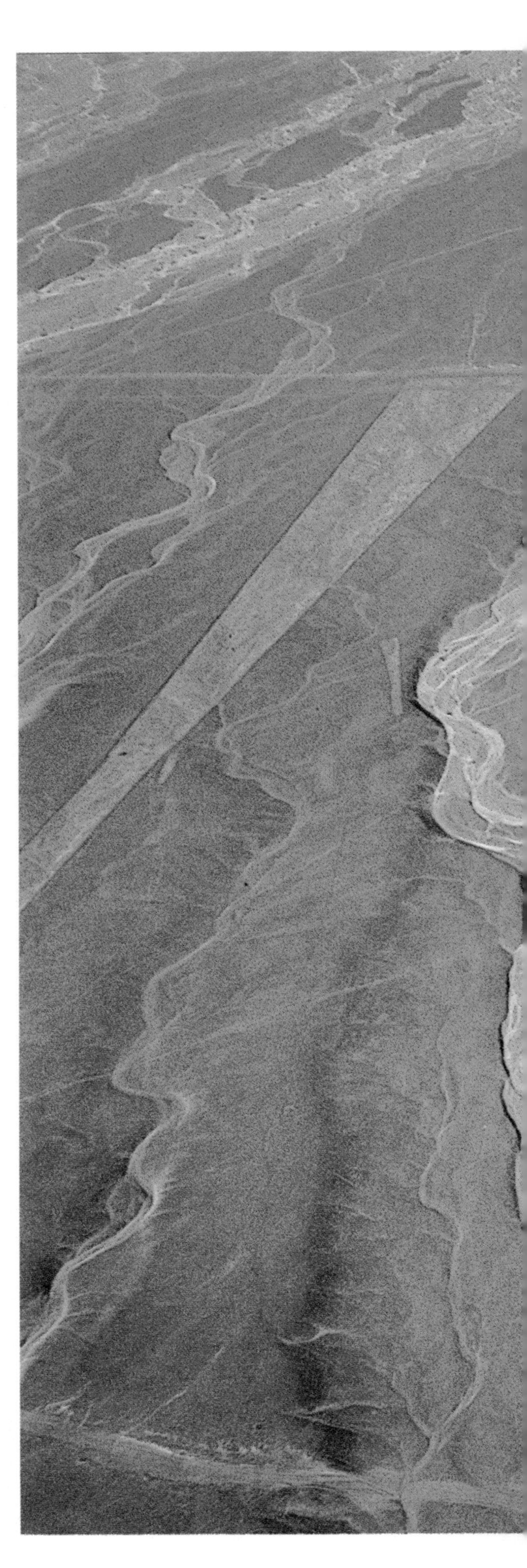

200–201 An aerial view of the desert reveals the long lines and geometrical figures that intersect like airport runways. Regardless of the number of attempts to solve the mystery of the designs, their interpretation is still uncertain.

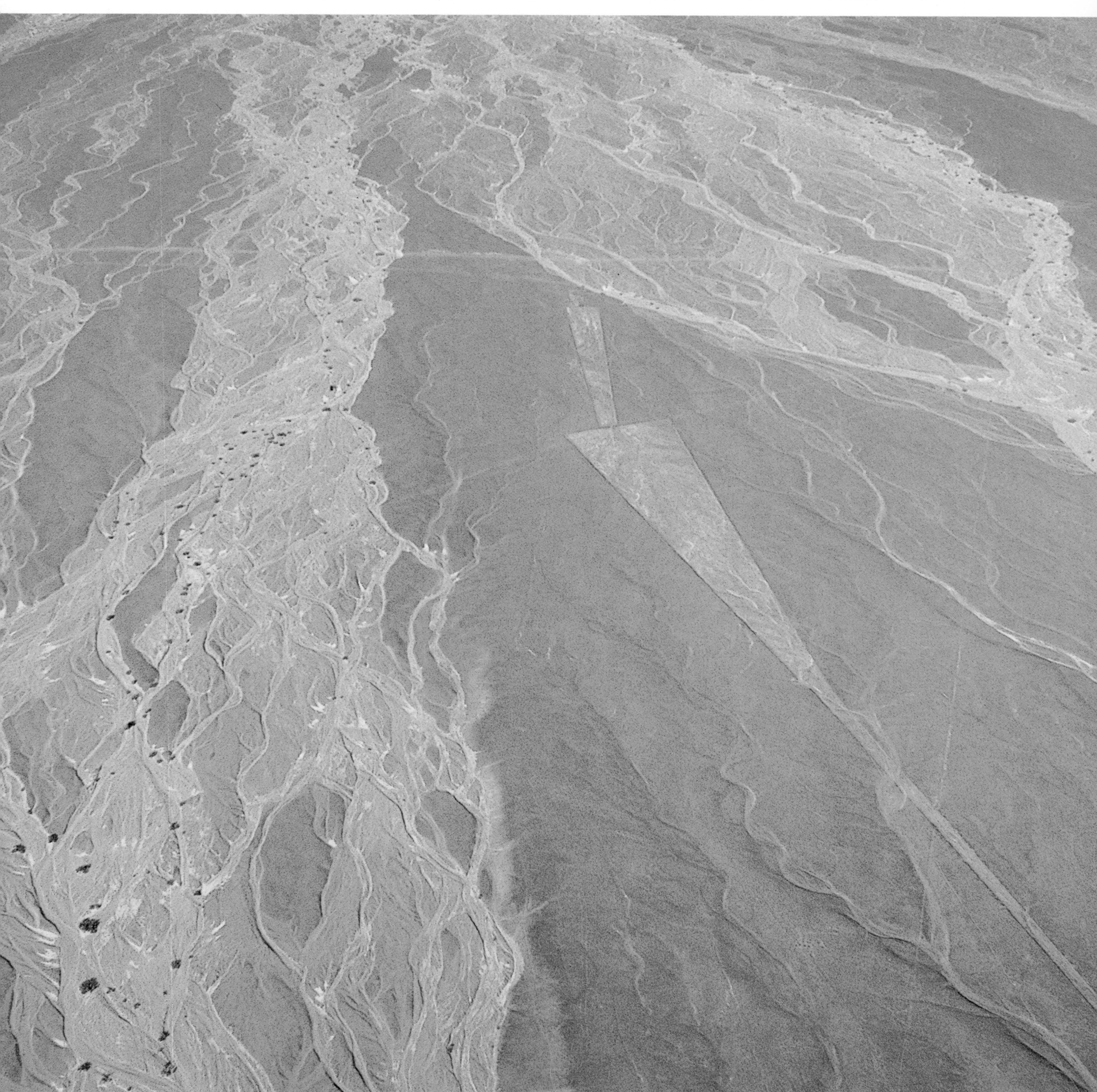

TIAHUANACO: CITY OF MEGALITHS

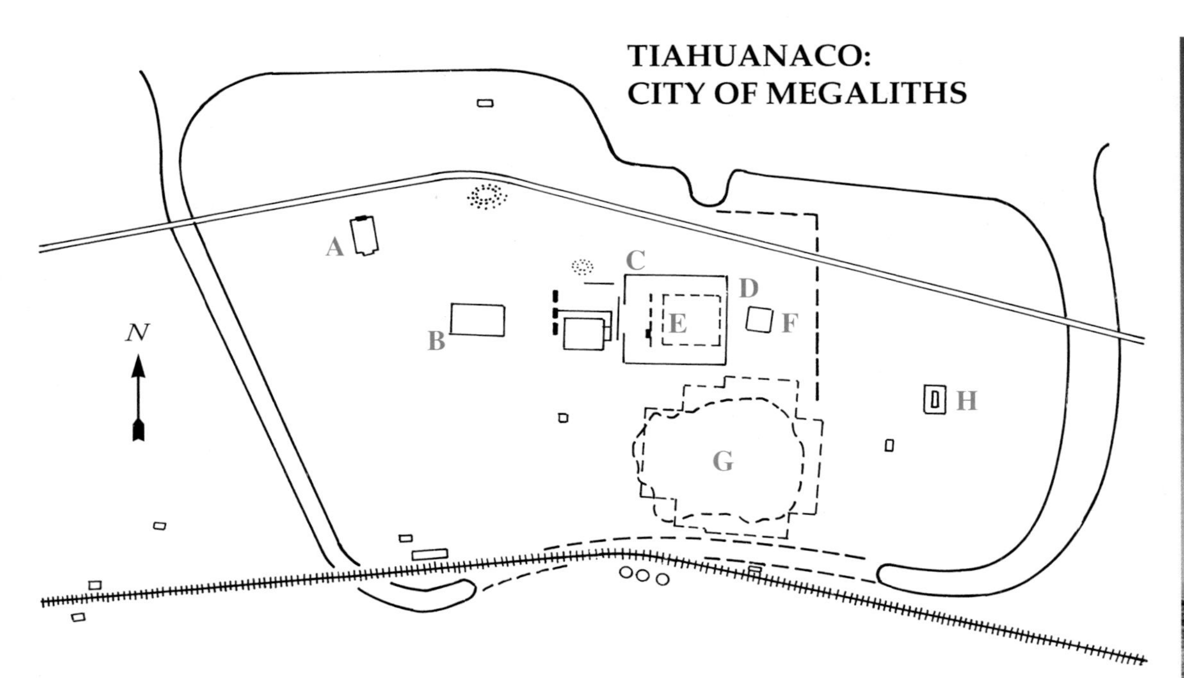

The site of Tiahuanaco covers an area of 400 hectares (990 acres) and lies at 3,850 m (12,600 ft) above sea level. Its various constructions, some of which are truly impressive, were built over several centuries, though several seem unfinished, as if the civilization that created them had been abruptly cut short. Due to its vast size and monumental buildings, archaeologists consider Tiahuanaco to have been a ceremonial centre for the worship of gods and cults associated with the stars. They also think that it was the probable successor to Chavín de Huántar. Many of the buildings are thought to have been built around AD 200, when the site had already been occupied for five centuries.

A Pantheon
B Palace
C Gateway of the Sun
D Kalasasaya
E Internal enclosure wall
F Eastern temple
G Akapana
H Kantatayita

202 (above) One of the most famous sculptures at the site of Tiahuanaco, the Ponce monolith is named after its discoverer.

202 (right) The interior walls of the Semi-Subterranean Temple at Tiahuanaco are studded with stone heads that resemble the tenoned heads of the temples at Chavín de Huántar. A link certainly existed between the cults worshipped at the two famous sanctuaries.

The religious area was probably built around AD 300. It is filled with stone temples, sunken squares, enclosed sanctuaries and gateways, such as the famous Gateway of the Sun. From around AD 500, the site expanded and rapidly became a town with a population of up to 50,000 inhabitants. It was the centre of a theocratic élite and an empire that extended its influence over the southern Andes until AD 1000.

Recent investigations have uncovered the boundary between the ceremonial centre and the surrounding residential areas, with their small houses made from adobe and river pebbles. One interesting fact that has emerged from the research is that neither the

202–203 A view of the enclosure wall of the Kalasasaya, which means 'Standing Stone' in Aymara.

203 (right) The Semi-Subterranean Temple in the foreground is a rectangular sunken court. It is enclosed by a wall made of large stone blocks interspersed with tenoned heads; in the middle are three monoliths. The Kalasasaya enclosure wall is visible in the background, with the Ponce monolith framed in the centre.

monumental nor the residential area contain any trace of storehouses or of the administrative buildings which would be essential to the infrastructure of an empire. The various buildings in the town have not yet given up all their secrets, however, and the function of many is a source of disagreement among archaeologists.

One of the most important, as well as one of the oldest buildings is the 'Akapana', a large platform formed of seven terraces, measuring about 200 m (650 ft) square and 17 m (56 ft) high and oriented to the four points of the compass. It was once thought to be a natural mound, but in fact the terraces were built from earth, clay and stones and were originally sheathed in carved stone. On the summit of the Akapana is a sunken paved courtyard lined with rooms that may have been used by the temple priests.

The remains of a large building, the 'Pumapunku', stand in a separate area to the southeast of the Akapana. This T-shaped platform, around 5 m (16 ft) high, consists of three sandstone terraces with a sunken courtyard on the top. Its eastern entry court has carved gateways and lintels and it is thought that the Gateway of the Sun once stood here. Other large buildings found in the vicinity of the Akapana include the Semi-Subterranean Temple, which consists of a large rectangular courtyard reached by a flight of steps on the south side. A series of round carved stone heads with stylized human features lines the sandstone walls. To the north of the Akapana is a strange complex, the Kalasasaya. The name means 'Standing Stone' and derives from the peculiarity of its structure. It consists of a low rectangular platform enclosed by a wall with large stone slabs. In the centre is a sunken court.

At the northwest corner of the Kalasasaya now stands one of the most spectacular of Tiahuanaco's monuments – the Gateway of the Sun. The massive structure weighs 10 tonnes and is famous for the images that decorate its architrave. Winged figures, perhaps demons or mythical beings, converge on a central figure who holds a staff in the shape of a snake in each hand and whose head is crowned by rays. There is an undeniable similarity between this deity and the ancient Staff God of Chavín de Huántar, suggesting some kind of cultural link between these two religious centres that were separate in both time and space.

The Bennett stela (named after its discoverer) was found in the centre of the Pumapunku but was later moved to the main square in La Paz.

204 (above left) Lines of winged demons, perhaps angels or messengers, converge on the Gateway God of the Gate of the Sun. There have been many interpretations of the cult related to this mysterious figure.

204 (left) This carved monolith is known as 'El Fraile'. The square and rigid figure has been sculpted rather roughly and its meaning is not known. It decorated the wall of the Kalasasaya.

204–205 The Gateway of the Sun is the symbol of Tiahuanaco. Today it stands in the northwest corner of the Kalasasaya but it was probably originally located in the Pumapunku. The central deity, identified by some scholars as Viracocha, is similar to the Staff God of Chavín de Huántar.

205 (left) One of Tiahuanaco's most interesting structures is the Kalasasaya, an Aymara word meaning 'Standing Stone'. It consists of a rectangular platform with a sunken court surrounded by a wall with large monoliths. The Gateway of the Sun is visible in the background.

206 A view of the ruins of the ancient ceremonial platform of the Pumapunku. Tiahuanaco is characterized by its megalithic architecture, the techniques of which were later inherited by the Incas.

206–207 These massive, square blocks forming a kind of enclosure are all that remain of the ceremonial building of the Pumapunku. The sockets in the stone base may once have held columns that supported the temple.

This stela is one of the tallest stone sculptures in the Andes, measuring over 7 m (24 ft) high, and was perhaps intended to glorify a local official or high priest. Two other monoliths, 'El Fraile' and 'Ponce', are similar in style and imagery. Rather than true sculptures in the round, these monoliths resemble massive pillars on which human features have been carved in low relief, with details of clothing and the objects held in their hands also shown. These rather austere images may represent rulers, but it is more probable that they were members of the priesthood of the cult which was perhaps the basis of the Tiahuanaco empire. The ruins of the 'Palacio' and the 'Gate of the Moon' lie close to the Pumapunku.

Scholars are still trying to interpret the images found on the monoliths and on pottery discovered in excavations at Tiahuanaco and in nearby areas, which resemble those associated with the Huari empire. Understanding these will be a major key to unlocking the puzzle of the two 'empires' that dominated the Andes during the Middle Horizon.

What surprised the Spaniards most when they saw the ruins of Tiahuanaco were the enormous sandstone and andesite blocks and slabs used to build the monuments, as well as the technical perfection with which they were carved and smoothed. The chroniclers describe how the stones were fixed together using T-shaped cramps of copper or bronze, but the question of how they were transported from quarries sometimes hundreds of miles away without the wheel is still a mystery.

207 (far left) A block from the ruins of the Pumapunku, one of the religious structures in the centre of Tiahuanaco.

207 (left) One of the many elegantly carved blocks from the Pumapunku. The motif of the stepped diamond may be linked to the worship of the sun; it is often found at Tiahuanaco and throughout the Huari region on textiles as well as in stone.

SILLUSTANI: THE TOWERS OF SILENCE

208–209 The burial towers of Sillustani are called chullpas *in Aymara. They were probably built by the Colla people from the region of Lake Titicaca and it is thought that they were collective graves, a practice that was later also adopted by the Incas.*

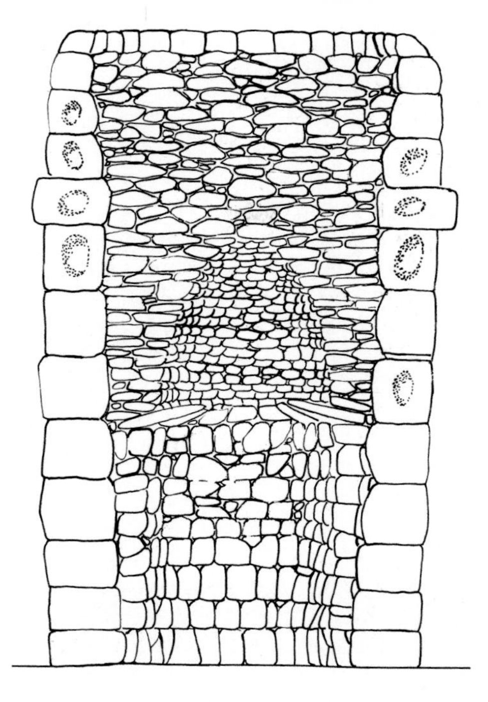

A cross-section of a chullpa *of Sillustani, showing the method of construction.*

Sillustani, west of the city of Puno, is about 8 km (13 miles) from the shores of Lake Titicaca. Today it is famous for a series of burial towers called *chullpas* in the Aymara language, a word that indicates a particular type of tomb. The Sillustani towers were built on a rocky peninsula that extends into Lake Umayo. These are not the only examples of such structures in the Andean highlands, indeed there are many of them, but others are simpler and less spectacular.

The Sillustani *chullpas* are usually cylindrical, though some have a square base. They stand on a sort of platform and flare slightly outwards as they rise. A cornice and a roof built using the corbel technique complete the structures.

Different techniques were employed in constructing the towers; some of the simpler ones were built using rough stones held together by a clay mortar, while others have a skin of perfectly carved and polished stones. The interior of even the most elegant *chullpas* is rough, made from uncut stones and clay. The burial chamber is always circular and topped by a slightly pointed corbelled vault. El Lagarto *chullpa* has a burial chamber 6 m (20 ft) in diameter and height. Access is through a curiously small opening, just large enough for a person to crawl through on hands and knees. It seems likely therefore that the voluminous layers of textiles were wrapped around the body once it was inside the chamber.

The first archaeologists to explore the Sillustani towers at the end of the 19th century noted that the chambers were used not for individual but for collective burial. Fray Bartolomé de las Casas recorded that, as with other tombs, the small door was only opened a year after burial, when the bodies had already been mummified.

A debate has arisen over a series of large circles traced on the ground near the *chullpas*. Once thought to be 'solar circles', that is sacred places used for rituals, today the more common view is that they represent the sites for other towers that were never built.

The culture that created the *chullpas* is still an unresolved problem. Some scholars believe that the towers were the work of the Incas, but a more widely accepted view is that they were the tombs of dignitaries and rulers of peoples who had settled around Lake Titicaca well before the Inca empire arose, possibly the Colla people. If so, once the Incas had subjected this area and its inhabitants, they adopted their funerary customs and built tombs of the same type though they perfected the construction techniques. None the less, this particular type of burial tower remained local to the highland regions and was not imported to Cuzco or other parts of the empire.

208 (opposite above) Circular stone walls are found throughout the Sillustani peninsula near the chullpas. *Some archaeologists think they are connected with solar cults, while others believe that they are the bases of unfinished* chullpas.

209 Two of the chullpas *of Sillustani, now partially collapsed. Originally they were covered with a roof built using the corbelling technique.*

ULASA: COFFINS IN THE CLOUD FOREST

210–211 Some of the large clay coffins at Ulasa, on which traces of the original paint are still visible. One has a human skull on the top of it as a trophy of war. The bodies found inside them were probably of warriors or people of high status.

211 Seven large anthropomorphic coffins made from clay cling to a cliff. These were created by the Chachapoyas people at the site of Ulasa, on the eastern slopes of the Andes. The Chachapoyas were one of the fiercest enemies of the Incas.

One of the many peoples to be subjected by the ambitious rulers of Tahuantinsuyu were the Chachapoyas who lived in the Amazonian region between the Río Marañón and the Río Huallaga. Archaeological research has recently demonstrated the existence of three successive cultural phases in development of the Chachapoyas culture, in the period between the 7th and 15th centuries.

These peoples are still shrouded in mystery and were described by the Spanish chroniclers as different from the other inhabitants of the Andes. The Incas were supposed to have been intrigued by their physical characteristics and took the Chachapoyas women away to the *Aclla Huasi* where they wove textiles and brewed chicha. Naturally, the different appearance of this Amazonian people has prompted scholars to formulate various theories, including that they had arrived from Europe before the Spanish Conquest, but no proof has been found. From an archaeological point of view, the Chachapoyas have left a series of impressive ruins that are without parallel.

The most famous site is Kuelap, which lies at an altitude of 2,970 m (9,750 ft). It consists of some 400 circular buildings enclosed by a large wall. It is thought that the site had ceremonial and religious functions rather than being a military fort as was once suggested.

The most typical remains of this people are funerary in nature. They created stone tombs, with painted or plastered walls, in the mouths of almost inaccessible caves on cliff faces. They also made large clay coffins in human form and placed them vertically in the mouths of caves dug out of precipitous cliffs.

In the 1980s an expedition of Italian and Peruvian archaeologists found groups of such coffins at the site of Ulasa in the valley of the Utcubamba river. The most spectacular group consists of seven statue-coffins situated halfway down the rock wall of a deep canyon. They are hard to reach due to their perilous location.

Examination of the coffins, their contents and the site has shed some light on the funerary customs of the Chachapoyas, whom the Spaniards described as proud, warlike and stubborn opponents of the Incas. The coffins, made of mud and straw over a framework of reeds, were not manufacture elsewhere and then brought to this spot, but were constructed directly on the rocky ledge. A small cavity protected them from the elements. Inside each coffin were the skeletal remains of a person, probably of high status – either a military leader or a member of the ruling class. The bodies were in a seated position and bound with cord. They were accompanied by offerings and funerary goods. On the heads of some of the effigies are skulls, perhaps of decapitated enemies defeated in battle.

The external surfaces of the coffins are usually painted white and decorated with stylized motifs in red, which, according to some experts, symbolize the plumage of birds. Two of the seven coffins have painted male genitalia.

TITICACA: THE SACRED ISLANDS

212 (opposite, above left) A panoramic view of the Island of the Sun, with the enclosure walls of the vast site known as the Temple of the Sun. Most of the structures visible here date from the Inca period but some traces of architecture in the Tiahuanaco style have been found.

212 (opposite, above right) This imposing gateway flanked by stone walls is the entrance to one of the ceremonial areas on the Island of the Sun. Lake Titicaca can be glimpsed in the background. The use of monolithic lintels is typical of the architecture of Tiahuanaco.

212–213 The archaeological remains found on the Island of the Sun are of great interest but have proved difficult to interpret. In this view, the ruins of the retaining walls of the artificial terraces for the Temple of the Sun can be seen.

The Island of the Sun and the Island of Coati on Lake Titicaca are now part of Bolivia. On both islands are the remains of sites dating from Inca times, which may have been inspired by existing buildings of the Middle Horizon. Ornamental elements are comparable with examples found at Tiahuanaco and Ollantaytambo. The most famous monument on the Island of the Sun is the 'Palace of Pilco Cayma'. It has been suggested that its corbelled vaults could have supported a second floor. The main façade is rather rigid and symmetrical: in addition to real doors it features large 'blind' niches.

The site on the Island of Coati has a large rectangular court surrounded by a series of rooms. The decorations are again similar to those found at Tiahuanaco and include a repeated sequence alternating false, stepped arches with rectangular ones, and blind doors with functional ones.

213 A series of terraces with the ruins of structures are all that remain today of the vast ceremonial complex on the rugged shores of the Island of the Sun. Although the site has been called the Temple of the Sun, very little is known of its precise function.

214 (opposite above) Agricultural terraces on the slopes of the Island of the Sun form a great bay, similar to those found in the most famous Inca centres. The Incas probably built their cult centres on the islands of the Sun and Coati on top of previous structures raised by the people of Tiahuanaco.

214–215 This view of the Temple of the Sun shows a long passage or corridor through a series of consecutive gateways topped by monolithic lintels.

215 (above right) Even more puzzling than the site on the Island of the Sun are the ruins of the Temple of the Moon on the Island of Coati. The unity of the façade of the building is broken up by a series of niches and false, stepped arches.

215 (right) One of the features of the Temple of the Moon on the Island of Coati is the series of false, stepped arches that resemble wall decorations at the Pumapunku in the city of Tiahuanaco.

CUZCO: THE CENTRE OF THE WORLD

216–217 The Colonial convent of Santo Domingo in the city of Cuzco was built on top of what remains of the ancient walls of the Coricancha, the Inca sun temple. The rooms and gardens of the temple were covered with gold foil but were completely ransacked by the Spaniards. The beautiful curved wall made from carefully fitted blocks of andesite is the most impressive surviving part of the temple.

Cuzco was the most famous city in the Inca world. Originally a small rural village set at 3,100 m (10,170 ft) above sea level in a slight depression surrounded by high peaks, it rapidly grew into the capital of the empire and became its ceremonial, political and administrative centre. The city was conceived as a sort of Axis Mundi, the 'omphalos of the world', to which all roads led. At the time of the Conquest, it was filled with squares, paved roads and elegant stone palaces and was equipped with a remarkable system for supplying water. Inca Pachacutec (Pachacuti) and his successors based the plan of Cuzco on models of ancient Andean cities such as Huari, Tiahuanaco and Chan Chan. Cuzco stretched between two rivers, the Huatanay and Tullumayo, in the shape of a puma, one of the totemic animals of the Andean civilizations.

216 (opposite, above left) *Some of the rooms of the Coricancha have been preserved inside the monastery of Santo Domingo. The large room in the picture has trapezoidal niches in the walls and a sacrificial altar.*

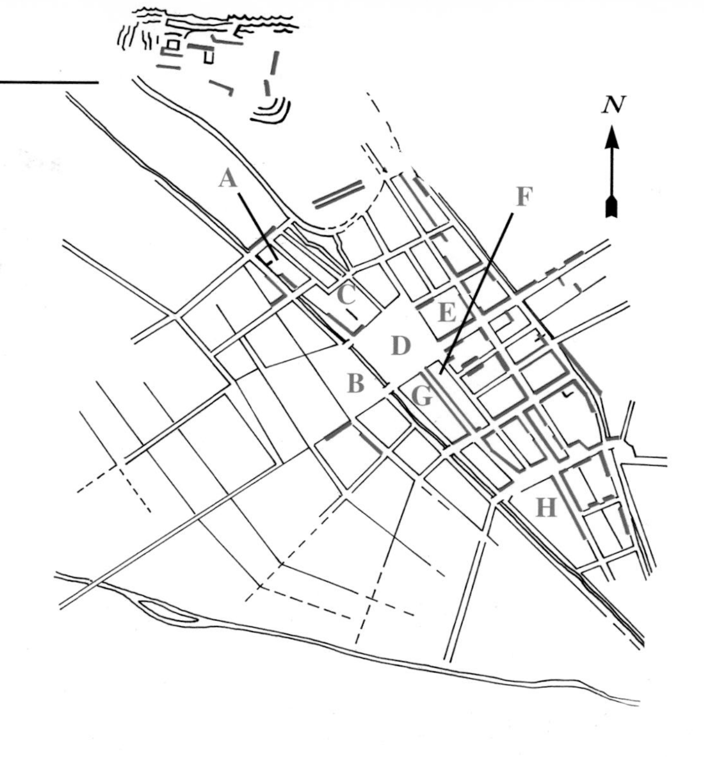

A Yachayhuasi
B Pachacutec's palace
C Inca Roca's palace
D Aucaypata (main square)
E Temple of Viracocha
F *Aclla Huasi* (House of the Chosen Women)
G Huayna Capac's palace
H Coricancha

Inca wall

216 (above right) *The Coricancha was dedicated to the Sun, but also to the Moon and the Stars. This is a part of the Temple of the Stars. Before the arrival of the Spaniards, the walls were entirely covered with gold sheet.*

Spanish chroniclers provide us with a picture of Cuzco as a wonderful place, where splendid, gold-covered palaces and gardens left no room for poverty. The largest stone buildings were the residences of the Sapa Inca (the One and Only Ruler), his family, the mummified remains of his ancestors and leading priests. The Inca himself was considered the descendant and incarnation of the sun god and, along with the nobles, was called 'Big Ears' by the Spaniards because of the elongation of their ear lobes as a sign of nobility. In summer, the kings and nobles would move to quarters along the Urubamba valley. Provincial governors also lived in Cuzco and their children attended the city schools and learned Quechua, the language of the élite.

The city of Cuzco was divided into two parts: the upper section, called Hanan Cuzco, and the lower, called Hurin Cuzco. These were subdivided into a series of *kanchas*, closed quarters of the city built around a four-sided square. At the heart of the city was a ceremonial centre based around a large trapezoidal plaza open to the southwest and connected to the Aucaypata, a smaller square. This open area was used for gatherings and important rituals. The modern-day Plaza de Armas and the Plaza Regocijo are the remnants of this ancient ceremonial centre. The royal palaces, residences of the élite and the temples were grouped around the central core, from which ran the four main roads that divided the Inca empire into four sections.

Accounts tell us that when a new ruler ascended to the throne, he built himself a palace that was larger and more sumptuous than all existing ones. Of Pachacutec's palace, described as the most impressive, only fragments of walls survive, incorporated into a modern restaurant. In addition to royal palaces, Cuzco boasted many public buildings such as the 'House of Knowledge', reserved for the education of the élite, various sacred buildings and the *Aclla Huasi*, the 'House of the Chosen Women'. Each year hundreds of girls were brought to the *Aclla Huasi* from every corner of the empire to weave fine cloth and prepare chicha. Part of the building was incorporated into the Monastery of Santa Catalina in the 17th century.

Almost all the palaces and residences were built with great blocks of cut stone fitted together so perfectly that they did not need any binding material. After the Conquest, remains of Inca walls and the constructions built by Pachacutec and his successors were reused and adapted, so that fragments survive.

Spanish chronicles describe in detail the most impressive and magnificent sacred building in the city centre. This was the Coricancha ('Golden Enclosure') situated in the lower city, the Hurin Cuzco. The name is derived from two Quechua words: *cori* meaning gold, and *kancha* meaning enclosed by walls. The walls of this splendid temple were covered with gold sheet and inside was a garden with statues, plants and animals also made of gold. This sumptuous building was dismantled and robbed of its treasures by Pizarro's men in 1534 and the Monastery of Santo Domingo was built on its foundations.

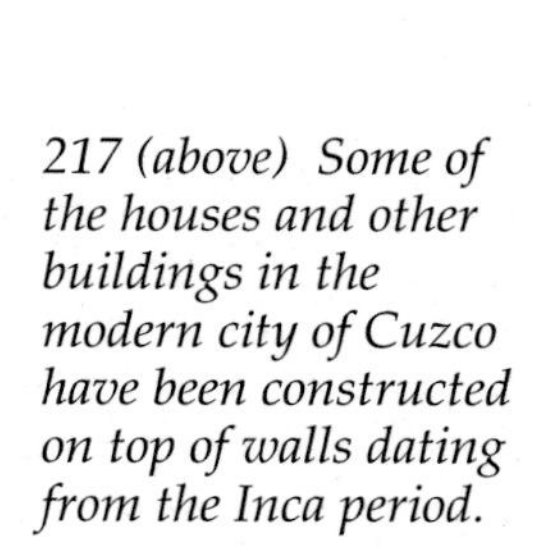

217 (above) *Some of the houses and other buildings in the modern city of Cuzco have been constructed on top of walls dating from the Inca period.*

217 (below) *The famous 'stone with twelve angles' in a wall in Cuzco survived the destruction of the colonial era. The enormous block of stone was precisely carved and perfectly fitted without the use of mortar.*

SACSAHUAMAN: THE TEMPLE-FORTRESS

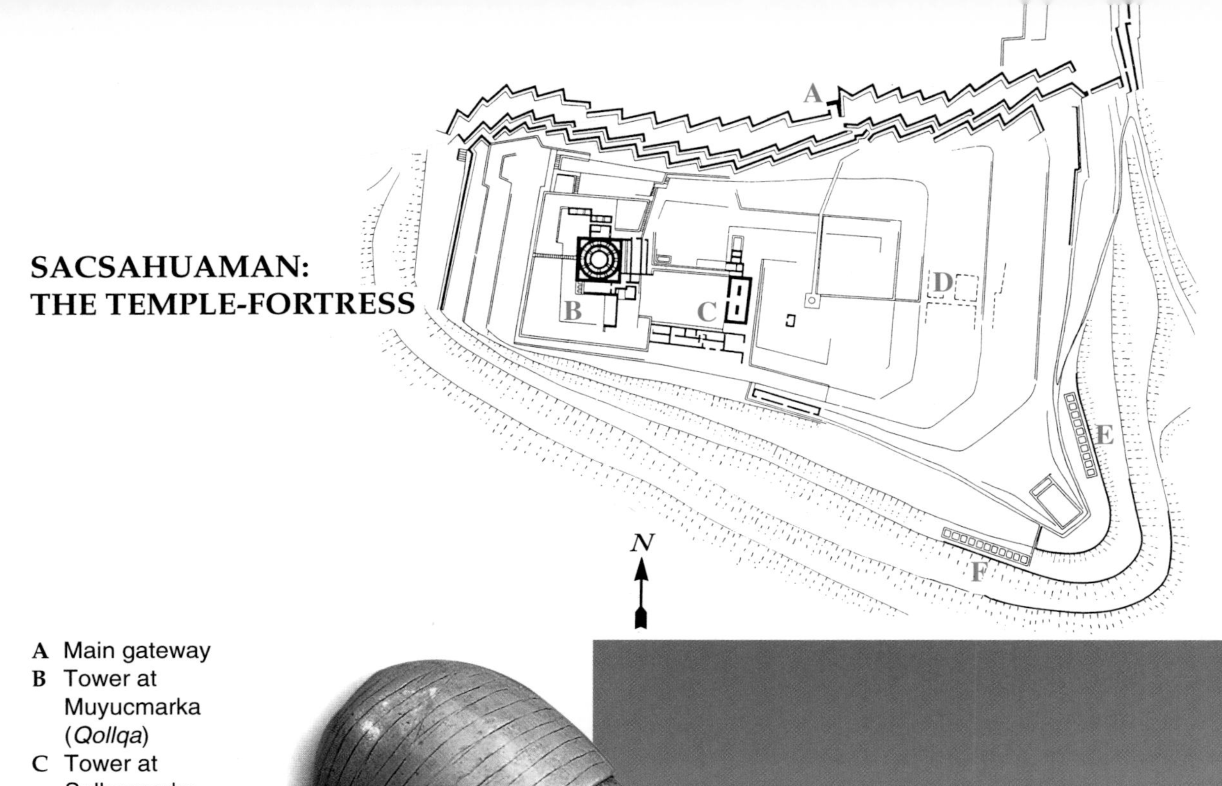

A Main gateway
B Tower at Muyucmarka (*Qollqa*)
C Tower at Sallacmarka
D Tower at Paucamarka
E Storehouses
F Storehouses

218 These silver figurines from the temple-fortress of Sacsahuaman are typically Inca in style. They were probably votive offerings.

218–219 The massive triple enclosure wall of Sacsahuaman stands out against the cobalt blue sky outside the city of Cuzco. Although it has a fortified appearance the structure was probably an ancient place of worship.

Unlike many other Inca cities, Cuzco was not built as a fortified centre and had no enclosure wall to separate it from the countryside. A few miles from the centre of Cuzco is a megalithic structure that was until recently thought to be a fortress, although different interpretations of its function have now been put forward.

Built by the Incas, the solid mass of the 'Fortress' of Sacsahuaman still

219 (left) The walls of the temple-fortress of Sacsahuaman were built with gigantic blocks of stone that were smoothed and fitted together perfectly.

219 (right) One of the monumental entrances in the enclosure walls of Sacsahuaman: the rounded walls on the right are a characteristic feature of Inca architecture.

dominates Cuzco. Three zigzag walls made of huge blocks of limestone – some of them are over 5 m (16 ft) high and one weighs around 128 tonnes – were built on three superimposed platforms that together reach a height of 18 m (60 ft). The giant blocks of limestone were transported from nearby outcrops.

Access to the interior is by a series of gates topped by monolithic lintels. At first glance Sacsahuaman appears to be an unassailable defensive structure, but closer examination reveals the presence of three mysterious buildings, now in ruins, which cannot have been part of a military complex. Some

accounts mention the existence of a temple dedicated to Inti, the sun god, at Sacsahuaman and it is possible that the site was not a fortress but an ancient place of worship, a temple complex to which the triple defensive walls were added at a later date. Some scholars have suggested that Sacsahuaman was an astronomical observatory, with access restricted to the Inca and priests-astronomers. Whatever the purpose of this impressive place, it still invariably amazes visitors.

A huge open space separates the 'temple-fortress' from a stairway cut in a spur of rock, called the 'Throne of the Inca'. According to the Spaniards, this was an *ushnu*, a sort of sacred altar – the Quechua word was used to indicate natural rocks of a particular shape or size. Many examples of *ushnus* are found around the empire and they were probably used as thrones or sacrificial altars.

220–221 The wall bastions that enclose the three platforms of Sacsahuaman have a clear zigzag shape. On the top of the platforms stand the remains of towers.

220 (opposite below) Sacsahuaman's huge blocks and massive lintels still impress today. Although it has the appearance of a fortification, it may have been a temple.

221 A flight of steps cut in the rock in front of the temple-fortress is known as the 'Throne of the Inca', although many scholars think it was a ceremonial altar.

KENKO: THE UNIVERSE IN STONE

222 (above left) Kenko is an exceptional example of Inca architecture and sculpture integrated into a natural rock setting. These steps form what is called the 'Throne of the Inca' though we do not know what its original function was.

222 (below left) This zigzag channel once emptied into a large stone tank that was placed on the edge of a sheer drop. Kenko, like Tambo Machay, was probably a centre of the cult of water and springs.

The archaeological site of Kenko is situated on a hill called Socorro. Everything about this fascinating site suggests that it was once a place of worship. Its name comes from the word *Q'enquo*, meaning 'line in the shape of a snail', a reference to the great carved rock that is one of the features of the site. The rock surface is entirely sculpted with steps, radiating lines, figures and a series of channels that join and separate, forming a mysterious pattern. At first sight these carvings look like natural irregularities in the rock and it requires a closer look to recognize them for what they are.

A small cave above the rock was adapted and used by the Incas as a place for sacred rituals. And in the northern part of the site is a feature known as the 'amphitheatre', a sort of elliptical courtyard that may have had a precise astronomical meaning. It is surrounded by a wall which originally had 19 niches, many of which are now destroyed. The wall is built of carved, regularly shaped stones. At the centre of the courtyard stands a monolith, 6 m (20 ft) tall, surrounded by a wall; its distinctive shape has given rise to its name, the 'Seated Puma'.

The sanctity of the site is evident everywhere, in the rock carved with mysterious symbols, and the huge monolith and its courtyard – features which bring to mind cults linked to the seasons and the sun. Perhaps the Incas once again incorporated into their own religion the remains of older cults, with their ancient beliefs and traditions.

223 (left) At Kenko a natural cave was transformed into a room for ceremonies and worship. A stone table, perhaps used as an altar, was carved from the rock.

222–223 One of the most curious aspects of Kenko is perhaps the monolith in the shape of a crouching feline that is enclosed by a stone wall.

224 (right) The so-called 'Inca's Bath' at Tambo Machay is formed by two artificial channels through which water from springs once flowed.

TAMBO MACHAY: THE CULT OF SPRINGS

There are many remains of Inca sites around Cuzco. One of the most picturesque is undoubtedly Tambo Machay, a few miles from Puca Pucara, although it is in a poor state of preservation. The name of this strange site is derived from two Quechua words – *tampu* or *tambo* (place of peace and provision) and *machay* (cave). Strangely, the name has nothing to do with the nature or function of the site as neither a cave nor any traces of a *tambo* have been discovered.

Tambo Machay's main feature consists of three fairly shallow terraces that were built into the side of the hill and surrounded by walls made of finely carved stone blocks decorated with trapezoidal niches. Steps connect the three terraces.

A spring gushes from the bottom of a wall to the left of one of the terraces and it is thought that this is linked to the function of the entire structure. The Incas channelled the flow of water to the next terrace where they made it disappear and then reappear in the form of a double waterfall which tumbles down to the last terrace. This is generally known as the 'Inca's Bath'.

The walls seem to merge into the rocks and, in another example of magnificent Inca stonework, a door frames a large rock that has had its corners modified to adapt it to the polygonal stones that surround it.

Some scholars believe that the site, with its mild climate and natural springs, was a sort of spa. A more probable interpretation is that the Incas modified a place that had previously been used for the practice of a cult of water and, as at Kenko, adapted it to their own architectural and religious traditions.

224–225 Tambo Machay, like Kenko, stands above the city of Cuzco. Large stone walls with polygonal blocks were built around a natural spring that was probably a cult site.

225 (above) The impressive enclosure walls at Tambo Machay: two channels carrying water cross the platforms and are usually known as the 'Inca's Bath'.

PACHACAMAC: THE ANCIENT ORACLE

Even the powerful kingdom of Chimú with its capital at Chan Chan was never able to prevail over the sacred city of Pachacamac, around 30 km (19 miles) from Lima. This large religious centre, like Chavín de Huántar and Tiahuanaco, was an important place of pilgrimage for many centuries up to the Spanish Conquest and was the site of an important oracle.

The Incas allowed worship to continue at the site and respected the cult. When the Spaniards reached Peru they learned that a large number of pilgrims still regularly visited the site, coming from distant territories to pay homage to Pachacamac, the oracle god. The pilgrims brought offerings in the form of gold and silver objects, pottery and fine textiles.

Chroniclers offer different versions of the name and origin of the deity worshipped, but all agree that the maritime cult had its roots in a much older age and that the Inca temples had been built over the ruins of other, destroyed, buildings. Some said that the name of the god had been 'Irma' or 'Vichma' and that it had been transformed to the Quechua word 'Pachacamac'. Whatever the truth, what is certain is that an important cult which had been created in the distant past was recognized by the rulers of Tahuantinsuyu.

226–227 (above) A panoramic view of the buildings at Pachacamac.

226 (opposite, below left) This building at Pachacamac is often called the Temple of the Moon, although according to the chroniclers it was the Aclla Huasi *or House of the Chosen Women.*

226 (opposite, below right) The Aclla Huasi *was built on different levels reached by steps; inside were courtyards, cisterns, ceremonial halls and small rooms used for daily life.*

227 (above left) This wooden figurine is a container for lime, which was mixed with coca. It resembles the 'oracle of Pachacamac', a tall carved wooden sculpture.

227 (above right) The Aclla Huasi *was built of adobe bricks, a material frequently used in coastal regions, with the addition of blind niches and trapezoidal doors in typical Inca style.*

A Tauri Chumpi sector
B Pyramid with ramp
C Temple wall
D Temple
E Temple of the Moon or *Aclla Huasi*
F Pilgrims' Square
G Temple wall
H Temple of the Sun

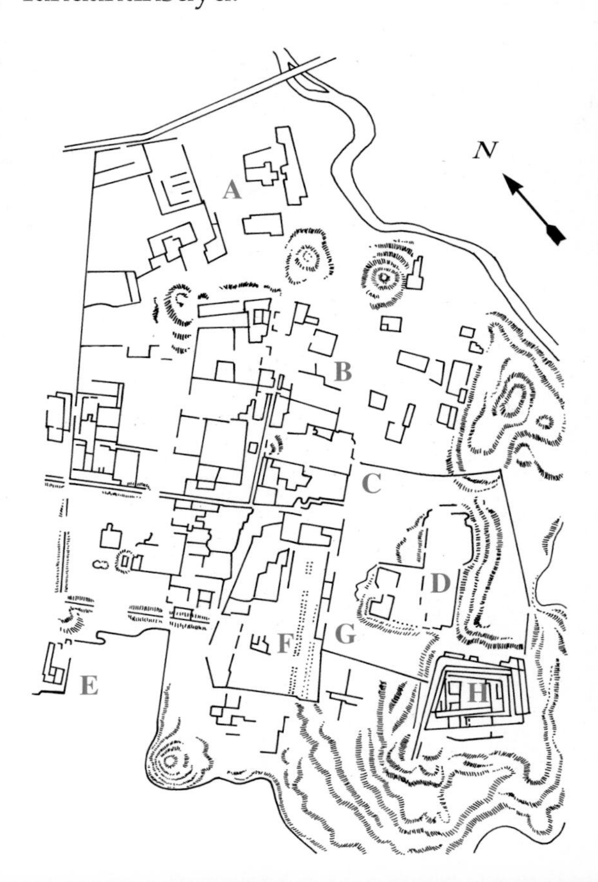

The different architectural styles at the site, as well as those of the votive and burial objects, show that the shrine was visited in various periods. Archaeologists have identified three clear styles that reflect strong external cultural influences: the Maranga style; the Tiahuanaco-Huari style, with regional characteristics; and the typical Inca style. The oldest style has characteristics typical of Chavín.

The buildings of Pachacamac stand in a flat desert area close to the sea. Several constructions of different periods have been identified in the many excavations at the site, including the Old Temple, the Polychrome Temple, the Temple of the Sun and the *Aclla Huasi*.

The Old Temple is the largest building at Pachacamac and stands on a rocky spur. Max Uhle led the first excavation here in 1903 and its current name was given to it by archaeologists in the 1960s. The structure was built of adobe bricks held together with clay; this technique, along with other design elements, has enabled archaeologists to date its construction to the Early Intermediate Period.

The Temple of the Sun may have been founded during the Inca period and is the best preserved building at the site. It is built in the form of a large stepped platform of five terraces using adobe bricks cemented with clay then plastered with layers of fine clay painted red. The temple stands on a base made of stones laid in regular rows. It is thought that the temple was built in 1450 when the Incas wanted to introduce the worship of their god, Inti (the Sun), to the people they had subjected.

Perhaps the most striking building at Pachacamac is the pyramidal Polychrome Temple, formed of nine terraces with red walls decorated with frescoes of plants and animals painted in greens, blues and pink.

Dating is made difficult by the fact that typically Inca architectural elements contrast with the style of the wall-paintings that appear to reflect older traditions. A second, older and smaller structure has been discovered inside the temple.

Among the other ruins at the site are those of the *Aclla Huasi* which was once mistakenly called the Temple of the Moon. Its clear Inca architectural style was later recognized and it was called the House of the Chosen Women, the accommodation for weavers and brewers, similar to the *Aclla Huasi* in Cuzco. The main features of the building are the large niches, trapezoidal doorways and Cuzco-type stones used in the construction of its base. Various walls and walkways were also built at different times.

Pachacamac developed into the most important sanctuary in the central coastal area during the Late Intermediate Period, though it later fell into ruins and was covered by the desert sands.

228 (left, above) A detail of the Temple of the Sun, which consists of five adobe terraces. Long flights of steps connect the different levels.

228 (left, below) Within the pyramid of the Temple of the Sun is a smaller pyramid from an earlier period, called the Pyramid of the Small Adobes.

228–229 (right) The adobe Temple of the Sun, with its walls punctuated by openings, is perfectly integrated into the landscape of Peru's central coast.

229 The Temple of the Sun is one of the most important and best preserved buildings at Pachacamac. Its adobe walls and stone platform were both originally painted red and some traces of this colour can still be seen.

OLLANTAYTAMBO: TEMPLES AND TERRACES

230 (left, above) A view of part of the site of Ollantaytambo. The trapezoidal niches of the building in the foreground are typical of Inca architecture.

230 (left, below) Many stone fountains are found at Ollantaytambo: the Incas may have considered natural springs as sacred places and they built ritual stone structures around them.

Sacsahuaman is not the only site near Cuzco whose architecture of monumental blocks and function appear mysterious and fascinating. One of the most famous is Ollantaytambo, situated on a rise at the mouth of the so-called 'Sacred Valley'. Chroniclers tell us that Ollantaytambo, together with Pisac, represented one of the strategic places from which the most important roads in the empire – those that led directly to Cuzco – could be monitored. The residential part of the site, at about 3,000 m (10,000 ft), includes the remains of an urban area of the Inca period on which the modern town is built.

The Inca city was organized on the same basis as Cuzco and elsewhere, with a trapezoidal ground plan divided rigidly into *kanchas*. It occupied a flat area on the banks of the river Patakancha, a tributary of the Urubamba. The outline of the ancient roads and the points where they intersected at right angles can still be discerned. In some areas, the

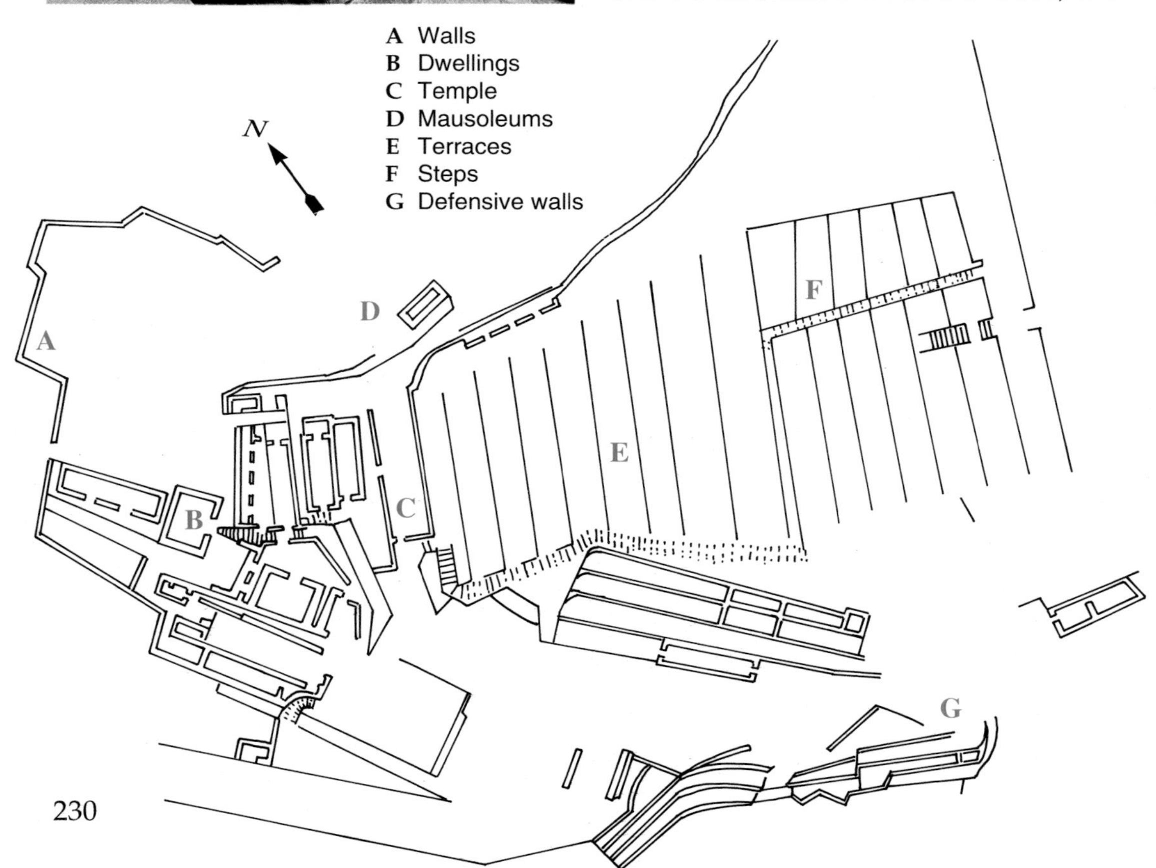

230–231 A series of seventeen terraces climbs the steep mountainside at Ollantaytambo to an unfinished temple at the top. A flight of steps rose through the centre and then to the left of the terraces.

231 (opposite, below left) Ollantaytambo may have been a residence of the Inca ruler or a ceremonial and administrative centre of the empire.

231 (opposite, below right) Fountains at Ollantaytambo may have been dedicated to the cult of water.

232 (above and below) A series of channels, tanks and steps cut into the rock make up the area known as the 'Inca's Bath'. It was possibly dedicated to the cult of springs.

232–233 Large, well-built terraces cling to the steep slopes at Ollantaytambo.

roads were blocked by gateways that opened on to huge squares. It is thought that the urban centre of Ollantaytambo had a population of around 1,000 people and that it was used as a secondary residence by the Inca and the ruling class and as an administrative centre.

The remains of another gigantic, almost threatening complex, construction of which was probably never completed, stand on the top of a rocky outcrop perched high above the river. The climb to the higher section of the site is up a long stone flight of steps set in the slope. The slope itself is formed into seventeen terraces with high retaining walls, which, the Spanish accounts tell us, were used to grow flowers of all colours for ornamental purposes. Several enclosed areas, walkways and flights of steps are found at the top of the terracing, as well as the most extraordinary set of ruins at the site. The most outstanding structure is called the 'Temple of the Sun', although its true function is unknown. What remains today is an impressive wall consisting of six huge rose-coloured rhyolite monoliths, 4 m (13 ft) high, with thin vertical sheets of the same material between. Protuberances on the surfaces of the blocks are of unknown significance, and a relief similar to a motif found on the monoliths at Tiahuanaco can be distinguished on the central block. This is perhaps further proof of a close link between the art and cultural roots of the Incas and the civilization that lived on the shores of Lake Titicaca.

The quarry from which the stones used at Ollantaytambo were extracted was on the other side of the river. A very ingenious method of transport was therefore required to transport the blocks across the river, then move them up and down the long, steep slopes.

As at Sacsahuaman, the Incas may have enclosed an ancient sacred area with walls and terraces. It is probable that construction was still in progress when the Europeans arrived and the project was brought to a halt. Some chroniclers give rather curious suggestions as to the possible interpretations of this site, which may contain a grain of truth. Garcilaso says that the place was imbued with magical and religious powers and so the viscera of dead rulers were buried here when they were mummified. He also says that gold statues, simulacra of the dead, were made and kept here. Cobo says that the ashes of sacrifices were thrown into the river from this

233 (far left) Remains of the Temple of the Sun at Ollantaytambo. The site is vast and complex and the function of all its buildings is not known for certain.

233 (left) Another unusual set of remains at Ollantaytambo consists of a large fountain carved from a single block of rock and decorated with a cornice.

234 (opposite, above left) Steep and narrow flights of steps link the different levels of the huge terraces at Ollantaytambo.

234 (opposite, above right) A massive wall encircles the Temple at Ollantaytambo. The perfectly cut blocks are precisely fitted together and include the typical Inca feature of trapezoidal niches.

234–235 Enigmatic structures and doorways originally formed the heart of the site's ceremonial centre, reached via the steps that lead up and down the steep terraced slope.

sacred spot because it was the wish of the creator-god Viracocha that they should reach the sea without contaminating the earth.

Ollantaytambo was also the site of an important battle between the Inca and Spanish troops when Manco Inca, attempting to take back power in 1536, besieged Cuzco and then won a notable victory over Pizarro.

Other important Inca monuments located in the immediate vicinity of Ollantaytambo attest to the great skills in rock carving and stoneworking of this civilization. The most important are the Intihuatana, with trapezoidal niches that were probably used to observe the sun, and the 'Princess's Bath', a fountain carved from a single large block of stone decorated with a cornice. Another curious structure is *la horca*, a small, four-sided tower built on the edge of a precipice.

235 (left) This trapezoidal door framed by massive stone blocks is the entrance to the ceremonial core of the site. Stone for the buildings at Ollantaytambo had to be brought from outcrops on the other side of the valley.

235 (top) Remains of storehouses cling together on the steep rocky slope at Ollantaytambo. The long, rectangular buildings have many windows and were originally covered by a roof. It is thought the buildings were used to store provisions.

235 (above) These 'blind niches' in the temple wall are a typical Inca feature.

236 (opposite, above left) The tallest of the rose-coloured rhyolite monoliths that formed the wall of the Temple of the Sun stands 4 m (13 ft) high and is 2 m (6.6 ft) wide.

236 (opposite, above right) A defensive wall, now mostly in ruins, was built along the hillside on which the ceremonial centre stands. The presence of such walls has suggested to some that the site was built as a fortress.

236–237 A view of the massive walls that perhaps once protected Ollantaytambo.

237 (top) These gigantic rose-coloured rhyolite monoliths, seen against the dark mass of the mountain, are all that now remain of the Temple of the Sun at Ollantaytambo.

237 (above) A wall of the temple at Ollantaytambo, one of the monumental constructions in the ceremonial centre at this complex and important site.

The residential area at Ollantaytambo
A Pata Calle
B Chaupi Calle
C Horno Calle
D Laris Calle
E Plaza de las Armas
F Patakancha River
1 First Street
2 Second Street
3 Third Street
4 Fourth Street
5 Fifth Street
6 Sixth Street
N
A
B
C
D
E
F
1
2
3
4
5
6

240 (right) A view of some of Pisac's most important and best preserved buildings: archaeologists think that the site is a temple complex, connected with the worship of the sun.

Ceremonies and rituals may have been carried out around the Intihuatana, the monolithic pillar which, according to Andean tradition, was the 'hitching post of the sun'.

240–241 Exceptional technical skill, even greater perhaps than that seen at other Inca centres, characterizes the architecture of Pisac. This spectacular site lies at an altitude of around 3,270 m (10,725 ft).

PISAC: THE FORTRESS OF THE INTIHUATANA

Pisac is another site that amazes visitors, both by its grandeur and because of the skill and mastery of the masonry techniques used in its construction. Situated high above the Vilcanota river, its ruins are considered among the finest examples of Inca architecture.

The Inca town stands on a rocky peak at 3,270 m (10,725 ft) above sea level, about 5 km (3 miles) from the modern market town of Pisac. One of its features is a series of *andenes*, artificial terraces created along the side of the mountain which at one time were held up by stone walls. As at both Machu Picchu and Ollantaytambo, the *andenes* were created for agricultural use.

The ruins of many groups of buildings are found in the 'city' or ceremonial centre but, as elsewhere, their precise function remains a mystery. Again like Ollantaytambo and also Sacsahuaman, the military and religious aspects of the architecture are closely linked and are often indistinguishable.

In the 1970s Peruvian archaeologists examined one of Pisac's most impressive ruins – the area known as the Intihuatana, a word meaning 'the hitching post of the sun'. The area has a fairly rigid layout, typical of Inca town planning, and comprises palaces, temples, stores, fortifications, observatories, roads, passages, tunnels and walkways.

241 (top) The skills of the Inca masons of Pisac are evident in this detail. The wall is built from finely carved blocks that are precisely fitted together, and is pierced by a trapezoidal doorway topped by a lintel.

241 (above) Massive walls with doorways and trapezoidal niches encircle the area of the Intihuatana at Pisac. As at Ollantaytambo and Sacsahuaman, the fortified appearance of the site was not related to a military function, rather the walls protected the important temple dedicated to the cult of the sun.

242 The mountain slopes at Pisac are covered by vast terraces used for agriculture. Inca terraces were often arranged in the form of an amphitheatre.

This entire sector is named after the large monolith called the Intihuatana, around which a structure of pink granite was built. The presence of this monument, and its impressive surroundings, suggest that the site may have been an important centre for the worship of the sun.

Next to the monolith are some of the better preserved buildings at the site, characterized by trapezoidal windows tapering towards the top, a typical feature of Inca architecture.

242–243 A panoramic view of Pisac shows the impressive complex of ruins that originally formed a large ceremonial area. In addition to the temple buildings, the site includes palaces, terraces, storehouses and walkways, all featuring typical Inca architectural elements.

The area of Pisac below the Intihuatana on the eastern slope of the mountain is also of great interest. Here the remains of numerous houses are laid out in thirty small walled areas, separated from each other and arranged in two concentric alignments around a semicircular area. This arrangement in fact follows the winding conformation of the mountainside on which the site stands and makes best use of the available space.

243 (above) The dramatic landscape around Pisac creates a stunning backdrop for the impressive walls and bastions that survive at the site.

244 (top) A view of the walls at Pisac, which are decorated with blind niches and elements that resemble the crenellations of fortifications in Europe. In the background, the peaks of the Andes stretch away into the distance against the blue sky.

244 (centre) The ceremonial area known as the Intihuatana, or 'hitching post of the sun', is the most important of the different centres at the site of Pisac and contains the remains of temple buildings.

244 (below) Pisac's immense walls are made from massive blocks that fit together perfectly. Elliptical towers, like the one seen here, stand at intervals along the walls.

244–245 Stairways and terraced platforms with towers crowd the ceremonial area of Pisac called the Intihuatana. This was probably a centre for the worship of the sun.

245 (left) Trapezoidal doorways and blind niches are typical features of all Inca centres, as seen here at Pisac. Scholars are still astounded by the ability of the Incas to transport and work the massive blocks of stone used in their constructions.

RAQCHI: THE DWELLING OF VIRACOCHA

246 (top) The site of Raqchi is situated south of Cuzco. Large quantities of volcanic stone are found in the surrounding area and this material was used by the Incas to build the ceremonial centre, the ruins of which are seen here.

246 (above) To the southeast of the complex known as the Temple of Viracocha is a residential quarter based on the kancha *system found in all important Inca centres. A number of circular structures, 8 m (26 ft) in diameter, have been found next to the square houses and were probably used for storage.*

At the site of Raqchi in the province of Canchis stand the ruins of a remarkable archaeological complex called the Temple of Viracocha. This structure was mentioned by several chroniclers and was explored for the first time by travellers in the 19th century.

Although the temple is named in honour of the creator-deity Viracocha, it is not known which god or cult was in fact worshipped at this imposing sanctuary. A large wall enclosed the site and some scholars think that the civil buildings whose remains surround the temple were used as barracks and storehouses for supplies.

The temple is truly impressive, with a tall central wall that looms over a vast flat expanse and remains of large columns. Its ground plan resembles that of other important buildings from the Inca period in the region of Cuzco, such as those found at Ollantaytambo and Machu Picchu. The central wall, around 90 m (300 ft) long and 12 m (40 ft) high forms the highest point of the roof. The roof was originally covered with straw which has since completely disappeared and has

been replaced by a modern structure to protect the remains. One column and fragments of others survive from the original colonnade which, like the central wall, originally rested on stone plinths.

The foundations on which the temple wall stands are made from blocks of volcanic rock 3 m (10 ft) high that have been shaped and smoothed. There are niches here and there, and wide bays that allow communication between the two naves of the sanctuary.

The upper part of the wall is made from adobe, which was originally plastered with red ochre, like the Temple of Pachacamac. The rooms have a curious T-shape, which was probably unintentional and due to the presence in the past of wood lintels that no longer exist. The presence of these lintels and the colonnade suggest that there was once an upper floor. At the end of the central wall there are traces of transverse walls built using the same techniques and materials.

246–247 A view of the large complex called the Temple of Viracocha at Raqchi. The roofs would have been made of a perishable material such as straw and have been replaced. The temple is one the largest examples of a roofed structure known from the Inca period.

247 (left) The Temple of Viracocha was built as a kallanka *or huge covered room. The central wall divided the structure into two sides, with doorways allowing movement between them.*

MACHU PICCHU: THE CITY IN THE CLOUDS

Of the many sites that demonstrate the power of the last Andean empire, Tahuantinsuyu, Machu Picchu must be the most compelling. This is largely because of its extraordinary, almost inaccessible location, up in the clouds. Although always known about by local people, it was rediscovered by the American historian Hiram Bingham in 1911. The astonishment experienced by the many tourists who visit the site each year can be nothing to what Bingham must have felt when he first reached it. Bingham was not an archaeologist by profession but a politician and experienced climber who loved the mysteries of the Andes. Basing his search on the accounts of the chroniclers, he succeeded in finding what might have been the 'Lost City' of fable, proving once again that behind literature and oral traditions there is often a background of fact.

Bingham's fabulous discovery was made on 24 July 1911 and is recounted in his fascinating book, *Lost City of the Incas*. Bingham's goal was to prove the existence of Vilcabamba, the legendary capital of the last Incas, the final stronghold of resistance against the invaders.

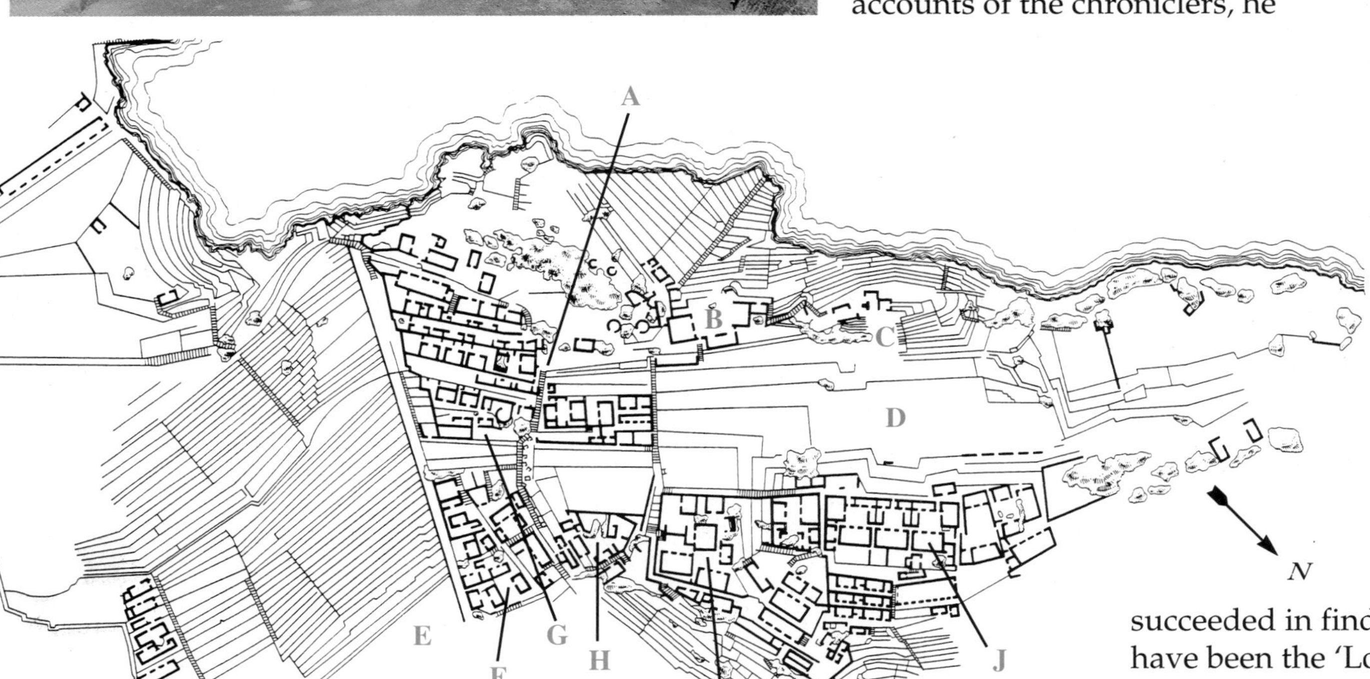

A Fountain Stairway
B Temple of the Three Windows
C Intihuatana
D Main square
E Southern agricultural terraces
F Sector of the People
G Sector of the Torreón
H Sector of the Prisons
I Sector of the Mortars
J Sector of the Three Gates

248 (top) The city of Machu Picchu contains numerous sacred buildings, squares, stairways and agricultural terraces. It is one of the most mysterious and grandest sites in the Andes.

248 (centre) The sacred or ceremonial area at Machu Picchu consists of the Main Temple and the Temple of the Three Windows.

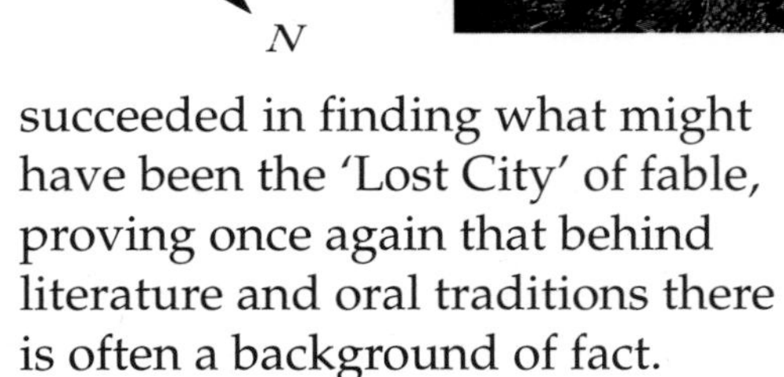

248–249 The ruins of Machu Picchu extend over a rocky saddle between the mountain summits named the 'Young Peak' and the 'Old Peak', which dominate the valley of the Urubamba river. The precise function of this mysterious city is still unknown.

249 (left) This doorway in the high wall that runs alongside a narrow paved road forms the entrance to the city of Machu Picchu.

250 (below) The Intihuatana, which means 'the hitching post of the sun', is perhaps the most important sacred monument at Machu Picchu. Similar examples are found in other Inca cities and they were perhaps the focus of ceremonies linked to the solstices and equinoxes.

250 (bottom) The Incas frequently carved sculptures from the living rock, as shown by this feature known as the 'Throne of the Inca'.

250 (right) This strange carved rock, called the 'Funerary Rock' may perhaps be an altar with steps.

250–251 Beyond the enclosure walls, with their strangely shaped crenellations, the extensive agricultural terraces of Machu Picchu are laid out on the steep valley slopes.

Having progressed beyond the almost impassable gorges of the river Urubamba, the explorer learned from a farmer called Arteaga that amazing ruins existed on the summit of Machu Picchu. Despite doubts and difficulties, Bingham asked to be accompanied to the site, where he found huge buildings in a state of complete abandon, almost submerged in thick vegetation. 'Suddenly we found ourselves in front of the ruins of two of the most elaborate and interesting buildings in Pre-Columbian America' – wrote Bingham – 'The walls were made of a lovely white granite with some blocks of a huge size, taller than a man. I was enchanted by the sight'. The excavations which Bingham himself supervised in the years that followed brought to light a large quantity of pottery and objects made from bronze, silver, copper and stone, all in the Inca style. But what was the function of Machu Picchu?

Machu Picchu is situated 112 km (70 miles) northwest of Cuzco at an altitude of nearly 2,805 m (9,200 ft) between two mountain peaks called Huayna Picchu (Young Peak) and

Machu Picchu (Old Peak). The 'imperial' style that was typical of other centres of the Inca empire is evident, though the site's location is so different. Machu Picchu stands in luxurious vegetation perched above the rushing waters of the river Urubamba in the valley below.

Many different theories have been put forward to account for the magnificent city, its strange and imposing buildings, its temples and its altars. Some question why the Inca rulers chose to build such a majestic complex on the borders of the Amazonian rainforest in a place that suffered from heat and humidity. One theory is that Machu Picchu was built as a strategic fortress in order to facilitate the subjection of the war-like peoples who lived in these wild territories. According to another theory, Machu Picchu was in fact 'Vilcabamba', the last refuge of the survivors of the ruling class after the rest of Tahuantinsuyu had been lost. Others believe that Machu Picchu was created as a secret refuge to hide Manco Inca (who was placed on the throne by the Spanish as a puppet king after the assassination of Atahualpa) when, in 1536, he turned against the Conquistadors and was forced to flee. Recent studies have led to new and interesting interpretations of function of the site, for instance that it was a place of worship linked to observation of the stars. The great Intihuatana, the

252 (left above) In addition to the public and ceremonial buildings at Machu Picchu, the city contains many residential areas. This is a detail of the so-called Guards' Houses near the enclosure walls on the edge of the terraced slope.

252 (left below) Different areas of Machu Picchu had different functions: this is the industrial area – also known as the Sector of the Mortars – which was probably where workshops, store-houses and markets were located.

252 (right above) The long, steep and spectacular Fountain Stairway was carved from the rock: this area of the city may have been a centre for a water cult.

252 (right below) A sophisticated water channelling system supplied water to Machu Picchu, with fountains and pools carved from the rock.

fountains, altars and other enigmatic buildings demonstrate that rites and ceremonies were practised here but their significance is still a mystery.

Machu Picchu's architecture is skilfully adapted to the natural form of the mountain tops on which the settlement stands. There are only around 200 buildings in all and they are arranged on wide parallel terraces around a vast central square that is orientated east–west. The square is built on different levels and divides the city into two parts corresponding to the two natural mountain tops.

The various *kanchas* or compounds are long and narrow in order to exploit the available space most economically. Extensive terraces were used for agricultural purposes and sophisticated channelling systems provided irrigation for the fields. Numerous stone stairways set in the walls allowed access to the different levels across the site.

One section of the city was probably residential, while the other, separated by the square, would have been for religious and ceremonial purposes. The ceremonial section, to the west, contains the building known as the Torreón, a massive semicircular tower with rounded walls, niches and windows. The windows in the centre look towards the point where the sun rises on the summer solstice. Despite its structure which resembles a European watchtower, many scholars think that the tower was an observatory. The rocky wall below the tower has a cleft and sort of cave in it. The cave was carved out to form a small room which can be reached by a diagonal stairway. The ceremonial area also includes architecturally unusual and highly accomplished structures, such as the Principal Temple, the Temple of the Three Windows, the Temple of the Sun and the famous Intihuatana ('the hitching place of the sun') at the summit of the entire site. This monolith sits on a trapezoidal rock and perhaps acted as a sort of a sundial, similar to examples found at other Inca sites. Mysterious carvings are found almost everywhere on the walls of small caves or on natural rocks, but their meaning remains an unsolved enigma.

The high level of craftsmanship involved in building the walls of these large structures is evident: the stones are cut, smoothed and placed on one another with great precision. The wall of the main temple is an example of the perfection found at the site, the blocks joining together flawlessly like pieces in a jigsaw.

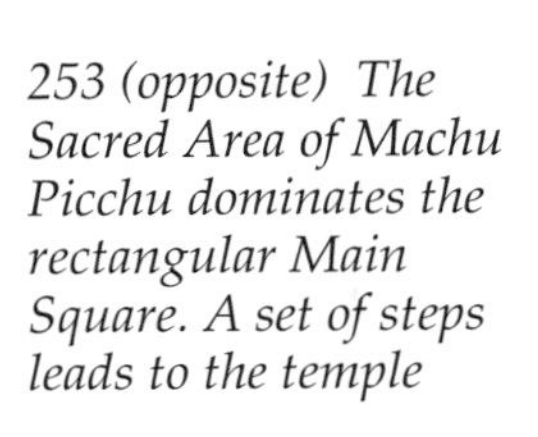

253 (opposite) The Sacred Area of Machu Picchu dominates the rectangular Main Square. A set of steps leads to the temple buildings on the summit of the rocky outcrop and to the Intihuatana, the monolith linked to the cult of the sun.

254 Perhaps more than at any other site, the architecture at Machu Picchu appears perfectly integrated into its natural setting, according to the Inca custom. The walls, pathways and terraces are laid out to follow the lines of the terrain on which they stand, until they merge with the rock.

255–258 The overall appearance of Machu Picchu has not changed greatly since the city was finally abandoned: only the roofs, which were made of perishable material, have disappeared and some walls have collapsed. This reconstruction recreates the site in its natural environment: extensive systems of terraces, today partially collapsed or hidden by vegetation, were created to maximize the agricultural land available and guarantee sufficient food to meet the needs of the population of the site.

259 The residential areas at Machu Picchu were aligned on narrow terraces or laid out in groups of four, six or ten around a central quadrangle. The roofs, which have not survived as they were made from perishable materials, had double overhangs.

260–261 *The massive Torreón resembles the towers of European fortresses but may have been an Inca temple or perhaps an astronomical observatory.*

261 (left above) *Machu Picchu is a complex site and its function and origins are not certain. It was perhaps a combination of a ceremonial centre with a defensive fort and an agricultural settlement.*

261 (left below) *This small fountain is cut from the rock at the foot of the complex that includes the Tower, the Royal Tomb and the Temple of the Condor, the ruins of which cling to the rock above.*

The residential area on the eastern side of the large main square includes pathways, flights of steps and small squares, and an efficient system for supplying water. The structures are usually single-storey rectangular buildings, often with enclosure walls called *huayrana*.

One feature of all the buildings is the trapezoidal shape of doorways, windows and niches which is typical of Inca architecture. Roofs consisted of a wooden frame covered with straw and with a single or double overhang. The roof frame was attached to the walls by stone projections. Although this was the residential area and the buildings did not have the grandeur of the ceremonial section, the techniques used in working the stone were remarkable: every structure is unique in its details. The local granite blocks used both for the houses and ceremonial buildings were probably polished using sand.

Machu Picchu, with its magnificent ceremonial buildings, temples, houses and monuments, is surrounded by precipices and walls that were designed to make access extremely difficult and which give the site the appearance of a city-fortress. Still today Machu Picchu never fails to amaze and intrigue archaeologists and visitors. Perhaps in the future it will yield the answers to some of its secrets.

261 (right above) *The beautiful curved walls of the Torreón stand above an unusual stepped chamber carved from the rock. This combination of sculpture and architecture resembles a crypt and is the reason why the feature was given the name the 'Royal Tomb'.*

261 (right below) *Many of the typical elements of Inca architecture at Machu Picchu and other large centres are visible here: the steps cut in the rock, walls made from huge, perfectly fitted blocks and imposing towers with trapezoidal windows and doors.*

262–263 (overleaf) *A spectacular view of Machu Picchu and its agricultural terraces descending the mountain into the Urubamba valley. The urban area sits on a saddle that joins the 'Old Peak' and the 'New Peak'.*

SIPÁN: TOMBS OF MOCHE LORDS

The varied terrain of present-day Peru runs down the Pacific coast of South America and extends inland to incorporate the central section of the Andes. In the past, this territory was the setting for one of the few original centres of New World civilization. The different peoples and distinct cultures that evolved here blended and merged for four thousand years before eventually coming to a tragic end with the conquest of the celebrated Inca empire by the Spaniards in the 16th century.

On the northern coast, one of the driest areas on the planet, the Moche (or Mochica) people lived between the 1st and 7th centuries AD. Their culture was typical of oasis dwellers, specializing in artificial irrigation which supported a dense and well-organized population. The Moche built large pyramidal monuments made from

264–265 The ruins of the structure that contained the tombs of the Moche nobles brought to light in 1987 lie in front of two tall pyramids. Once the tombs of the Lord and the Priest had been excavated, the tomb of an old Moche noble was uncovered in the southern section, as seen here.

264 (opposite, below left) A long period of hard work that seemed to bring no progress finally led us to the discovery of the first royal tomb, that of the young Lord.

264 (opposite, below right) The bones of the person we named the 'Old Lord' were removed and placed in specially modelled foam rubber.

265 (above) The large, square, tightly fitting adobe bricks were an unmistakable sign that we were near to an important tomb: that of the Lord of Sipán.

265 (left) This embossed ornament is one the many pieces of jewelry found in the tomb of the 'Priest', though it contained fewer items than those of the two Lords.

adobe and mastered sophisticated metalworking techniques, such as the fusion of copper, silver and gold and the gilding of copper. Although they had no system of writing, the Moche left an impressive legacy of pictorial scenes depicting their religious, mythical and daily life in the form of realistic and expressive pottery vessels. The Moche, like other cultures including the Incas, buried their dead with the goods and objects they had possessed in life, a practice that resulted in the constant plundering of the tombs over the centuries. It is with one of these many robberies that the story of the Lord of Sipán begins.

In February 1987 'gold fever' gripped the inhabitants of Sipán, a rural village in the Lambayeque valley. Dozens of farmers began to scrabble in the earth of an ancient adobe platform searching for fragments of gold that might have been left by a band of *huaqueros* (tomb-robbers). A few days before, the robbers had plundered the tomb of a high-ranking figure of ancient Moche culture. The local police, although they moved quickly, were able to repossess only a small part of the robbers' extraordinary and beautiful haul. Among the objects found in the house of one of the tomb-robbers was a realistic and luminous gold head with silver eyes and pupils made from lapis lazuli, and the large and expressive masks of two pumas or jaguars with open mouths revealing sharp fangs of red shell. The other items from the tomb disappeared on to the black market and into the hands of collectors in America and Europe, with the result that a valuable page of the Pre-Columbian history of Peru and South America was lost for ever.

Having overcome the initial resistance of the tomb-robbers – who were of course reluctant to give information – and with few resources but full of enthusiasm, we finally managed to get a small team to the site. After four months of excavation work during which we removed tons of earth, we finally found the untouched burial chamber of a Moche lord in the centre of the adobe structure. This amazing find turned out to be one of the most important for New World archaeology. For the first time, a ruler of ancient Peru was

266 (centre) One of the many sets of pottery objects found in the platform lay near the southwestern side of the Lord's burial chamber; it consisted mostly of anthropomorphic vessels with the features of soldiers and prisoners.

266 (below left) Niches containing votive pottery vessels were found at the sides of the Lord's burial, which was also flanked by the skeletons of two men lying in opposite directions. In addition, the skeletons of three females and a young boy were found at the feet and head of the dead nobleman.

266–267 This artist's reconstruction of the Lord's tomb shows the positions of the people with whom he was buried, which could be deduced from the arrangement and distribution of their bones. The niches containing the anthropomorphic pottery vessels are visible next to the body. The structure of the tomb and the materials used in creating the coffins and the funeral chamber are visible.

267 (left) This copper crown partly covered the skull of one of the women who accompanied the Lord of Sipán. It is not very well preserved but it is still possible to see that it is decorated with an image in the shape of a mask with ear ornaments.

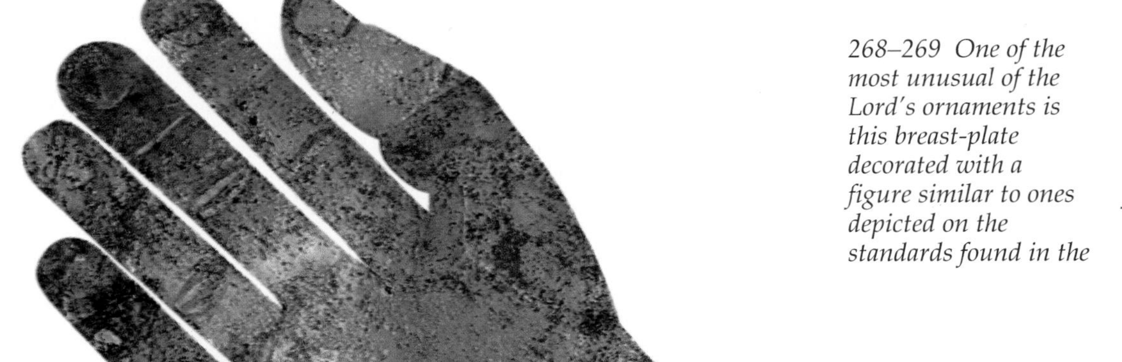

268–269 One of the most unusual of the Lord's ornaments is this breast-plate decorated with a figure similar to ones depicted on the standards found in the tomb. In this case, however, the figure is placed in the centre of a headless anthropomorphic figure with raised arms, cut from a sheet of gilded copper.

seen in all his magnificence. His tomb represents an inestimable contribution to our knowledge of the social organization, religion and daily life of those times.

Eight skeletons of retainers and warriors flanked a wooden coffin which contained the remains of the occupant of the tomb. The treasure accompanying him included ornaments, head-dresses, emblems and coverings made from gold, gilded copper and semiprecious stones. More than simply a collection of exquisite objects made by metalworkers of great skill, the contents of the tomb were the symbols of power of a dignitary who had been dead for 1600 years and whom we agreed to call the 'Lord of Sipán' (*Siec* meaning 'lord' in the extinct Moche dialect).

It took around ten months to complete the work of clearing and systematically recording the burial chamber. Day after day, in great heat and dust, more finds and new information were brought to light.

When we began, our excavations were restricted to a low stepped platform in front of two large pyramidal constructions which rose about 30 m (100 ft) in height in the middle of the sugar cane fields. The platform was built using sections of adobe bricks like columns placed on top of one another. By cleaning the deep and irregular hole dug by the robbers, we recovered some vessels, ornaments and an impressive copper-alloy sceptre. The sceptre-head took the form of a model of a Moche palace decorated with mace heads, human heads and a depiction of a creature, half-feline, half-reptile, copulating with a woman on the crescent moon. It perhaps represents the myth of the creation of the world or the origin of the Moche people.

After these initial finds, we began to excavate the central and upper levels of the platform. Below the debris and other modest tombs belonging to later peoples, we found a group of intact blocks inside which there was an area filled with earth and decomposed wooden beams. It was like a small room that had been filled with sand and earth filtering through the roof. Within this chamber was a deposit of 1,137 pottery vessels containing the remains of food, four copper crowns, remains of sacrificed llamas and the skeleton of a man. All had probably been offered to honour the gods or a high-ranking dead person and this was our first clue that we were in the presence of his tomb.

Slowly, as we continued to clean the eastern section of the platform, another four-sided earth fill began

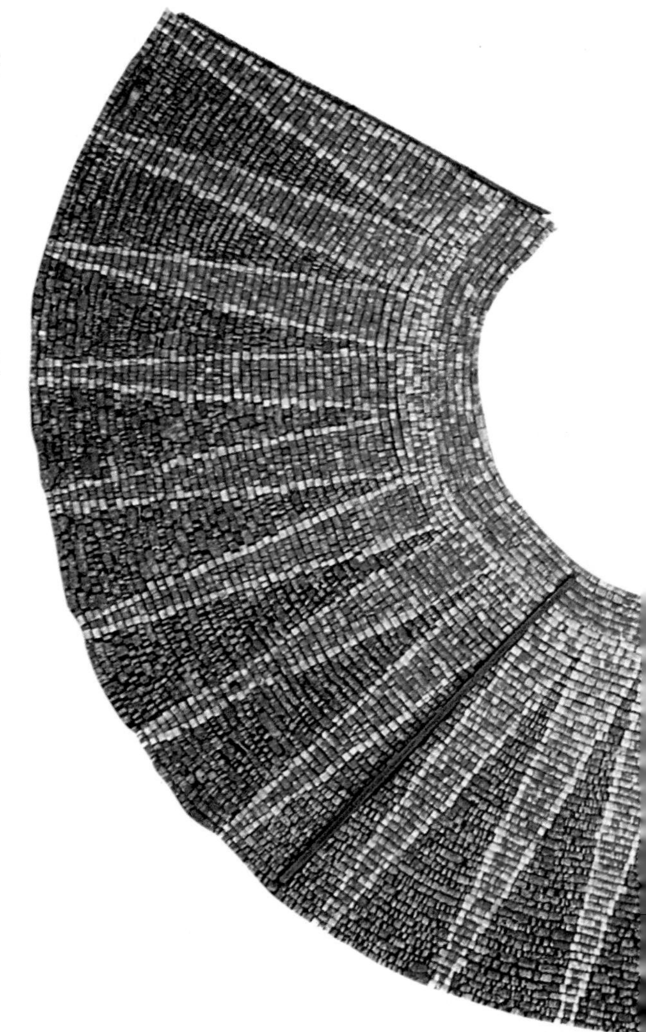

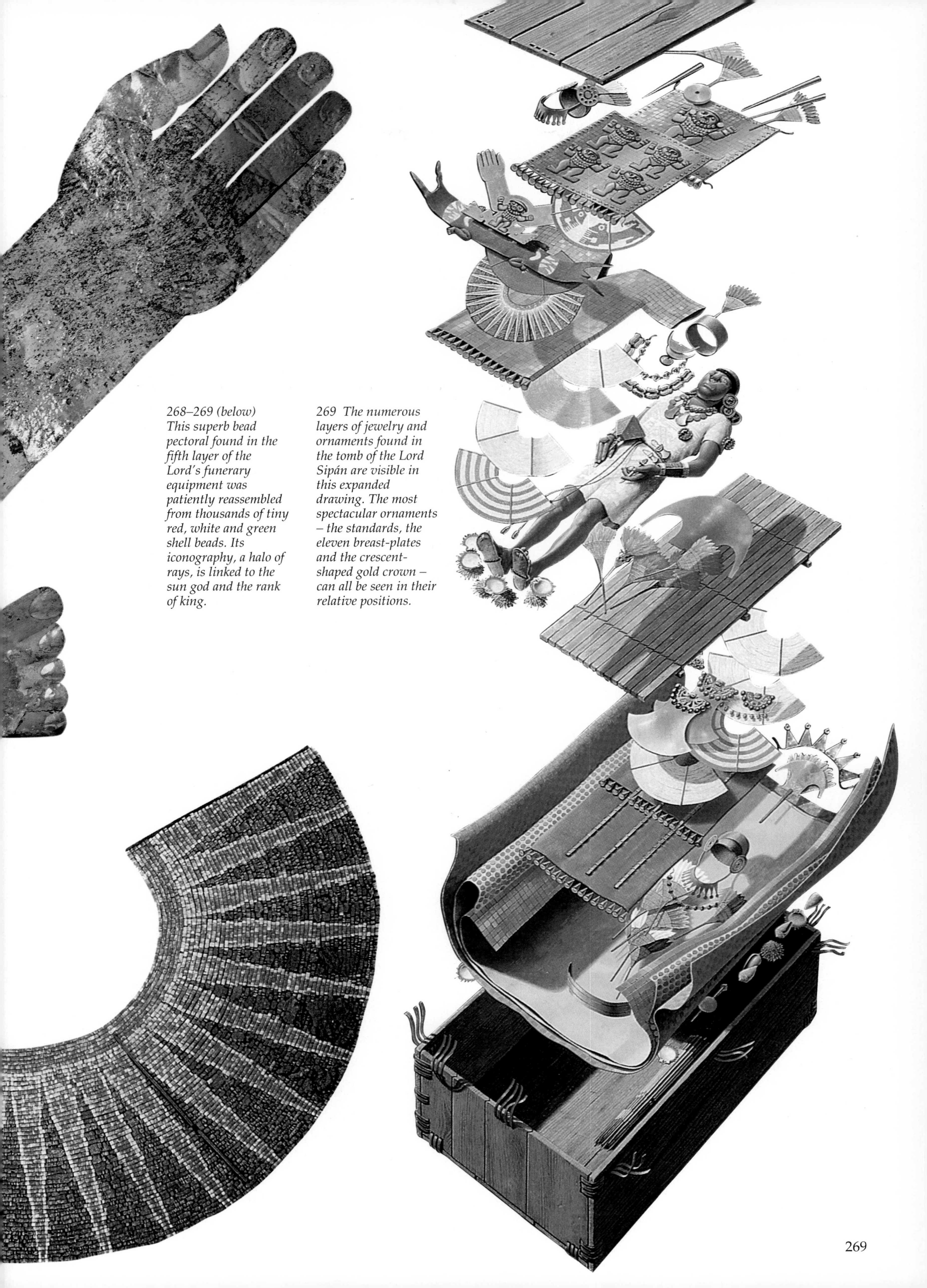

268–269 (below) This superb bead pectoral found in the fifth layer of the Lord's funerary equipment was patiently reassembled from thousands of tiny red, white and green shell beads. Its iconography, a halo of rays, is linked to the sun god and the rank of king.

269 The numerous layers of jewelry and ornaments found in the tomb of the Lord Sipán are visible in this expanded drawing. The most spectacular ornaments – the standards, the eleven breast-plates and the crescent-shaped gold crown – can all be seen in their relative positions.

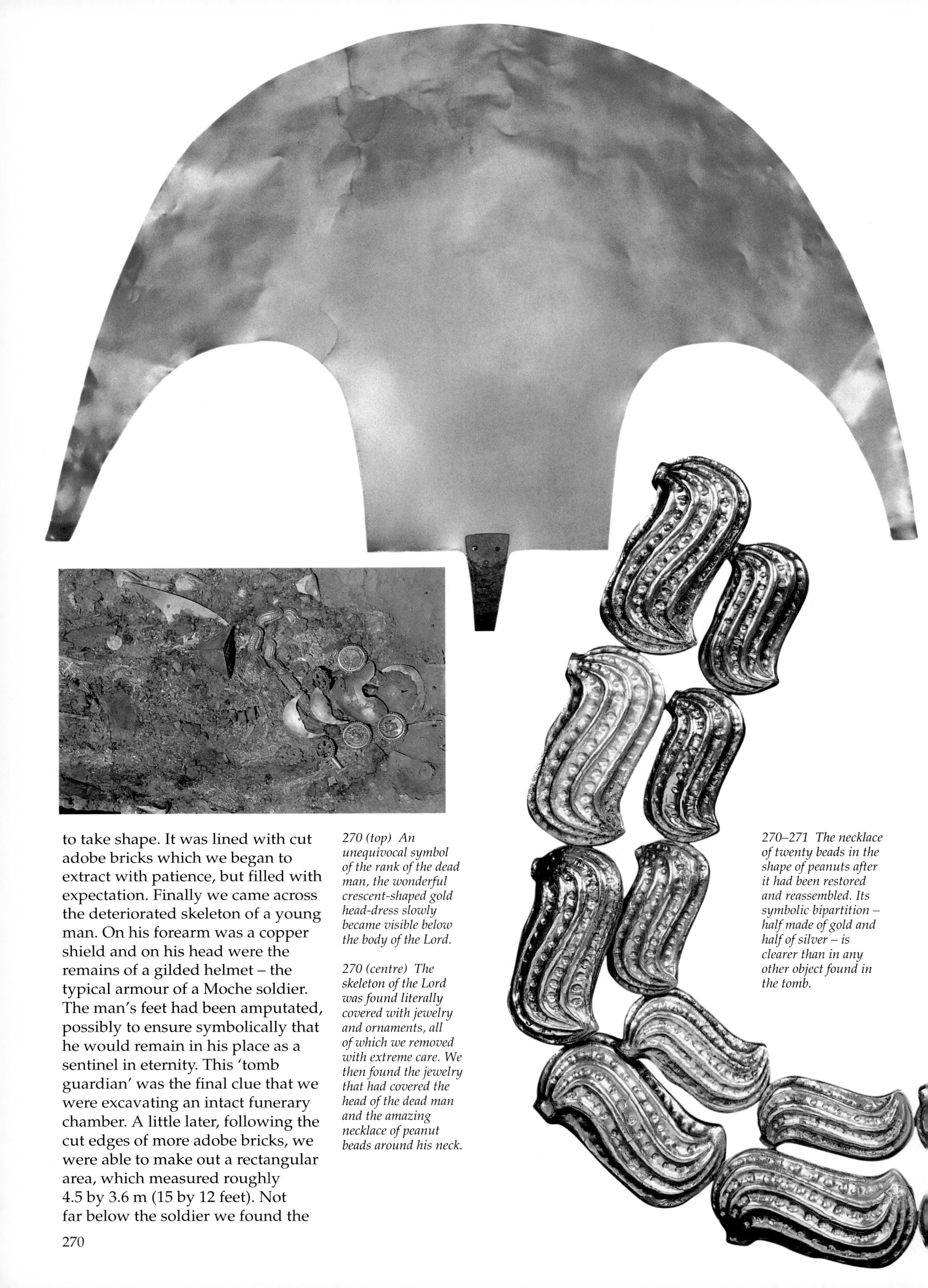

to take shape. It was lined with cut adobe bricks which we began to extract with patience, but filled with expectation. Finally we came across the deteriorated skeleton of a young man. On his forearm was a copper shield and on his head were the remains of a gilded helmet – the typical armour of a Moche soldier. The man's feet had been amputated, possibly to ensure symbolically that he would remain in his place as a sentinel in eternity. This 'tomb guardian' was the final clue that we were excavating an intact funerary chamber. A little later, following the cut edges of more adobe bricks, we were able to make out a rectangular area, which measured roughly 4.5 by 3.6 m (15 by 12 feet). Not far below the soldier we found the

270 (top) An unequivocal symbol of the rank of the dead man, the wonderful crescent-shaped gold head-dress slowly became visible below the body of the Lord.

270 (centre) The skeleton of the Lord was found literally covered with jewelry and ornaments, all of which we removed with extreme care. We then found the jewelry that had covered the head of the dead man and the amazing necklace of peanut beads around his neck.

270–271 The necklace of twenty beads in the shape of peanuts after it had been restored and reassembled. Its symbolic bipartition – half made of gold and half of silver – is clearer than in any other object found in the tomb.

remains of seventeen parallel wood beams that had originally formed the roof of a sealed chamber but had disintegrated over the centuries and thus let earth in. In the centre, scraping away the soil, we found a series of oxidized copper strips tied in knots as though they had been strips of leather. Eventually, we freed eight of these, defining a space 2.2 m long by 1.25 m wide (7 ft 2 in by 4 ft 1 in). At that moment we realized that we had come across the first wooden coffin in American archaeology. Opening the coffin was like a surgical operation as the contents were compressed in several layers of sediment and material that had covered the chamber. During this operation our tangible tension turned into amazement when the powerful, miniature and perfect face of a small gold man dressed in a turquoise tunic appeared beneath our staring eyes. A breath of air blew away the dust from this small sculpture which represented a Moche soldier wearing a crescent-shaped crown on his head and a mobile ornament suspended from his nose. Around his neck were tiny owl heads held by gold thread, and small rattles hung from his belt. The realism of the sculpture was such that even the contraction of his leg muscles was depicted; in his right hand he held a war club and his tiny shield had just slid off his left forearm. This delicate human figure was the central part of a circular ear ornament edged with small gold balls; two soldiers appeared in profile at the sides, created in mosaic from minute inlays of turquoise and gold.

Beginning with this object, all the finds took on a surprising sequence and the small effigy turned out to be almost premonitory. From the resemblances between the details of ornaments and head-dresses and the skeletons of the two soldiers that flanked the person buried in the coffin, it seemed that the miniature figure actually represented the dead man. The archaeologist Luis Chero, my first assistant Susana Meneses and I agreed to call the person we were raising from his long oblivion the 'Lord of Sipán'.

Every foot we progressed we uncovered surprising head-dresses, emblems and regalia. Full clearance of the first layer revealed two more pairs of gold and turquoise ear ornaments placed on either side of the head. Three sharp lances and several copper discs were also found and in the centre lay a solid gold ingot. The Lord wore silver sandals and his body was wrapped in layers of textiles, two of them with added gilded copper platelets. All around him were Spondylus shells from the Gulf of Guayaquil, highly prized in ancient Peru.

Next to be discovered were more head-dresses and coverings, including two square standards made from cloth with gilded copper plaques attached depicting one and

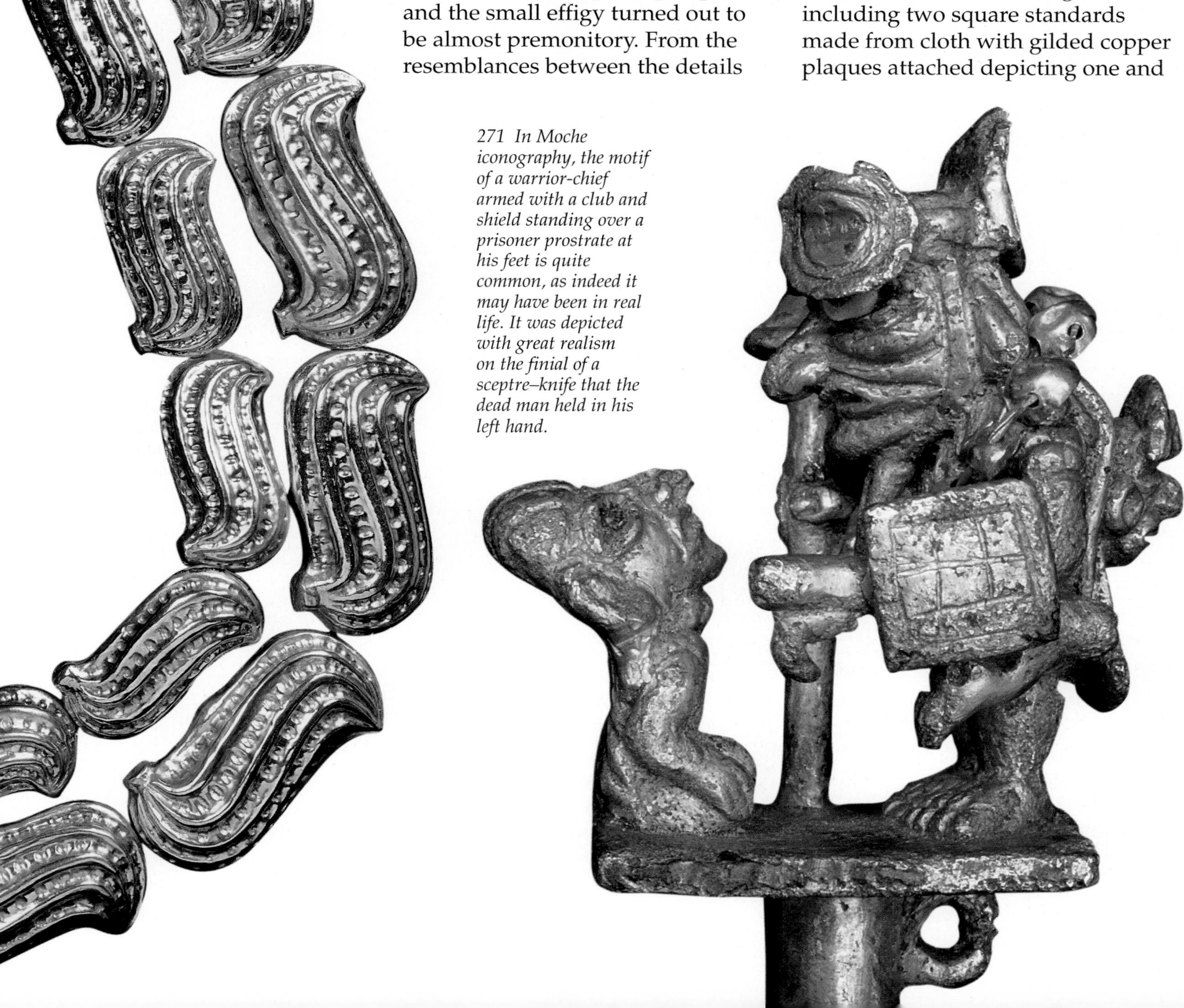

271 In Moche iconography, the motif of a warrior-chief armed with a club and shield standing over a prisoner prostrate at his feet is quite common, as indeed it may have been in real life. It was depicted with great realism on the finial of a sceptre–knife that the dead man held in his left hand.

four human figures respectively. A figure in the same pose, arms raised and fists in the air, also appeared in the centre of a gilded copper plaque in the form of headless figure with its arms outstretched and hands open in the shape of a 'V'.

The dead man's skull was partially hidden by a pair of gold eyes, a gold nose and a gold chin protector which was intended to cover his face up to the cheeks like a sort of helmet. Two light gold nose ornaments, *narigueras*, were placed near the face and a gold plate or cap contained fragments of his cranium.

Thousands of cylindrical beads made from red, white and orange shell formed a total of eleven pectorals on the man's chest, legs or below the skeleton. We also found various head ornaments in very poor condition that resembled fans made of feathers with a copper handle; on his arms, hundreds of minute turquoise, shell and gold beads formed the chief's bracelets.

On his chest, two rows of metal peanuts, amounting to twenty in all, gradually appeared. To our surprise, we realized that the ten on the right were made of gold, while the other ten were silver or copper. This was the first sign of the duality or bipartition that turned out to be an important and constant factor of the burial objects. For example, a silver ingot lay in the man's left hand and a gold one on his right.

In his right hand he held the most important symbol of social power and hierarchy: a sceptre with a gold terminal in the form of an upside-down pyramid. The sides were embossed with a scene depicting a richly dressed man holding a prisoner by the hair and pointing a war-club towards his face. This dramatic representation relates to the capture, torture and sacrifice of prisoners by Moche warriors.

The left hand of the dead man held a silver sceptre-knife with the same image modelled in miniature.

He also wore a necklace of sixteen gold discs, which no doubt once shone like miniature suns. At his throat was a collar of 71 gold balls graduating in size from the largest in the middle, decreasing towards the ends. On his chest there lay two knives, a gold one on the right and a silver one on the left. Here again was the bipartition of metals that was a regular feature and probably represented balance or duality, perhaps symbolizing east and west, day and night, purity and impurity, life and death, the sun and the moon, positivity and negativity, and all those concepts that are at the same time opposite and complementary. We observed with interest that the man was lying as if his body was a fulcrum, balancing the forces represented.

His bones were in very poor condition and to retrieve the fragments we consolidated them with acrylic resin which allowed us to remove the skeleton as if it were a fossil. The thousands of beads from his pectorals were also stuck to pieces of cotton cloth using resin.

Under his body we found a large, crescent-shaped gold head-dress,

61 cm (24 in) across. In Moche iconography such head-dresses are worn by people of the highest rank.

Below a wooden bed reduced to dust lay two gold semicircular rattles, finely cut out and embossed with an image of one of the most important Moche deities, Ai Apaec 'the decapitator'. This supernatural being is shown holding a *tumi* knife in one hand and a human head in the other. Close by were some of the Lord's most spectacular metal ornaments, a backflap of gold, 45 cm (18 in) tall and weighing about 0.77 kg (1.7 lb), and another, identical in shape but made of silver. At the top of each is again the impressive image of Ai Apaec. More ornaments in copper, gilded copper and feathers were found in the layer of earth below the man, who probably died at the age of about 35.

Excavating around the four sides of the now-empty coffin, we found an orderly and symbolic arrangement of skeletons. At the head and foot of the coffin were the burials of two young women who were not even twenty years old at the time of their deaths. One of them wore a copper crown and faced west whereas the other lay facing the other direction. The skeletons of two men were found lying on their backs, head to head with the two women. A shield, copper head-dress and club identified one as a soldier. The other wore a breast-plate of shells and metal pendants and between his legs was a dog. A third woman lay below the first, while a ten-year-old child was found in a seated position in the southwest corner. Finally there were two llamas which must have been the first sacrifices to be put in the chamber. On three sides of the chamber were five niches or *hornacinas*, containing 212 small pottery vessels and food offerings. The vessels, mostly jars representing warriors, prisoners or seated figures, were positioned in a way that suggested a ritual arrangement.

Once we had completed this extraordinary excavation, it was clear that the finds contained a huge amount of information concerning the Moche people, their culture, organization, religious beliefs and technological achievements. The tomb of this great Lord lacked nothing any king of the Old World

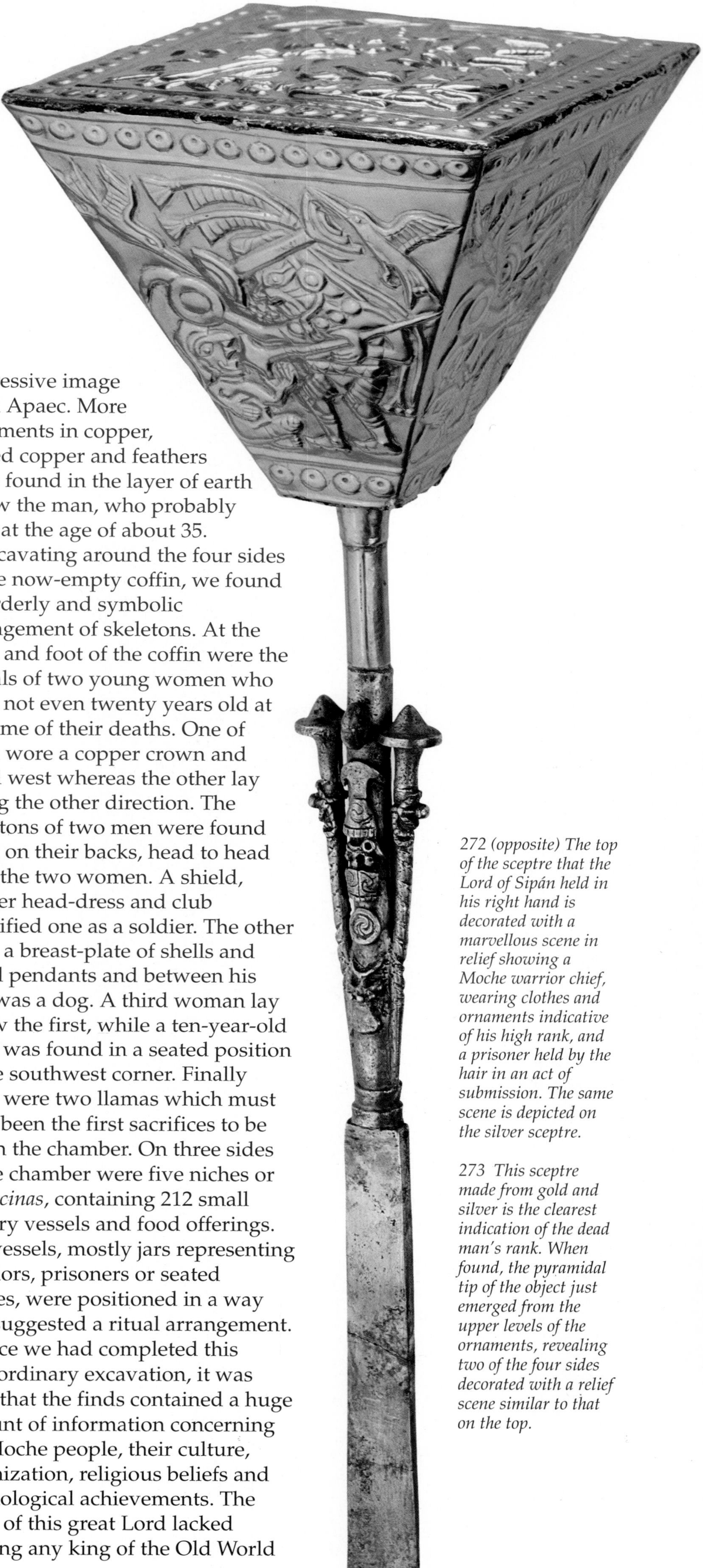

272 (opposite) The top of the sceptre that the Lord of Sipán held in his right hand is decorated with a marvellous scene in relief showing a Moche warrior chief, wearing clothes and ornaments indicative of his high rank, and a prisoner held by the hair in an act of submission. The same scene is depicted on the silver sceptre.

273 This sceptre made from gold and silver is the clearest indication of the dead man's rank. When found, the pyramidal tip of the object just emerged from the upper levels of the ornaments, revealing two of the four sides decorated with a relief scene similar to that on the top.

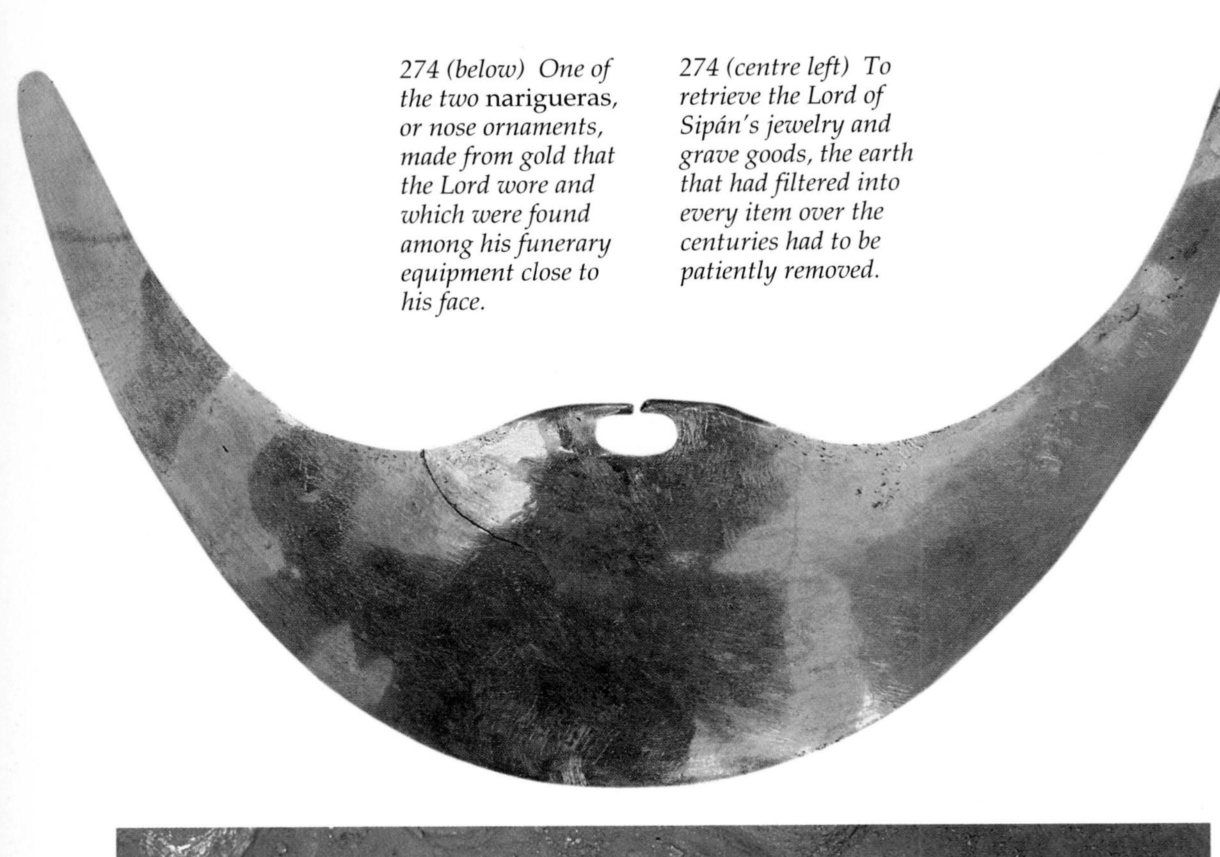

274 (below) One of the two narigueras, *or nose ornaments, made from gold that the Lord wore and which were found among his funerary equipment close to his face.*

274 (centre left) To retrieve the Lord of Sipán's jewelry and grave goods, the earth that had filtered into every item over the centuries had to be patiently removed.

could have boasted. Exotic materials had been brought from hundreds of miles away–turquoise from Argentina or southern Peru, lapis lazuli from Chile, shells from Ecuador, gold from the eastern slopes of the Andes and cinnabar from the highlands. We had no doubt once we had recorded the contents of this magnificent tomb that we had found the grave of a Moche ruler.

Moche art is essentially figurative and religious, and numerous examples of images, motifs and scenes are known in which humans or supernatural beings appear. Some of the most complete and characteristic depict a ritual sacrifice in which a richly dressed individual receives offerings and honours and is venerated during an investiture. Before the discovery of the Lord of Sipán's tomb, archaeologists and scholars of Moche art assumed that these scenes were purely mythical, but when the various ornaments and emblems of rank from the tomb were examined, it was discovered that they corresponded exactly to those associated with the important personage in such scenes. Our discoveries had proved the actual existence of the individual depicted and a new key was given to the understanding of Moche society.

After this spectacular find, the team continued excavating carefully

274 (centre right and below) A bird motif appears on a pair of circular ear ornaments made from gold and turquoise.

275 (opposite) This magnificently made miniature Moche warrior chief was one of another pair of ear ornaments. His club, shield, necklace and belt are removable.

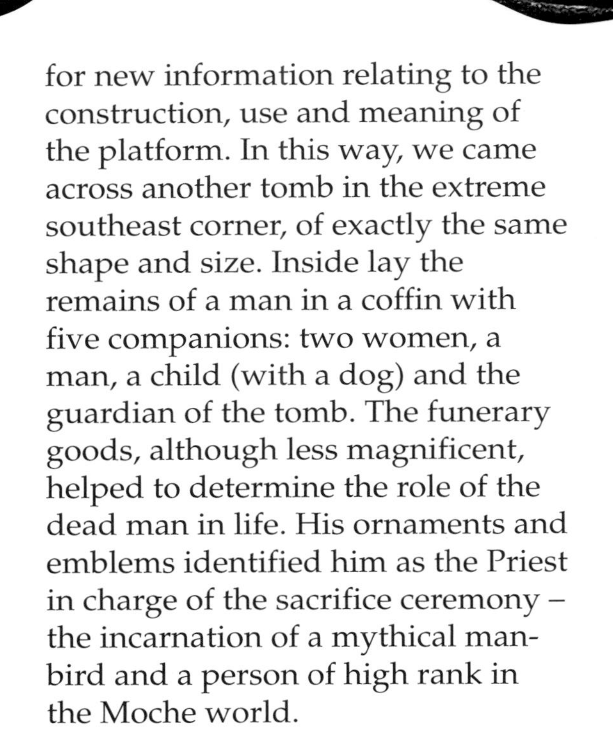

for new information relating to the construction, use and meaning of the platform. In this way, we came across another tomb in the extreme southeast corner, of exactly the same shape and size. Inside lay the remains of a man in a coffin with five companions: two women, a man, a child (with a dog) and the guardian of the tomb. The funerary goods, although less magnificent, helped to determine the role of the dead man in life. His ornaments and emblems identified him as the Priest in charge of the sacrifice ceremony – the incarnation of a mythical man-bird and a person of high rank in the Moche world.

Moving on to the southern section of the platform, we discovered sets of offerings and sacrificial remains a little below the surface. There were groups of small vessels, skulls and llama bones which had probably been deposited as offerings in the most recent phases of Moche civilization. We then came upon small adobe enclosures in which hundreds of ceramic pots, llama bones and miniature copper models of implements and ornaments had been laid out with care. Beside them were human amputated arms and feet, probably sacrificial offerings.

Retrieving and recording these offerings, sealed in earth that had hardened to rock, required patience and skill. Each element or impression had to be meticulously drawn and photographed as the layers of sediment and rubbish were slowly removed. It was during this process, at about 5 m (16 ft) below the actual surface, that we came upon the earliest level of the construction of the platform, when it rose only about 6 m (20 ft) above the ground.

A strange mark led us to some ceramic vessels which did not immediately seem be the prelude to another important discovery. Yet, further down, brushing away a layer of slightly darker earth, a priestly face made from gold shone in the sun once again. It decorated the abdomen of an exquisitely fashioned spider, also made from gold, and was just one element of a necklace of ten identical beads. This impressive necklace had been placed as the final article on the curved upper surface of a funeral bundle formed of gilded copper plates. Additional ornaments had

276 (opposite above) This necklace of nine human-head beads made of gilded copper was found around the neck of the man we called the Priest. The grinning faces, revealing teeth made of white shell, are possibly linked to religious symbolism. The individual beads had to be carefully cleaned to remove all traces of oxidation.

276 (opposite centre) At an advanced stage of the excavation of the Priest's tomb, the silhouette of an owl became visible. The bird, with outspread wings, formed a spectacular head-dress, one of the most important ornaments among the funerary goods of this high-ranking person.

been placed around the remains of what we identified as another Moche leader. We named him the 'Old Lord of Sipán' due to his earlier date – he was probably a predecessor by several generations of the first and younger nobleman discovered. He was accompanied by ornaments, head-dresses, clothes and symbols of military, civil and religious power, demonstrating that that the various branches of authority had been held in the hands of a single person in his time.

As we cleaned the rectangular burial depression, we realized that it had been dug when the first version of the platform had been constructed. It was also clear that although this tomb was smaller and simpler than Lord's, it too belonged to a man of the highest rank. The differences between the Old Lord and the Lord of Sipán were perhaps representative of important changes in funeral rituals between two phases of the same culture.

The body, originally wrapped in a cotton burial shroud that had disintegrated, lay in the centre. On both sides were 26 white-painted vessels containing the remains of food offerings. The vessels were decorated with the faces of people and the heads of dogs or owls, images linked to funerary beliefs and rituals.

At the dead man's feet were symbols of his military rank – the copper sheathing of lances, a war mace and a shield that had been folded or crushed in a ritual manner. His warrior status was also confirmed by the bundle of long wooden lances, sheathed in gilded copper, that lay to his right.

276 (opposite below) Photographs taken during excavation were essential in recreating the exact layout of the burial chamber and its contents later on. This is a view of the tomb of the Priest, with his badly preserved skeleton surrounded by ornaments and votive objects.

276–277 A detailed reconstruction of the Priest's burial: he was accompanied by two young women, a man, a child with a dog, and a llama.

Thirteen layers of ornaments, head-dresses and metal insignia were discovered slowly over a period of eight months before we finally reached the man's skeleton. The skull, which was badly preserved, had been covered by a life-size gilded copper burial mask, missing one of the white shell inlay eyes. The mask wore a necklace of owls' heads – perhaps a symbol of the god of night or death.

A thick layer covering the dead man's chest was found to contain a series of decorative elements made from pieces of gilded copper and silver arranged as a pectoral. This large, complex ornament ended in eight scrolls with the lower tips curled in a clockwise or an anticlockwise direction to represent the tentacles of a mythical octopus.

Other complex and enigmatic figures or deities also emerged, such as a strange creature

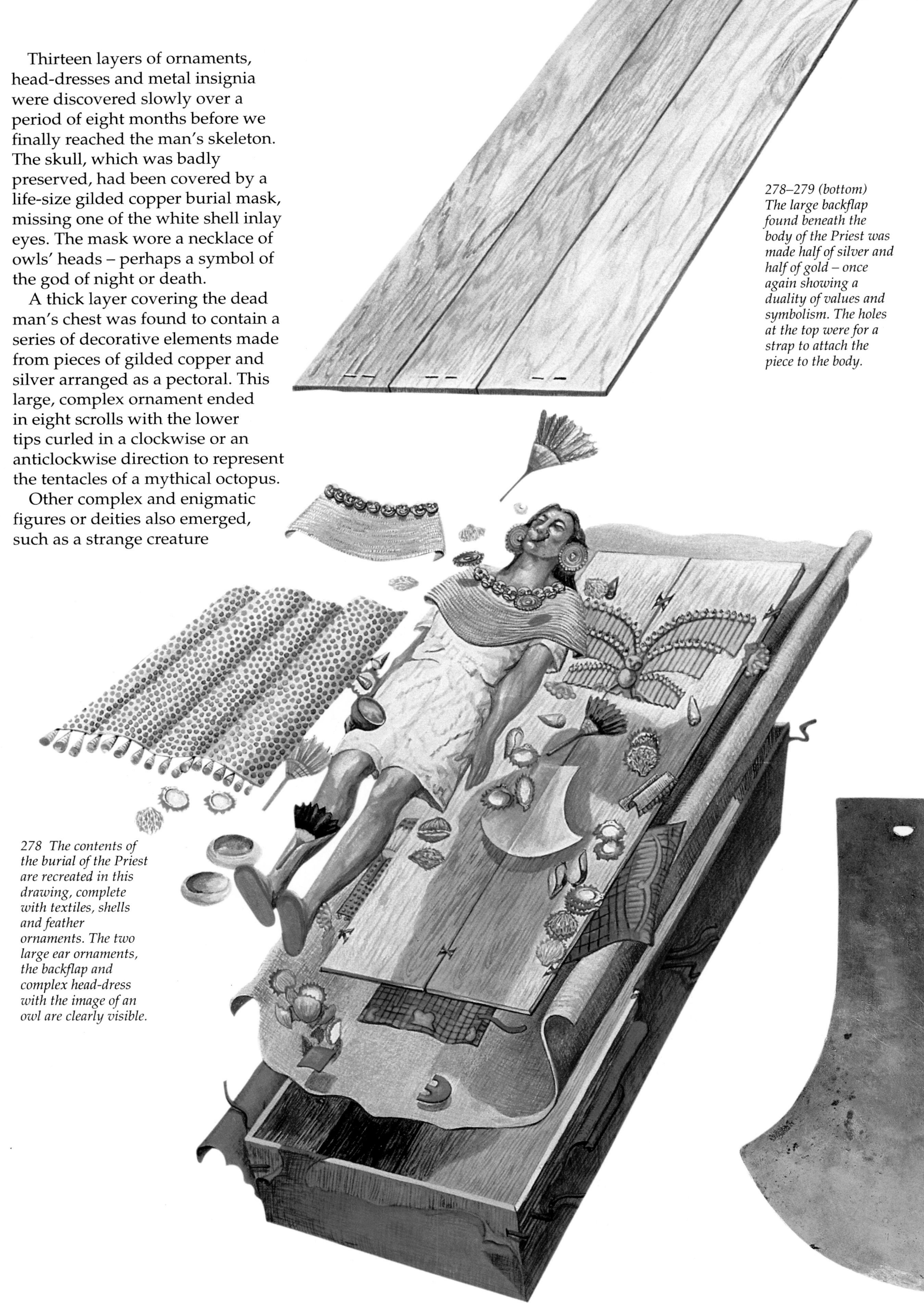

278–279 (bottom) The large backflap found beneath the body of the Priest was made half of silver and half of gold – once again showing a duality of values and symbolism. The holes at the top were for a strap to attach the piece to the body.

278 The contents of the burial of the Priest are recreated in this drawing, complete with textiles, shells and feather ornaments. The two large ear ornaments, the backflap and complex head-dress with the image of an owl are clearly visible.

279 *This cleaned and restored ear ornament is one of a pair found in the tomb of the Priest. Like those found in the Lord of Sipán's tomb, it is made from gold, turquoise and gilded copper. The contrast in colours highlights the tiny human face in the centre.*

with the head and legs of a man and the body and claws of a crab. Perhaps the most spectacular was an anthropomorphic feline with sharp copper talons. The fierce face of this figure retains its shell teeth and on the forehead are two snakes, one with two fish heads and another with two bird heads. On the figure's head is a diadem formed of a snake ending in feline heads with protruding tongues. In Moche religion this figure was associated with the rainbow or the celestial serpent. Once the entire piece had been restored, we could admire its original and thrilling beauty. Both these metal figures, the crab and the feline, were unknown previously in Moche art. They measure 62 cm (24 in) and 56.5 cm (22 in) respectively and are made up of various elements of embossed and gilded copper. They were intended to be seen frontally and may originally have been attached to cotton fabric, forming standards that accompanied the magnificent military parades and religious ceremonies of the élite of the Moche world.

The passing of the years and the chemical composition of the soil had oxidized the copper of the pieces and they had also suffered a high degree of internal corrosion. To save them, delicate restoration processes

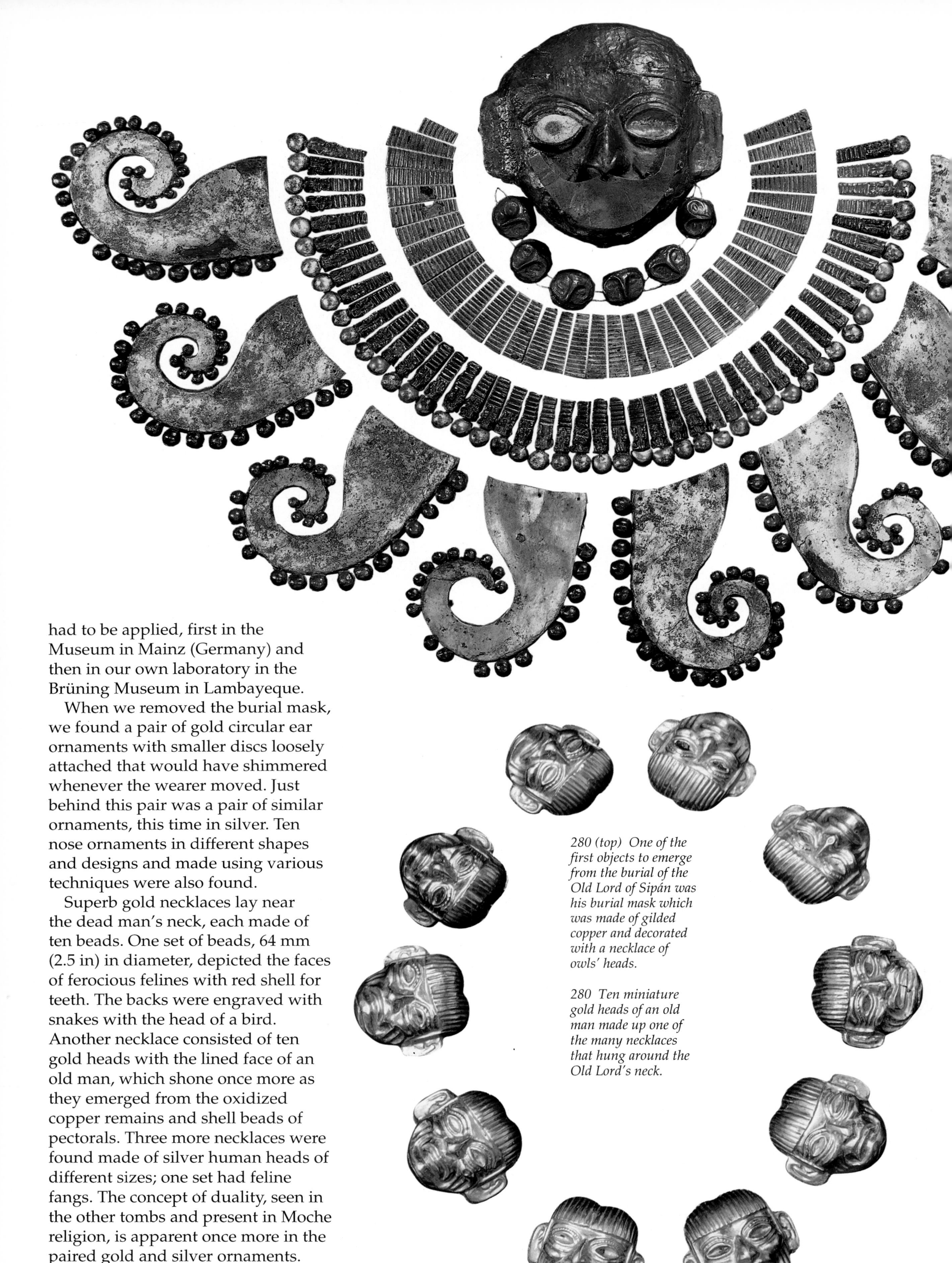

had to be applied, first in the Museum in Mainz (Germany) and then in our own laboratory in the Brüning Museum in Lambayeque.

When we removed the burial mask, we found a pair of gold circular ear ornaments with smaller discs loosely attached that would have shimmered whenever the wearer moved. Just behind this pair was a pair of similar ornaments, this time in silver. Ten nose ornaments in different shapes and designs and made using various techniques were also found.

Superb gold necklaces lay near the dead man's neck, each made of ten beads. One set of beads, 64 mm (2.5 in) in diameter, depicted the faces of ferocious felines with red shell for teeth. The backs were engraved with snakes with the head of a bird. Another necklace consisted of ten gold heads with the lined face of an old man, which shone once more as they emerged from the oxidized copper remains and shell beads of pectorals. Three more necklaces were found made of silver human heads of different sizes; one set had feline fangs. The concept of duality, seen in the other tombs and present in Moche religion, is apparent once more in the paired gold and silver ornaments. Many religious concepts are superbly

280 (top) One of the first objects to emerge from the burial of the Old Lord of Sipán was his burial mask which was made of gilded copper and decorated with a necklace of owls' heads.

280 Ten miniature gold heads of an old man made up one of the many necklaces that hung around the Old Lord's neck.

281 A tiny Moche warrior advances in a menacing way. Found in one of the upper levels of the Old Lord's tomb, this soldier is made from gilded copper.

illustrated in the finds from these royal tombs, which also demonstrate the superb technological skills of the ancient Moche metalworkers.

During the careful but exciting task of cleaning the objects that lay on the chest of the Old Lord of Sipán, we came across small shell objects that partially covered one of the most spectacular finds in this tomb. Slowly, the miniature sculpture of a Moche war chief, exquisitely made from gold and silver, emerged. We were amazed at the degree of detail achieved in this object, a nose ornament, just 119 mm

281 (centre) As in the Lord of Sipán's tomb, the Old Lord's burial contained a gold sceptre. Less elaborate than the first one found, the Old Lord's sceptre is topped by a spherical finial, perhaps a fruit.

281 (left) The figure of the gilded copper anthropomorphized crab is probably a representation of an important deity. The object was found in pieces in the burial of the Old Lord.

(4.6 in) tall. The warrior gripped a war club in his right hand and a shield in his left; his tunic was made of minute squares of turquoise and on his head he wore a gold crown in the shape of an owl with extended wings outstretched. Small hanging discs completed the decoration, while tiny rectangular plates formed the feathers of the bird. The warrior's eyes were made of turquoise set with brilliant black stones for pupils. He even has his own nose ornament, below which the beautifully rendered mouth expresses a forceful personality.

A true work of art of the Moche goldsmiths, this nose ornament displays great creativity and imagination. It might well be considered as one of the most beautiful and fascinating objects found anywhere in the American continent.

Various silver and gilded copper ornaments were found above the bones of the pelvis. Ten crescent-shaped ceremonial bells made of gold were also found, decorated with the face of the god Ai Apaec, 'the decapitator'. Although smaller, they were similar to those of the first

282 (opposite above) A figure from a standard or banner is surrounded by a circle of embossed plaques depicting ulluchus, *a fruit that is now extinct.*

282 (opposite below) One of the most surprising of the Old Lord's ornaments is this threatening representation of an anthropomorphic feline. It is an enigmatic deity from the Moche pantheon.

282–283 The largest of three standards found in the tomb of the Old Lord, this example features the same figure as on the other banners, framed by a line of ulluchus.

283 (below) When discovered, the anthropomorphic feline shown opposite was in very poor condition and had to be restored.

tomb discovered. Next to the pelvis, we found a backflap 29 cm (11 in) high. Decorated with the image of the same god, this backflap was very similar to that of the younger lord. Nearby there were others, simpler in design and lighter, made from gilded copper.

Perhaps in order to distribute evenly all the ornaments the Lord had used during his life, four pectorals were placed over his legs. Skilfully made from small pieces of shell, they formed perfect circles.

After an initial cleaning of the most important artifacts found on the body, we replaced them in their original positions to photograph them. It could not have been more impressive: there were 54 items made of gold, along with dozens of other ornaments made of gold and gilded copper.

The Old Lord was buried with two sceptres. One was made of gold and had a spherical rattle at one end; its knife-shaped shaft was perhaps used to cut the arteries of sacrificial prisoners or animals during sacred royal ceremonies that are often depicted in Moche art. To complete the duality, his other sceptre was made of silver, and ingots of both metals were found around his body: gold ones in his mouth and near his head and silver ones on his chin.

Turning over his forearm, we found hundreds of cylindrical beads made from gold, turquoise, lapis lazuli and shell measuring just 2 mm in diameter that were the elements of his bracelets. Only in the lower corner of the bundle did we find a few remains of the cotton the body had been wrapped in; the rest had disintegrated due to the action of the salts and humidity of the soil. Eight pieces were found after weeks of

284 (below) Ai Apaec is one of the most frequently represented Moche gods at Sipán. He is shown on many of the Old Lord's rattles, holding a head in his right hand and a sacrificial knife in the other.

284 (above left and centre) A gold backflap, visible in the centre of the Old Lord's burial, was decorated with the representation of the 'decapitator' god.

284 (above right) A distinctive sign of rank, the Old Lord was accompanied by a pair of gold orejera, *or ear ornaments. The two discs are decorated with two concentric circles of tiny shining sequins.*

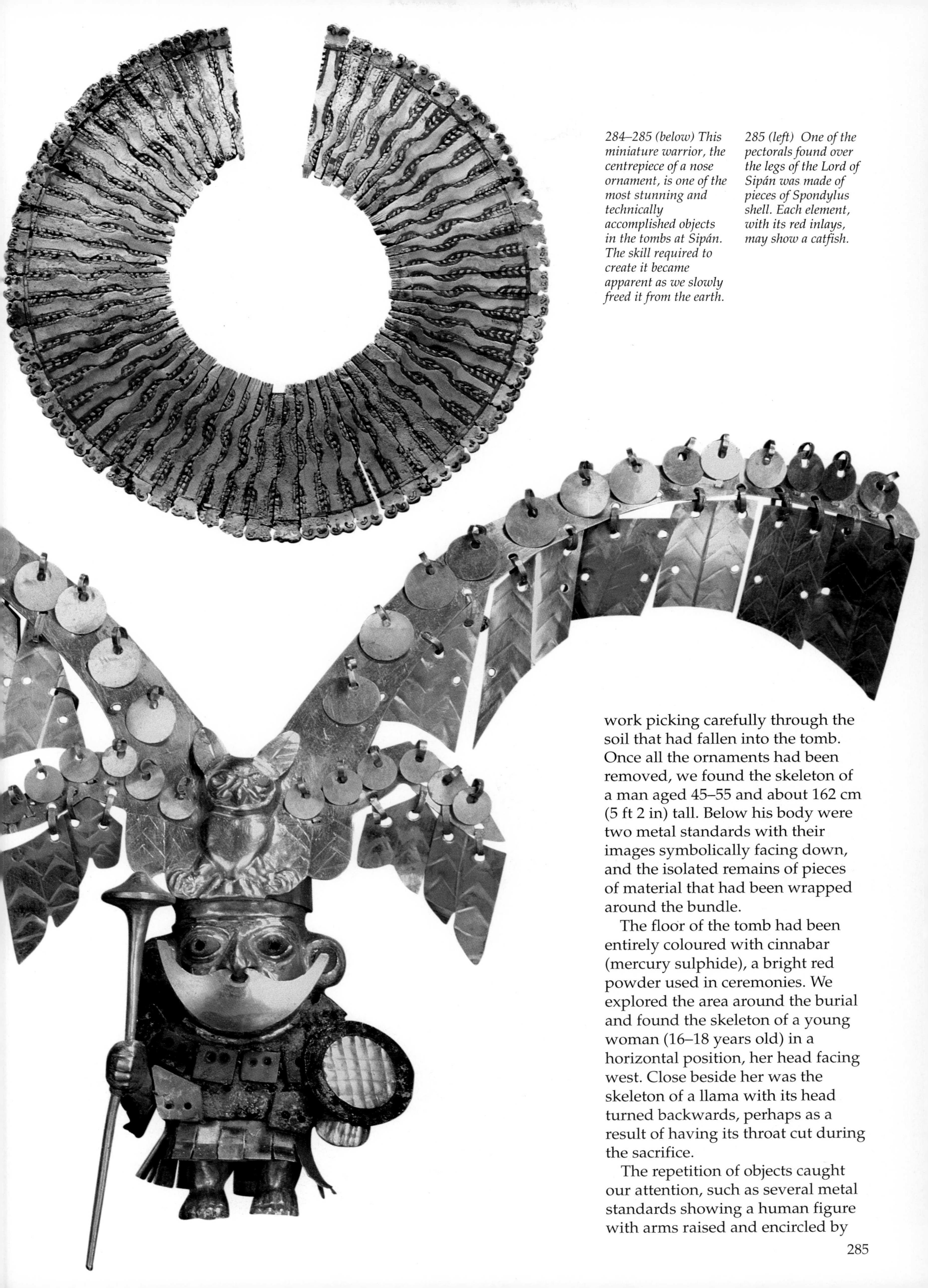

284–285 (below) This miniature warrior, the centrepiece of a nose ornament, is one of the most stunning and technically accomplished objects in the tombs at Sipán. The skill required to create it became apparent as we slowly freed it from the earth.

285 (left) One of the pectorals found over the legs of the Lord of Sipán was made of pieces of Spondylus shell. Each element, with its red inlays, may show a catfish.

work picking carefully through the soil that had fallen into the tomb. Once all the ornaments had been removed, we found the skeleton of a man aged 45–55 and about 162 cm (5 ft 2 in) tall. Below his body were two metal standards with their images symbolically facing down, and the isolated remains of pieces of material that had been wrapped around the bundle.

The floor of the tomb had been entirely coloured with cinnabar (mercury sulphide), a bright red powder used in ceremonies. We explored the area around the burial and found the skeleton of a young woman (16–18 years old) in a horizontal position, her head facing west. Close beside her was the skeleton of a llama with its head turned backwards, perhaps as a result of having its throat cut during the sacrifice.

The repetition of objects caught our attention, such as several metal standards showing a human figure with arms raised and encircled by

286 (above) *The funerary bundle of the Old Lord was flanked by terracotta vessels. Around his neck was a large gold necklace of ten beads depicting a spider with a body in the form of a human head.*

286 (below left) *Susana Meneses has identified six construction phases of the platform that contained the tombs. The reconstruction drawing shows how the dimensions of the levels progressively increased.*

plaques with embossed images of a fruit resembling a European fig. The fruit is called the *ulluchu* by scholars of Moche iconography and is often connected with motifs of war and sacrificial rituals. There had been much speculation as to the precise identification and size of this fruit which is now extinct, and, to our surprise, we found actual examples behind the plaques.

A brief comparison of the richness of adornments and the symbols of power of the 'Lord of Sipán' and the 'Old Lord of Sipán' showed that the two were of a similar rank. Differences in variety and number of offerings, a greater quantity of religious images, the absence of a coffin, the smaller quantity of pottery and the fact that there was only a single woman in the tomb of the Old Lord would indicate that changes in religion and perhaps a progressive consolidation of power took place. The older individual had held both political and religious power, which were later separated.

The research into this exceptional archaeological site was not limited to the exploration and recording of the contents of the tombs: much

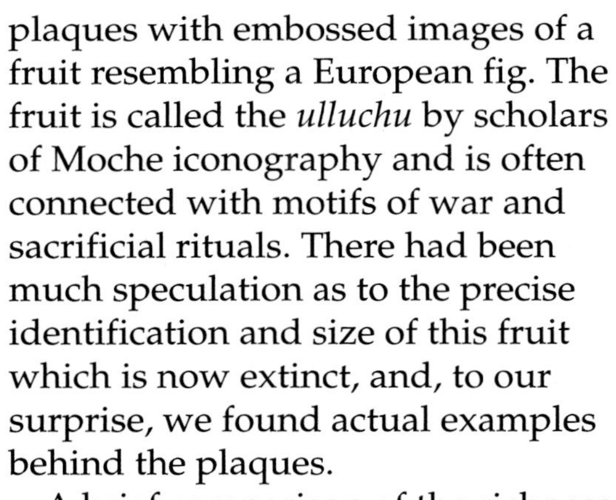

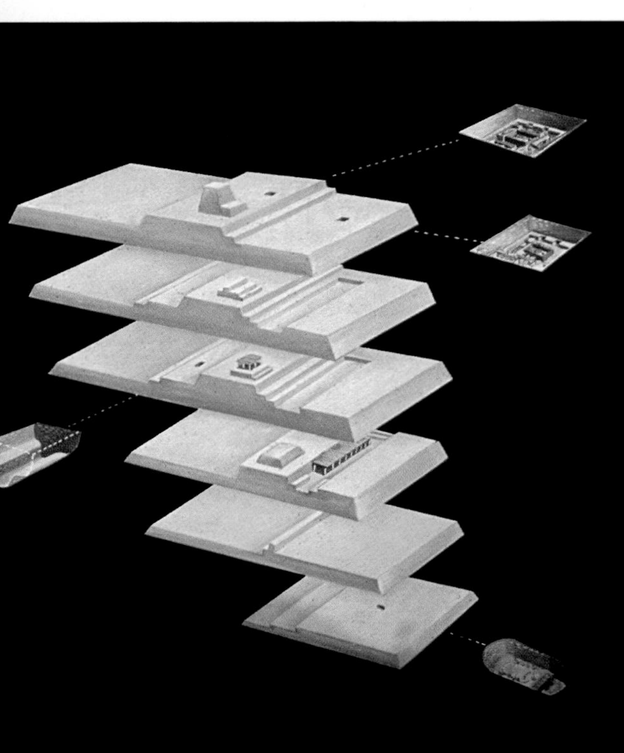

time was also spent in studying the architecture of their construction. Dozens of drawings and plans describe in detail every architectural element and any alterations. Susana Meneses has identified six phases of construction of the funerary mound. Beginning with a simple stepped platform, the Moche seem to have progressively enlarged and raised the levels. The façades of the modified and superimposed structures faced north; at least two of them were decorated with polychrome wall paintings that had been totally destroyed. The tomb of the 'Old Lord of Sipán' was clearly associated with the earliest level, whereas the tombs of the Priest and the 'younger' lord were linked with the uppermost level.

Twelve tombs have so far been discovered. Their relative positions and different contents reflect cultural changes and a complex hierarchy of Moche nobles with specific roles and functions. These included rulers with semi-divine powers, priests who administered the religious aspects of Moche life, and warrior-chiefs. The ordinary people must have been buried in cemeteries located in the surrounding areas.

Today there are fields of crops around the site and, in the distance, canals in what are now desert areas, showing that the Moche farmed more fields than are in use today. These abandoned fields also contain the remains of the houses of the ordinary people – the farmers and craftsmen whose efforts supported the development of the fascinating Moche culture.

286–287 Unusual in iconography and surprising in their manufacture, the beads of the Old Lord's gold necklace appeared in all their splendour after restoration. Small human faces have been embossed on the backs of spiders sitting on webs made of thin gold threads. The circular hollow base of each bead also has embossed decoration.

287 (below) A reconstruction of the Old Lord's tomb: he was accompanied on his final journey by a large number of funerary goods, though perhaps less remarkable than those of the younger Lord. In addition to the jewelry, ornaments and votive objects, the remains of a woman and sacrificed llamas were also found.

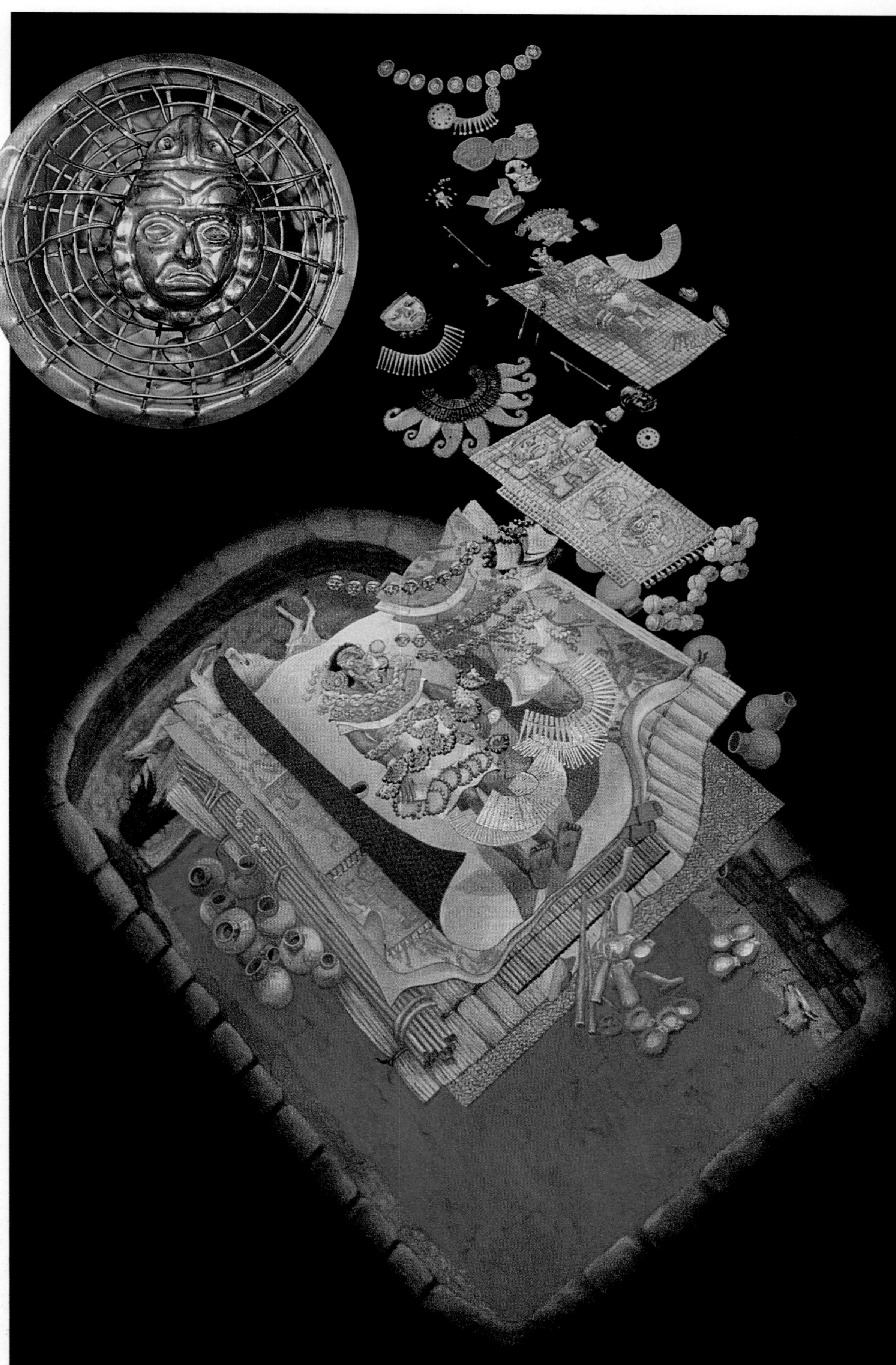

GLOSSARY

ACLLA HUASI A Quechua expression that means 'House of the Chosen Women': an Inca institution where females chosen to serve the emperor were brought to weave and brew chicha. They lived almost completely enclosed.

ADOBE A Spanish word meaning sun-dried clay; in the form of mud bricks it was the principal building material in arid desert areas.

ARYBALLO A container with a narrow base and tall open top, used to hold water or other liquids for libations in the Inca world. The shape of the container is similar to the Greek vase of the same name.

CUCHIMILCO A votive terracotta figurine, usually in human or animal form, typical of the Chancay culture of the central coast.

FARDO Large funerary bundles, most typical of the Paracas and Nazca cultures. The bundle contained the mummy and offerings wrapped up in many layers of woven textiles or vegetal fibres.

HORNACINA Adobe brick niche in the side of a royal tomb that usually contained votive objects.

HUAQUERO A robber or plunderer of Pre-Columbian tombs.

INTI The name of the Inca sun god, worshipped as their principal deity.

INTIHUATANA A Quechua term from combination of the words *inti* ('sun') and *huatana* ('attach or bind'), translated as 'hitching post of the sun'. It refers to a monolith, usually carved from the natural rock, found in many Inca centres and connected with the cult of the sun.

KERO A container in the shape of a cylindrical beaker, usually made from wood, and often painted with pictorial scenes. They were typical of the Huari, Tiahuanaco and Inca civilizations and continued to be produced in the Colonial era.

MITA A system of obligatory labour used by the Incas.

MONEY-AXE A copper plate in the shape of an axe head probably used as a means of exchange between Pre-Columbian peoples of Ecuador in the period just before the Spanish Conquest.

NARIGUERA Nose ornament made to hang from the cartilaginous membrane between the nostrils. It was usually worn by high-status males.

OREJERA A disc-shaped ear ornament, often quite large and decorated.

POPORO A small bottle, made of metal, which held the lime powder to be mixed with coca leaves to heighten the hallucinogenic effect. Some of the finest examples were made by Quimbaya goldsmiths.

QUECHUA The official language spoken and imposed throughout the Inca empire.

SPONDYLUS A large shell found off the coast of Ecuador and highly valued by the ancient peoples of Peru.

STROMBUS A large spiral shell used as a trumpet by Pre-Columbian peoples.

TOCAPU Complex geometrical pattern that decorated fabrics and wooden containers during the Inca period. It has been interpreted by some as a system of writing.

TUMBAGA An alloy of gold and copper, frequently used by Andean goldsmiths.

TUMI A Quechua word meaning 'knife'. Used in particular to signify the ceremonial knives used by coastal cultures of northern Peru.

ULLUCHU An indigenous fruit, now extinct, with religious, symbolic and ritual meanings. It may have had anti-coagulant properties.

UNKU A Quechua word for a sleeveless tunic worn by the Inca people.

USHNU A type of monument carved from the rock and probably used as a sacrificial altar or throne. Examples are know from many Inca sites.

SELECT BIBLIOGRAPHY

HISTORY OF THE ANDEAN CIVILIZATIONS

Bankes, G., *Peru before Pizarro*, Oxford, 1977

Bernand, C., *The Incas. Empire of Blood and Gold,* London and New York, 1994

Bruhns, K. Olsen, *Ancient South America*, Cambridge, 1996

Cieza de León, P., *The Incas of Pedro de Cieza de León*, trans. H. de Onis, Norman, 1959 (1553)

Fagan, B., *Kingdoms of Gold, Kingdoms of Jade. The Americas before Columbus*, London and New York, 1991

Garcilaso de la Vega, Inca, *Royal Commentaries of the Inca and General History of Peru*, trans. H.V. Livermore, Austin, 1966 (1604)

Haas, J., Pozorski, S. and Pozorski, T. (eds), *The Origins and Development of the Andean State*, Cambridge, 1987

Hagen, A. von and Morris, C., *The Inka Empire and its Andean Origins*, New York, 1993

Hagen, A. von and Morris, C., *The Cities of the Ancient Andes*, London and New York, 1998

Hagen, V. von, *The Royal Road of the Inca*, London, 1976

Hemming, J., *The Conqest of the Incas*, Harmondsworth, 1983

Lumbreras, L.G., *The Peoples and Cultures of Ancient Peru*, Washington DC, 1974

Lumbreras, G., *Arqueología de la America Andina*, Lima, 1981

Moseley, Michael E., *The Incas and their Ancestors*, London and New York, 1992

Richardson, J.B., *People of the Andes*, Washington DC, 1994

Squiers, E.G., *Peru: Incidents of Travel and Exploration in the Land of the Incas*, Cambridge, MA, 1973 (1877)

Various Authors, *Circa 1492*, Washington, 1992

DAILY LIFE, ART AND RELIGION OF THE ANDEAN PEOPLES

Baudin, L., *Daily Life in Peru under the Last Incas*, London, 1961

Benson, E.P., *The Cult of the Feline*, Dumbarton Oaks, Washington DC, 1972

Bonavia, D., *Mural Painting in Ancient Perù*, Bloomington, 1985

Donnan, C.B., *Moche Art and Iconography*, UCLA, Los Angeles, 1976

Donnan, C.B., *Early Ceremonial Architecture in the Andes*, Dumbarton Oaks, Washington DC, 1985

Hyslop, J., *Inka Settlement Planning*, Austin, 1990

Lanning, E.P., *Ceramic Archaeology of the Andes*, in *Quaternaria*, Vol. III, Rome, 1966

Meisch, L.A., et al., *Traditional Textiles of the Andes*, London and New York, 1997

Pollard Rowe, A., *Warp-patterned Weaves of the Andes*, Washington, 1977

Stone-Miller, R., *To Weave for the Sun. Andean Textiles in the Museum of Fine Arts*, London, 1994

Stone-Miller, R., *Art of the Andes, from Chavín to Inca*, London and New York, 1995.

Various Authors, *Power of the Sun. The Gold of Colombia*, Antwerp, 1993

AN ARCHAEOLOGICAL JOURNEY THROUGH SOUTH AMERICA

Alva, W., *Sipán*, Lima, 1994

Alva, W. and Donnan, C.B., *Royal Tombs of Sipán*, UCLA, Los Angeles, 1993

Bingham, H., *Machu Picchu: A Citadel of the Incas*, New Haven, 1930

Bingham, H., *Lost City of the Incas ... The Story of Machu Picchu and its Builders*, London, 1951

Burger, Richard L., *Chavín and the Origins of Andean Civilization*, London and New York, 1995

Hadingham, E., *Lines to the Mountain Gods: Nazca and the Mysteries of Peru*, New York, 1987

Heyerdahl, T., Sandweiss, D. and Narvaez, A., *The Pyramids of Túcume. The Quest for Peru's Forgotten City*, London and New York, 1995

Hyslop, J., *The Inka Road System*, Orlando, 1986

Kauffman Doig, F., *Perù-Inca*, (edited by Giancarlo Ligabue) Venice, 1993

Kendall, A., *Aspects of Inca Architecture. Description, Function and Chronology*, Vol. II, London, 1985

Kolata, A., *Tiwanaku: Portrait of an Andean Civilization*, Oxford and Cambridge, MA, 1993

Morris, C. and Thompson, Donald E., *Huánaco Pampa. An Inca City and its Hinterland*, London and New York, 1985

Moseley, M.E. and Day, K.C., *Chan Chan: Andean Desert City*, Albuquerque, 1982

Paredes Botoni, P., *La Huaca Pintada o El Templo de Pachacamac*, in *Boletín de Lima*, Lima, 1985

Protzen, J.-P., *Inca Architecture and Construction at Ollantaytambo*, New York and Oxford, 1993

Reinhard, J., *The Nazca Lines: A New Perspective on their Origin and Meaning*, Lima, 1988

Shimada, I., *Pampa Grande and the Mochica Culture*, Austin, 1994

Tello, Julio C., *Paracas*, Lima 1979

ILLUSTRATION CREDITS

Antonio Attini / Archivio White Star: pages 10–11, 44, 48–49, 164 below, 164–165, 165 below, 166, 167, 168, 168–169, 169 below, 194, 195, 196, 197, 198, 199, 200, 201, 202, 203, 204 top, 204–205, 206, 207, 208–209, 209, 212, 213, 214, 215, 216, 217, 218–219, 219 top and below, 220–221, 222, 223, 224 below, 225, 226 below, 226–227, 227 above, 228, 229, 230, 231, 232, 233, 234 above, 234–235, 235 below left, 236, 237, 240, 241, 242, 243, 244, 245, 246, 247, 248, 249, 250, 251, 252 above left, 252 right, 253, 254, 259, 260, 261, 262–263.

Archivio White Star: pages 60, 62, 63 left, 63 above right, 64, 66 right, 67, 80, 82, 83, 84, 85 below right, 86 above left, 86 below right, 87 below, 88 above right and left, 89, 143 above right, 154 left, 156 below.

Marcello Bertinetti / Archivio White Star: pages 224–225, 235 below right, 250 below left.

Massimo Borchi / Archivio White Star: pages 12–13, 41 right above, 99 below left, 106 above, 107 below, 108 above, 152–153 above, 157 above, 162–163, 164 above, 170–171, 171 below, 172 below, 172–173, 173 above, 174, 175, 178, 179, 180, 181, 182, 183, 184–185, 186 left, 186–187, 187 left, 193 below.

Dirk Antrop: pages 1, 31 below, 36, 37, 43, 47, 48 above, 56 right, 57, 58 above right, 80 below, 86 above right, 87 above left, 90 centre, 91 above, 96 above, 100, 101, 102, 104 above, 106 below, 107 above, 108 below, 110–111, 111 above, 118, 132 below, 132–133, 138 left, 144 above, 145, 146 above, 147, 149 above, 150, 151, 152 centre, 160 below, 161, 171 above, 173 below, 227 below, 292.

Massimo Borchi / Atlantide: pages 204 below, 205 below.

Giovanni Dagli Orti: pages 2–3, 6, 7, 38, 46, 58–59, 65, 69 above centre and right, 70 left above, 71 left, 71 right above, 72 right above, 78–79, 80–81, 87 above right, 90 above right, 92, 93, 94, 114 above, 115 above, 116 above left, 116–117, 120 above and below, 130 below right, 135 below, 136, 137, 140 left, 143 below, 148 above, 149 below, 153 above, 160 above, 187 below, 188–189, 190–191, 208 above, 218 left.

Massimo Cappon: pages 210–211.

Centro Studi Ricerche Ligabue: pages 28, 30, 58 below left, 66 left, 81 above, 110 above, 148 below, 155 above, 159 above left, 159 centre, 211, 235 above right.

Double's: pages 31 above, 48 below, 69 above left, 88 below, 69 above left, 88 below right, 95 left, 104 above, 53 below.

Archivio fotografico Erizzo: pages 33 below, 99 centre.

E.T. Archive: pages 86 below left, 119 below left, 159 below.

Charles Lenars: page 190 below.

Foto Mayr & Cabal: pages 9, 77, 123, 124, 125 right, 126, 127, 128–129.

Henri Stierlin: pages 8, 32, 33 above, 34, 35, 39, 40, 40–41, 41 below left, 42, 45, 49 below, 50, 51, 52, 53, 54, 55, 72 left below, 73, 74, 75, 76, 80 above, 96 centre and below, 97, 98, 99 above left, 103, 104 below, 106–107, 109, 112, 113 right, 116 below right, 117 below, 119 above right, 120–121, 121 right, 122, 125 left, 130 above right, 131, 134 below, 138 right, 143 above left, 152 below, 155 below, 157 below.

Agenzia Fotografica Luisa Ricciarini: pages 140 left, 141 right, 142.

R. Sheridan – The Ancient Art & Architecture Collection: pages 130 left, 135 above, 156 above.

Mireille Vautier: pages 16, 17, 60–61, 68, 69 left below, 70 left below, 70 right, 71 right below, 85 above and below left, 90 below, 91 below, 113 left, 132 above, 134 above, 154 above right and centre, 154 below, 158, 159 above right, 188 above, 189.

Werner Forman archive – Index Firenze: pages 56 left, 59 right, 63 right, 81 below, 114 below, 115 below, 139 above, 144 below.

MUSEUMS AND ART COLLECTIONS

Banco Central de Reserva Museum, Lima: pages 32, 34, 35, 42 right, 55 above, 72 left below. 73, 74–75 above, 97, 98, 103.

Banco Central Museum, Quito: pages 78–79, 94 right.

Banco del Pacifico Musuem, Guayaquil: page 75 below,

Barbier-Mueller Museum, Geneva: pages 50 above.

Brüning National Archaeological Museum, Lambayeque: pages 1, 4–5, 8, 9, 132, 133, 264, 265 , 266, 267, 268–269, 270, 270, 271, 272, 273, 274, 275, 276, 279, 280, 281, 282, 283, 284, 285, 286, 287.

Casa de Cultura, Guayaquil: page 8.

Cuzco Museum: page 113 left.

Dallas Art Museum: page 139 above.

E. Poli Collection, Lima: page 90 above right.

Foundation Guayasamin, Quito: page 94 left.

Gold Museum, Bogotá: pages 76, 131.

Gold Museum, Lima: pages 2–3, 6, 40–41, 45, 54, 55 below, 120 above and below, 130 below left, 135 below, 137.

Ica Regional Museum: pages 49 below, 50 below, 96.

Museum für Volkerkunde, Berlin: pages 56 left, 59 right, 63 right, 81 below, 114 below, 115 below, 146 below.

Museum of Archaeology, La Paz: pages 80–81.

Museum of Ethnography, Geneva: page 41 left below.

Museum of Ethnography, Götheborg: page 114 above.

National History Museum, Buenos Aires: page 71 right above.

National Library, Madrid: page 65.

National Museum of Archaeology, Lima: pages 7, 33 above, 38, 39, 40, 41 right, 42 above left, 46, 48 below, 51, 52–53, 58–59, 88 below right, 90 below, 91 below, 95 left, 99 above left, 104 below, 106 above, 107 below, 109, 119 below left, 136, 141, 142, 143 below, 148, 149 below, 227 below.

Pedro de Osma Museum, Lima: pages 16, 17, 60–61, 68.

University Museum, Cuzco: page 218 left.

Versailles: page 69 above centre.

Map by Betty Vandone

INDEX

Numbers in *italics* refer to captions

292 A Chimú textile decorated with figures of prisoners who have had their weapons and clothes taken away and are tightly bound by a noose around their necks. The decorative motifs in the border depict a two-headed snake and a jaguar. Both were sacred images found in the art of many cultures throughout ancient Peru.